W9-ABN-881

A LITTLE WAR THAT SHOOK THE WORLD

A LITTLE WAR THAT SHOOK THE WORLD

GEORGIA, RUSSIA, AND THE FUTURE OF THE WEST

RONALD D. ASMUS

palgrave
macmillan

A LITTLE WAR THAT SHOOK THE WORLD
Copyright © Ronald D. Asmus, 2010.
All rights reserved.

First published in 2010 by PALGRAVE MACMILLAN® in the United
States—a division of St. Martin's Press LLC, 175 Fifth Avenue, New York,
NY 10010.

Where this book is distributed in the UK, Europe and the rest of the world,
this is by Palgrave Macmillan, a division of Macmillan Publishers Limited,
registered in England, company number 785998, of Houndmills,
Basingstoke, Hampshire RG21 6XS.

Palgrave Macmillan is the global academic imprint of the above companies
and has companies and representatives throughout the world.

Palgrave® and Macmillan® are registered trademarks in the United States,
the United Kingdom, Europe and other countries.

ISBN: 978-0-230-61773-5

Library of Congress Cataloging-in-Publication Data
Asmus, Ronald D.
    A little war that shook the world : Georgia, Russia, and the future of the
West / Ronald D. Asmus.—1st ed.
        p.   cm.
    Includes bibliographical references and index.
    ISBN 0-230-61773-5
    1. Georgia (Republic)—Military relations—Russia (Federation)
2. Russia (Federation)—Military relations—Georgia (Republic)   3. South
Ossetia (Georgia)—History, Military—21st century.   4. Abkhazia
(Georgia)—History, Military—21st century.   5. Caucasus, South—History,
Military—21st century.   6. Russia (Federation)—Foreign relations—
Georgia (Republic)   7. Georgia (Republic)—Foreign relations—Russia
(Federation)   I. Title.
DK676.9.R8A86   2010
947.5808'6—dc22

                                                          2009037705

A catalogue record of the book is available from the British Library.

Design by Letra Libre

First edition: February 2010
10 9 8 7 6 5 4 3 2 1
Printed in the United States of America.

CONTENTS

PREFACE

T his timely and important book, useful to policymakers and interested citizens alike, sheds a bright light into the shadows of a pivotal episode in the evolution of post–Cold War Europe, Russia, and American foreign policy. In short, Ron Asmus has put the "little war" of the title into a big picture of geopolitics.

Vladimir Lenin famously reduced history to the question of "who/ whom," as in, "Who prevails over whom?" He saw the defining events of national and international life as win-lose contests of political will and armed might. The big conclusion that Ron draws from the "little war" of his title is that it had no winners and multiple losers.

Georgia was a loser for three related reasons: (1) its de facto dismemberment became de jure, insofar as Russia has recognized South Ossetia and Abkhazia as ostensibly independent states and claims it is prepared to protect them as though they were part of Russian territory; (2) Georgia's prospects of eventually joining the European Union and NATO were set back insofar as it will be, for a long time to come, harder than before for that historically unlucky country either to meet the criteria for European Union membership or to qualify as a stable, unified state that can plausibly contribute to the security of the Atlantic alliance; and (3) its current leadership, led by President Mikheil Saakashvili, damaged its reputation in the West when it allowed itself to be sucker-punched by a Russian leadership—led, in this instance as in many others, by Prime Minister Vladimir Putin.

The United States, too, was a loser. The George W. Bush Administration championed Georgia's Western orientation and its eligibility for NATO. At the same time, the administration tried to induce Russia toward more responsible international behavior. Georgia was the most salient and precarious test case of the United States' ability to continue expanding a democratic peace in Europe while developing a genuine, multifaceted partnership with Russia.

Yet for months—indeed, years—before Russian tanks rolled through the Roki Tunnel, powerful players in Moscow were looking for a pretext for an invasion, occupation, and virtual if not literal annexation of Georgian territory. For many in Russia, this outcome would serve both as an assertion of their claim to a "sphere of privileged interest" in the former Soviet space and as payback for the U.S.-led campaign that led to the international recognition of Kosovo as an independent state.

As Ron demonstrates in detail, as Russian-Georgian relations turned increasingly tense in 2008, American working-level diplomats were trying to prevent a military confrontation. But there was not the sort of high-profile, full-court press that the crisis called for.

I recall that during the weeks leading up to the invasion, I felt as though I was watching a familiar movie. Nine years earlier, in 1999, when I was in the State Department, I was involved in American efforts to defuse a similar eruption of tensions between Russia and Georgia. Back then, the proximate cause was Russia's desire to conduct hot pursuit and bombing runs against Chechen guerrillas who sought refuge in the Pankisi Gorge, which is in Georgia.

However, an underlying, chronic, and exacerbating factor was the Russians' detestation of Eduard Shevardnadze, Saakashvili's predecessor as leader of Georgia. As seen from Moscow—especially by Boris Yeltsin's heir apparent, Vladimir Putin—Shevardnadze's sins included his responsibility, as Mikhail Gorbachev's foreign minister, for the dissolution of the Soviet Union, compounded by his friendliness toward the West. Russians I dealt with made no secret of their hope that the man we in Washington called "Shevy" would, one way or another, disappear from the scene. There was widespread suspicion that Russian special services were involved in several attempts to assassinate him.

President Bill Clinton and Secretary of State Madeleine Albright used their good relations with both Yeltsin and Shevardnadze to mediate and sent me to the region to reenforce their messages in Moscow and Tbilisi and to keep the situation from spinning out of control.

By contrast, nine years later, the Bush Administration was neither as attentive nor as engaged as it should have been in what might be called preemptive diplomacy focused on both sides.

The Europeans were losers, too, since, if anything, they were even less foresighted and proactive than the Americans. For months before the war broke out, Georgia pleaded in vain with the European Union to put monitors on the ground to stabilize the situation before it exploded. Once the war broke out, President Bush—instead of committing American prestige and energy to stop it—abandoned the diplomatic field to President Nicolas Sarkozy, whose mission to Moscow had the combined appearance of grandstanding and too-little-too-late. The result was an unjust peace riddled with ambiguities that Moscow has exploited ever since.

Finally, another loser in the war of August 2008 was its self-proclaimed winner: Russia. True, the armed takeover of South Ossetia was a walkover from a military standpoint. But the political—and economic—results were anything but good for Russia over the short term, not to mention the long term. The operation occasioned a worldwide wave of condemnation and concern about Russia's return to the bad habits of its Soviet (and Czarist) past. That damage to Russia's reputation was accompanied by loss of investor confidence. A selloff in the Russian stock market increased the country's vulnerability to the ravages of the global financial crisis.

The land grab was also short-sighted strategically. Putin and his comrades may have thought that by invading Georgia, they were killing two birds with one stone: punishing their bête-noire Saakashvili while at the same time sending a message to leaders (and would-be, future leaders) in other former Soviet republics about what might happen to them if they, like Saakashvili, continued to turn westward and press for admission to Western institutions, first and foremost NATO. In fact, however, the invasion provided an object lesson in why Russia's neighbors should *want* the protection of membership in Western political, economic, and security institutions. In this respect, Russia's move was Pyrrhic—and, to use the Washingtonian euphemism for "stupid," counterproductive.

That is true in another respect as well. Russia has set back its own chances of integration into the political West. Never mind that Putin and other Russians now in the catbird seat are downplaying if not dismissing any such aspiration. I'm enough of an optimist to believe that they are making these noises for a tactical reason. With apologies to Groucho Marx, they don't want to knock on the door of any club that won't let them in. Whatever their real views, we can hope that their successors will one day be realistic enough to see that isolationism (or its post-Soviet variant, Eurasianism) is not a real long-term option, and is certainly not a good one.

The Russian Federation will, eventually, have to integrate into the international community, which means playing by its rules, not breaking them. Otherwise, it will go the way of the USSR. Russians may come to regret their support for separatism in Georgia in 2008 when that same force raises its ugly head again inside Russia, notably including in the North Caucasus. The Chechen crisis is not over; it is merely dormant. Nor is the Chechen crisis unique or contained. It has its analogues elsewhere in the North Caucasus—and beyond. It is quite likely that Moscow's muscle-flexing and bullying in August 2008 did not intimidate separatists within Russia's own border. Indeed, it may have done the opposite.

It is in the context of what will happen in the future that Ron's book is especially pertinent and compelling. He leaves no doubt that the real casus belli for "the tanks of August" was not so much Saakashvili's insistence on regaining control and sovereignty over South Ossetia and Abkhazia as his desire to join the political West. To squeeze to its essence a point that Ron makes with considerable sophistication and persuasiveness in his conclusion, Russia needs not only to stop fighting that desire of its neighbors but to adopt it as a Russian objective as well.

A final point about Ron himself. He has been a thought-leader in the Washington policy debate both inside and outside government. Even though he currently lives in Brussels, his voice resonates in Washington. In the 1990s, when he and I worked closely together in the State Department, he was instrumental in designing and then implementing the strategy and diplomacy that built bridges across what had been the Iron Curtain to Central and Eastern Europe, in particular the Baltic states. An early and powerful advocate of NATO enlargement, he was no less adamant and effective in pressing the need to develop a cooperative NATO-Russia partnership as well as strengthening pan-European structures like the Organization for Security and Co-operation in Europe to help draw Russia into a Western orbit. He has told that story authoritatively in his 2002 book *NATO's Open Door.*

In the work he has done for the German Marshall Fund of the United States over the past seven years, he has continued to be on the forefront of transatlantic brainstorming on European security issues, with considerable focus on the Southern Caucasus and wider Black Sea region.

What Ron has to say in the pages that follow should—and I'm confident will—have influence on the Obama Administration, as well as in Georgia and in Europe.

I can even imagine it will have resonance in Moscow, where thoughtful but well-connected and in some cases well-placed Russians are—quietly and cautiously—pondering the lessons, consequences, and implications for the future of their government's constant troublemaking in the Caucasus and, in particular, its mauling of Georgia in August 2008.

Strobe Talbott

Map of Georgia showing the autonomous republics of Abkhazia (de facto independent) and Adjaria, and the de facto independent region of South Ossetia.
Courtesy of United Nations Cartographic Section

A LITTLE WAR THAT SHOOK THE WORLD

INTRODUCTION

It was August 7, 2008. I was in Varna—a Bulgarian resort town on the western edge of the Black Sea that was the site of a 1444 battle with the Ottomans, which set the stage for the subsequent fall of Constantinople in 1453—visiting a colleague, Ivan Krastev, one of Europe's leading political scientists and thinkers on Russia. We had gotten together during the dog days of summer to relax and compare notes on trends in Russia, a country we both saw as increasingly autocratic at home, assertive abroad, and newly challenging to the West. Little did we know that the events of the next five days would underscore just how important those questions were.

We were sitting in a villa on a bluff enjoying an exquisite view of the western edge of the Black Sea. The scenery was peaceful, but my Black-Berry was purring with a stream of text messages and phone calls from Georgia at the eastern end of what the Greeks and Romans once called the hospitable sea. There, life was far less peaceful and the question of Russia's foreign policy ambitions less theoretical. Georgia and Russia were about to go to war. For months tension had been building between them. Relations had long been frosty, but Moscow had been escalating its pressure on Tbilisi since the beginning of the year following the West's recognition of Kosovo's independence and NATO's Bucharest summit, at which the Atlantic Alliance had declared that Georgia and Ukraine would one day become members.

Moscow had warned Georgia many times that its desire to "go West" would have consequences and that any cooperation on resolving the separatist conflicts in Abkhazia and South Ossetia would depend on Tbilisi's deference to Russian demands. Georgia had refused to buckle under Russian pressure but now Moscow was upping the ante. It had responded to the West's recognition of Kosovo and NATO's granting Georgia a promise of eventual membership by strengthening links with the separatist provinces in what looked like a strategy of creeping annexation. It was illegally moving troops and arms into the region and building the kind of infrastructure that very much looked like preparations for a military invasion. Was the empire getting ready to strike back?

Tbilisi had been trying to raise alarm bells. It had pleaded with the West to intervene with Moscow directly to halt this escalation, to put truly neutral observers or peacekeepers on the ground in the separatist regions instead of Russian ones, and to change the existing formats to give life to a moribund peace process in order to halt the downward spiral taking place. But the West, disinclined to push Moscow and reluctant to assume the risks of expanding its presence on the ground, was not eager to take such steps. Many thought that the Georgian fears were exaggerated and that Tbilisi was crying wolf. Others feared that pushing Moscow to accept new arrangements would simply be too hard. While Russia often stirred the pot in these separatist provinces to mischievously keep Georgia unstable and Tbilisi off guard, few thought that Moscow would actually go so far as to invade. That was assumed to be beyond the pale in post–Cold War Europe—or so it seemed. In any case, Europe was preoccupied with other issues and was preparing to shut down for the summer holidays with many leaders in or en route to the opening of the Beijing Olympics.

The mood in Washington was not much different. President George W. Bush was a lame duck and was winding down his second term. The president had been perhaps Georgia's strongest supporter in the West, but Washington's attention was also diverted elsewhere. The administration was focusing on its "surge" in Iraq and trying to nail down progress in the Middle East in its waning months. Key satellite and intelligence assets had been moved to focus on other priorities, leaving the United States largely blind to what was happening on the ground and giving Moscow a free hand to pursue its buildup. When the war broke out, the U.S. intelligence community, too, was caught by surprise and was initially unable to provide a clear picture of what was happening on the ground to the White House.

Politically, the U.S. election campaign between Barack Obama and John McCain was moving into high gear. It was absorbing everyone's time and attention in Washington as both candidates were getting ready for their respective conventions. Georgia was clearly not on their minds either. Over the spring and summer months I was one of several observers who wrote op-eds and position papers urging the West to get more involved in Georgia in order to prevent the worst from happening. It did not matter. Washington, too, was preoccupied with other issues and with itself.

In early July, I took part in a long dinner with Georgian president Mikheil Saakashvili at the seaside terrace at the Excelsior Hotel in the Dalmatian coastal city of Dubrovnik on the margins of a conference hosted by a Croatian government seeking to burnish its credentials for its NATO candidacy. Swedish foreign minister Carl Bildt, U.S. assistant secretary of state Dan Fried, Bruce Jackson from the Project for Transitional Democracy, and a handful of other leading think-tank personalities from both sides of the Atlantic were there. As the sun set, the scenery was spectacular but the discussion sobering. We talked openly about the risk of a Russian invasion that summer. Saakashvili had a few weeks earlier sent Russian president Dmitry Medvedev a secret peace proposal on Abkhazia and was hoping to see him the following day in Kazakhstan to test his reaction. He was oscillating between putting his faith in the latest Western diplomatic initiatives and trying to acquire modern weapons such as Stingers on the black market in case the situation came to war.

Everyone at the table urged him not to fall for a Russian provocation or start a war he could never win. He acknowledged the danger and pledged to avoid it, but he also made clear that he could not simply stand by and do nothing if Moscow moved to take these two separatist provinces. U.S. secretary of state Condoleezza Rice was scheduled to arrive in Georgia in a few days to attempt yet again to get a peace process underway. Saakashvili then asked us what we thought the West was willing to do in concrete terms to stop the drift to war. Would we intervene diplomatically in Moscow to halt the escalation or put neutral observers on the ground to stabilize the situation? No one had a good answer. Saakashvili and I would meet again several weeks later in the Crimean resort city of Yalta at another international gathering. Over lunch I told him the most dangerous window for Moscow to move was probably mid-August. I was off by a week.

Sitting in Varna on August 7, my BlackBerry buzzed again. It was Temuri Yakobashvili, the Georgian minister in charge of handling the "frozen conflicts" in Abkhazia and South Ossetia, the two separatist provinces largely controlled by Russia and its separatist proxies—and where the war was about to break out. In practice, these enclaves were run largely by Moscow's military and intelligence services, who had steadily transformed them into pawns of Russian policy—and Moscow was now using them to bait Tbilisi into a war. Temuri was a friend, a former NGO activist and think-tanker who had recently joined the Georgian government of Mikheil Saakashvili. His voice was tense. He was en route to Tskhinvali, the capital of South Ossetia, on a last-ditch diplomatic mission to find out what was happening and try to prevent the worst. He described his fear that something big and ominous was brewing. He was worried that things were spinning out of control.

I could not help but feel that I was watching a bad movie whose ending I knew, yet I was somehow hoping against hope that it would come out differently. The momentum for a Georgian-Russian clash had been building for months if not years. I had seen and felt it during my trips to Georgia as well as the separatist provinces. It was now coming to a head. That evening Saakashvili declared a unilateral ceasefire to try to halt the escalation and stabilize the situation. Would it hold? After a final set of phone calls with Georgian friends and a check of Russian websites by my friend Ivan, I went to bed in Varna hoping that the worst-case scenario had been averted. The following morning I woke up to discover those hopes dashed. Russia and Georgia were at war.

The Russo-Georgian war of August 2008 lasted a mere five days. Casualties were modest. By the standards of modern warfare, it was a little war. It was nevertheless a little war that shook the world. It sparked the greatest crisis in European security since Serbian dictator Slobodan Milošević unleashed the dogs of ethnic cleansing in the Balkans in the 1990s and brought Russia and the West to the edge of a new cold war. Moscow did not just invade a neighbor for the first time since the Soviet invasion of Afghanistan in 1979. It broke the cardinal rule of post–Cold War European security that borders in Europe would never again be changed by force of arms. In August 2008, Russia showed an ugly neo-imperialist side of its policy that many in the West had hoped was gone. No one should look at

Vladimir Putin's Russia in the same way after this conflict as it did before. It showed that Russia once again is prepared to use military force to pursue its interests vis-à-vis its neighbors.

The war's impact was felt first and foremost across the wider Black Sea region. Western diplomatic intervention came late and rescued a democratically elected Georgian government teetering on the edge of disintegration. A wider escalation of the conflict across the region or into a new East-West military confrontation or a new cold war was prevented. In that sense, Western diplomacy can claim to have prevented regime change in Tbilisi as well as a new East-West crisis. Yet the United States and Europe failed to reverse Moscow's military gains on the ground or restore the political status quo ante as it had first hoped. A close partner of the United States and a candidate country for NATO was invaded, and neither Washington nor the Atlantic Alliance did much to come to its assistance.

The ceasefire brokered by Paris with Moscow was also unjust. The West has been unable to compel Russia to fully implement the provisions it agreed to or to prevent Moscow from subsequently recognizing these separatist provinces against the will of the international community. One year after the war, Georgia's future remains uncertain and the conflict between Moscow and Tbilisi continues unabated. Bloodied, battered, and with its prospects for going West undoubtedly set back by the war, Tbilisi still continues to pursue a pro-Western course. Moscow seems equally determined to stop it and is still pursuing its goal of regime change as well as discrediting Georgia's Western aspirations through other means. The region today is less stable than it was before and the likelihood of another conflict between Russia and Georgia remains real.

But this was a war that was aimed not only at Georgia but at Washington, NATO, and the West more generally. It was also aimed against a European security system Moscow had come to see as tilted against itself and which it believed encouraged or enabled countries like Georgia to go West against its interests. Moscow's goal was to kill any chance of NATO ever expanding to Georgia or anywhere else along its borders and to dissuade other neighboring countries from getting too close to the West. That can be seen in everything from the way the war was portrayed in the Russian press, to the graffiti left behind by Russian soldiers in Georgia, to the way Russian general officers on the ground talked about their mission to both Georgian and Western journalists. Russia's response was designed to not only teach Georgia a lesson but also the West. It was intended to demonstrate that Moscow was again a force to be reckoned with and that the days of Russian strategic retreat were over.

The war was a watershed for another reason as well. Following the fall of the Iron Curtain twenty years earlier, the West and Russia had worked together to build a new cooperative European security architecture. The result was a series of agreements and policy decisions that, in Western eyes, were designed to end the geopolitical division of Europe and build a new democratic peace that would lock in stability and security once and for all. It was an attempt to produce the functional equivalent of a new peace treaty to seal the end of the Cold War. That process had begun with the signing of the Charter of Paris and had been carried forward with a series of subsequent agreements reached under the auspices of the Organization for Security and Co-operation in Europe (OSCE).

At the center of those "rules of the game" was a pledge not to change borders through the use of force and to accept the right of all states large and small to enjoy equal security and to choose their own security alliances. The rules also demonstrated the rejection of old-fashioned spheres-of-influence thinking. They constituted in a sense a kind of bill of rights for a new European security order. It was an attempt to create a democratic peace across Europe that transcended the Cold War's bipolar division of the continent and old patterns of geopolitical rivalry and replaced them with a new pattern of cooperative security. Russia was a full partner to and participant in those negotiations, and these agreements all bear the signature of the President of the Russian Federation.

The problem from Moscow's perspective was that those same rules of the game also ended up legitimating the enlargement of NATO and the European Union to its borders. For, given the chance to choose their own path, nearly all of the countries of the former Soviet empire immediately opted to try to go West and seek the same kind of alliance with the United States and obtain the same kind of the security and prosperity Western Europeans had enjoyed for decades. In response, the West drew up its own dual-track strategy of opening its doors to these new members while offering Russia a parallel set of arrangements that would draw it closer to the West as well. The logic behind the Western strategy was to anchor and integrate Central and Eastern Europe but also pull Moscow closer into the Western orbit at a pace both sides could manage. Thus, the West offered Moscow new partnerships with NATO and the European Union as well as a strengthened OSCE as part of an overall strategy of creating a Europe whole, free, and at peace.

Moscow initially bought into that strategy under President Boris Yeltsin, albeit reluctantly. But that strategy eventually failed. Why it did so is a question we will come back to later in this book. But by the summer of 2008 Moscow had not only turned its back against the West; an increasingly nationalistic and revisionist Russia was also rebelling against a European system that it felt no longer met its interests and had been imposed on it during a moment of temporary weakness. The agreements that Moscow had signed over the previous two decades about the rights of all countries to choose their own alliances no longer meant anything to the Kremlin. They were simply pieces of paper to be ignored as Moscow decided it would not let its neighbors go West.

In other words, the Russo-Georgian war may have been small, but it raised some big questions about the future of European security. That European security system diplomats had spent two decades developing failed in August 2008. The norms, principles, and mechanisms that were supposed to prevent future conflicts were too weak to stop this one. Moscow's justification for the war laid claim to precisely the kind of sphere of influence on its borders this system was supposed to ban. One reason why past security arrangements in twentieth-century Europe failed was that when the tough cases arose—and they often involved far-away countries with complicated names and poorly understood geography—the major powers opted not to go to bat to enforce the rules because either the problem was considered too hard, the country not important enough, or one party involved too powerful not too accommodate. There are echoes of each of these causes in the run-up to the Russo-Georgian war.

Given the swirl of controversy that continues to surround the questions of how and why this war started, how it ended, and what it means for the future, I decided to write this book in part to help clarify the historical record. I have also written it because of my conviction that we need to look more deeply into what went wrong and what it means for our own policies and for Europe writ large. Much of my professional career over the past two decades has been spent working, initially as a thinker but then as a practitioner, on developing that cooperative European security order that I believe failed in August 2008. I hope this book helps the West look in the mirror and understand the reason for this larger failure.

A hard look at U.S. and European strategy is, in my view, essential if we are to draw the right lessons for the future. This war represents a deep failure with implications that go well beyond Georgia and Russia. We need to understand how and why it happened. This war still matters today—and not just because of the many unresolved issues it left in its wake. It matters because we need to draw the right lessons for the future of European security. It raises core questions about how the United States and Europe should deal with young democracies, the future of Western alliances, how we deal with a more assertive Russia determined to reassert its control over its neighbors, and whether the rules of European security need to be rewritten yet again for a new era.

The argument of this book can be summarized in five main theses. First, this war was not fought over territory, minority rights, or the future status of the separatist provinces Abkhazia and South Ossetia. Russian claims that its invasion was a response to Georgian aggression in South Ossetia and that it was simply defending its peacekeepers and citizens in the separatist provinces do not hold up to scrutiny. To be sure, Russo-Georgian relations were troubled and these conflicts real. But the root cause of this war was geopolitical. Georgia was determined to go West and Russia was determined to stop it from doing so. In that struggle, Moscow took these conflicts hostage and instrumentalized them as part of a broader Russian strategy to keep Georgia off balance and dependent on Moscow's good will and to undercut Tbilisi's Western aspirations.

Russia deeply opposed and resented Georgia's effort to escape its historic sphere of influence and anchor itself to the West. It feared the impact that Georgia's pro-Western democratic experiment could, if successful, have in the Southern Caucasus and potentially across the border in the Northern Caucasus within Russia itself. The fact that countries like Georgia or Ukraine had experienced genuine democratic elections as opposed to having their elites preselected by a ruling oligarchy set a dangerous precedent, from Moscow's perspective. Even worse, oligarchic regimes in these countries had been unseated by civil society acting from below. If Ukraine and Georgia could embrace liberal democracy and successfully become part of the West, the Russian ruling class's narrative about its own "sovereign democracy" at home and the reestablishment of Russian power abroad might be exposed as hollow.

This conflict was not only a function of the age-old dilemma that Russia has tended to feel secure only when those on its borders are under its control and feel insecure. It was also tied to the growing importance that the export of energy played as an instrument of power in Russian foreign policy. Moscow's goal was to dominate the energy sources and supply routes to Europe, and Tbilisi was part of the coalition trying to circumvent that by creating an alternative way to bring Caspian energy to the West bypassing Russia. The Kremlin openly told Tbilisi it had to decide whether they were on the side of Moscow or the West and that Moscow's attitude on resolving the frozen conflicts in Abkhazia and South Ossetia would be driven by Georgia's answer to that central question. Had Georgia abandoned its Western aspirations and acquiesced to Russian demands, this war would in all likelihood have never happened. But Georgia would not, so the two countries were set on a collision course that made this conflict almost inevitable.

What happened on August 7 was but the final act in a longer, complicated drama. Russia had de facto declared war on Georgia well before hostilities broke out in the summer of 2008 as Moscow concluded that Tbilisi would not bend. This war was the culmination of a broader Russian strategy of rollback, fueled by rising nationalism and petrodollars, and designed to reestablish its dominance over its neighbors. A resurgent Russia was determined not to "lose" Georgia and to reassert its will over the Southern Caucasus. That is why what happened in this small country of some five million people on the eastern edge of the Black Sea mattered so much to the Kremlin. It is why Tbilisi's defiance of Russia produced such resentment and rage in the Kremlin. It is why, from Moscow's perspective, Tbilisi's democratic experiments had to be undercut, demonized, and, in the final analysis, destroyed.

Second, Georgia also made plenty of mistakes that led to this war. As we will see, there is a logic that leads to President Saakashvili's decision to fight on August 7. His action was a desperate response to what he believed was the imminent threat of the ethnic cleansing of tens of thousands of Georgian citizens, the possible loss of South Ossetia and Abkhazia once and for all, a possible Russian assault on Tbilisi itself—along with his conviction that he would never survive politically if he stood by and did nothing. That still does not mean it was a wise choice. President Saakashvili began a war his allies had warned him not to start, a war that they would not support, and a war that he could not win. The armed forces Georgia sent into battle were neither trained nor equipped to confront the Russian army. It is an old adage of military strategists that it is far easier to start a war than to successfully end one—as Tbilisi found it when it was subsequently forced to acquiesce to an unjust peace to survive.

The list of Georgian mistakes goes on and on. Tbilisi's handling of its relations with Russia, destined to be difficult, could have been better. Luke-warm European support for Georgia was not just a function of appease-ment, as Georgian officials sometimes suggested. It reflected real doubts about Tbilisi's democratic reforms at home and the weaknesses of Georgian diplomacy. In its desperation to somehow resolve the frozen conflicts, Geor-gian strategy oscillated between threatening to delegitimize the Russian po-sition and presence in the region to offering secret deals with Moscow over the heads of separatist leaders that accepted that presence. At times Tbilisi seemed to be pursing what Richard Nixon once called the "madman theory" of foreign policy—threatening to act irrational to get someone's attention—in this case threatening to go to war with Russia in a desperate attempt to get the attention of the West.

Georgia certainly had a difficult hand to play. Its road to the West was destined to be longer, steeper, and stonier than the path Central and Eastern Europe had followed to the European Union and NATO a decade earlier. That difficulty reflected geography and stronger Russian opposition. Geor-gia was also weaker and had much farther to go in terms of reforms. It had teetered on the edge of being a failed state before the Rose Revolution in No-vember 2003. The leaders of the Rose Revolution were saddled with frozen conflicts they had not created. Abkhazia and South Ossetia constituted an albatross around Tbilisi's neck that made its Western quest so much more difficult. Given these obstacles and hurdles, Tbilisi had little margin for error. Given the hurdles Tbilisi faced and the forces aligned against it, success required statecraft, high-caliber diplomacy, and a prudent and consistent long-term approach. Unfortunately, prudence and consistency were often in short supply in Tbilisi. It was a paradox: this government that was so pro-Western and reform oriented at home and which proudly flew the EU flag as a symbol of its pro-European orientation could work with Washington, but it could never translate those sentiments into a relationship of mutual trust and confidence in dealing with the European Union.

Third, war erupted because the existing international involvement and mechanisms on the ground in Abkhazia and South Ossetia proved woefully inadequate for keeping the peace, let alone resolving conflict effectively. This, too, represented a failure of Western political will and strategic imagination. The United Nations had a mission in Abkhazia and OSCE has a sister mission in South Ossetia. Both were established in the early 1990s to monitor ceasefires in Abkhazia and South Ossetia. Unfortunately, these efforts were never transformed into the kind of support systems that could produce an authentic peace process or support reconciliation. Instead, over time they were used by Russia as a cover for its own goals. Yet no one in the West was willing to call Moscow to account for its abuse of them. It was a failure of the international community to not resist and correct this trend. Instead, the West regularly extended the arrangements that locked in Russian domination and allowed Moscow to block any initiative it did not like.

One need only compare—or rather contrast—the level of interest and the investment of political will and resources the West made in trying to resolve conflicts in the Balkans as opposed to Georgia and the Southern Caucasus. In the former case, the international community—led by the United States and Europe—undertook a massive initiative to bring peace and stability to the region. Here was a full-fledged, UN-blessed effort at peacekeeping, conflict resolution, and political and economic reconstruction led by the United States, the European Union, and NATO. The conflicts in Georgia received a tiny fraction of such attention or resources. There the UN and OSCE missions observed but had no real authority or influence on the ground. The peacekeeping structures created were not neutral but dominated by a country that was party to the conflict and bent the rules for its own ends.

The West always spoke about the indivisibility of security across Europe and OSCE documents held that phrase up as an important principle. But in reality geography did matter to the West, and what happened in the Balkans mattered more than what happened in the wider Black Sea region. Had the international community mounted a peacekeeping effort in Georgia comparable in scope to what was done in the Balkans, or had they been willing to push for truly neutral peacekeeping forces on the ground, this war might never have happened. This represents a failure on the part of the international community. One example illustrates the point. After the war the European Union was able to quickly deploy several hundred officers to patrol and monitor the ceasefire. Had it deployed the same monitors the previous spring—as the Georgian government had urgently requested—the course of history could have been different.

Instead, over a period of over fifteen years a serious peace process failed to materialize. It is difficult to point to a single serious peace initiative from Moscow throughout this period. Tbilisi tabled a long list of initiatives, none of which ever gained traction, but several of which had real potential. On at least two occasions, it put forth far-reaching secret proposals, on South Ossetia in 2006 and on Abkhazia in 2008, that could have provided a basis for serious negotiations. Those initiatives were immediately leaked in the Russian press and killed or rejected without a hearing. Some blame undoubtedly falls on the Georgian side for the way they presented them. But the record suggests that Moscow had little interest in a resolution of these conflicts, which could have allowed Georgia to go West even faster. The same is true of their separatist allies, whose future would be iffy to say the least if these conflict zones ever opened up to an outside world.

Fourth, the West, too, needs to look in the mirror. Our mistakes and disunity also accelerated the path toward war. One factor was the recognition of Kosovo's independence despite Moscow's warnings that it would respond by taking steps to recognize Abkhazia and South Ossetia. Another was NATO's handling of Georgia and Ukraine at the Bucharest summit in the spring of 2008. These provided Moscow with a double pretext to act against Georgia. In both cases the West had no plan to shield Tbilisi from the consequences of its own policies. Many will point to Georgia's own shortcomings, or to the combustible personality of its president, as the primary reason why Tbilisi did not enjoy more trust and did not have more international or Western support. Either may be true. But our commitment to the core principles of the Charter of Paris—the right to territorial integrity, sovereignty, equal security, and to choose one's own alliance affiliation— were supposed to be the bedrock of a new post–Cold War security order. These principles were not supposed to be conditioned upon a president's personality or the effectiveness of a country's internal reforms or foreign policy. They were written to protect small states from the predatory behavior of more powerful ones. These principles needed to be upheld when challenged if that post–Cold War order was to be credible. They were not—both because the necessary trust between Georgia and the West did not exist and because many key Western powers did not care enough.

That was precisely the rub. As Georgia and Russia edged closer to war, too few people saw this coming war as a challenge to the very foundation of Europe's post–Cold War order or as Moscow's simply casting aside a key part of the rule book on how differences in Europe were to be resolved. Instead, too many saw it as a faraway conflict in a country that didn't affect them with difficult-to-pronounce names in a region they were not even sure was part of Europe or that they wanted to embrace anyway. They were worried about being dragged into a conflict on Russia's doorstep. They did not believe the key issue was standing up for a small beleaguered country but rather were afraid of disrupting their relations with Moscow unnecessarily. Why they felt this way is another issue this book will explore. Western weakness and disunity after Iraq, Europe's growing dependency on Russian energy, and sheer lack of interest are all parts of the answer.

The fifth and final thesis of this book is that the Russo-Georgian war underscores the need for rethinking and overhauling the Western strategy toward Russia and our European security architecture in general, enlargement and outreach to the European neighborhood in particular. This war shattered many of the old assumptions that had guided Western policy for the past fifteen years and that led to the enlargement of the European Union and NATO to include countries stretching from the Baltic to the Black Sea. That enlargement redrew the map of Europe for the better and produced a continent that is more democratic and more secure now than at any point in recent history. It was at the core of our attempt to build a new pan-European security architecture that also locked in a new partnership with Russia as part of building a Europe that is whole, free, and at peace.

But the same decade and a half produced a revisionist and anti-Western Russia convinced that the West sought to humiliate and take advantage of its weakness. Whether that Russia is a consequence of Western policy or of that country's own domestic dynamics and whether it would have emerged anyway is a question I will address later in this book. But the Russo-Georgian war was also in a sense a revolt against this system by a new revisionist regime in Moscow. It was no accident that one of Russian president Medvedev's first moves after the Georgian war was to table a proposal to rewrite the rules of the European security system because they are seen in Moscow as being too Euro-Atlantic and tilted to the advantage of the West.

What is nonetheless clear is that the consensus in the West behind our own strategy has also grown progressively weaker as enlargement has moved farther eastward; subsequent classes of candidate countries have proved weaker and less attractive; and Russian resentment and opposition to enlargement and the West in general has grown. Signs of enlargement fatigue were visible before the Georgian war. Today they are unmistakable. If enlargement is to remain a viable strategy, it needs to be rethought and adapted to new circumstances. It requires a new reason as to why it is needed, a practical framework for how it can be accomplished in today's very different world and, above all, a fresh approach for dealing with Moscow.

This book tells the story of why and how the war in Georgia happened. But that story must also be embedded in the broader narrative of the decline of the transatlantic relationship and the breakdown in relations between the West and Russia. To tell it, one has to look both backward and forward. We need to look back and examine the breakdown of relations across the Atlantic as well as where and why our relationship with Moscow went wrong. We must also look forward; a new policy toward Russia must recognize the reality of a more assertive Russia determined to follow its own path. The West needs a strategy that engages Russia in areas where we can find common ground yet does not betray the values we believe in or abandon those principles we are convinced constitute the ultimate foundation for peace and stability in Europe.

Such a strategy will require the United States and Europe to again come together and renew a transatlantic partnership. The Georgian war came at a time when the transatlantic relationship was at a low point. The breakdown during the past decade of the strongest Alliance in the history of the Western world also contributed to this conflict. The election of Barack Obama as president has raised hopes that the United States and Europe can come back together to meet the challenges of a new era. In addition to the major national security challenges we face in Afghanistan and Pakistan and the wider Middle East or the rise of China in East Asia, this administration needs to repair a fractured Alliance and forge a new strategy toward Europe's East.

One book inevitably cannot answer all such questions. I have decided to focus on the issues I consider most germane and about which I am most knowledgeable given my own role in the debates of the past two decades over European security and my own involvement in Georgia and the frozen conflicts. The evidence presented in these pages is like a mosaic—a collection of individual pieces of data that alone may not seem decisive but when put together start to reveal a clear pattern. I believe a clear picture of what happened on August 7 emerges. Finally, the reader deserves to know about my own involvement with Georgia before continuing with this book.

I tell this story as someone fortunate enough to know many key individuals as well as to have had a ringside seat at some of the debates described in these pages. The reason goes back some twenty years when, as a young man, I found myself in Central and Eastern Europe as Communism collapsed. I became an early proponent of NATO enlargement and was subsequently recruited by the Clinton Administration in the mid-1990s to help implement that policy. I was involved in the diplomacy that led to the first round of enlargement as well as the establishment of the 1997 NATO-Russia Founding Act and the effort to draw Russia closer to the West.

If someone had asked me then whether Georgia and Ukraine would ever be serious candidates for NATO membership, I would probably have said no. Our vision at that time was focused solely on Central and Eastern Europe from the Baltic to the western edge of the Black Sea and building a new partnership with Moscow. That changed with the Rose Revolution in Georgia in November 2003 and the Orange Revolution in Ukraine the following year. Both reinforced the sense that democratic breakthroughs were possible deeper into Eurasia and the Southern Caucasus and that we needed a strategy to respond to them. In the spring of 2004, my former State Department mentor Strobe Talbott and I had lunch with Mircea Geoana, the former ambassador to Washington and then foreign minister of Romania. Geoana made an impassioned plea that enlargement not stop at the western edge of the Black Sea with Romania and Bulgaria but be extended across the sea to countries like Georgia and Ukraine.

I sat there conflicted. I understood the case he was making, but I also knew this task would be harder than it had been in Central and Eastern Europe and could consume the next decade of my life. Was this the next logical step in the vision of democratic enlargement I had helped develop—or was it mission impossible? Several months later I was on my first flight to Tbilisi to take a look. Like many Westerners, I arrived at the airport wondering whether Georgia was capable of making the leap from the former Soviet Union to the Euro-Atlantic community. Within a day or so I had met President Mikheil Saakashvili, Prime Minister Zurab Zhvania, and Nino Burjanadze, the head of parliament. It soon became clear that the Georgians themselves had few doubts about their European destiny even if we in the West did.

Traveling around the country I discovered a young generation of pro-Western democratic-minded Georgians determined to go West regardless of their odds of success or our level of support. It reminded me of my early trips to Central and Eastern Europe or the Baltic states when many questioned whether they were capable of making the leap and ever becoming members of NATO or the European Union. I was soon captivated—and not only by the tasty food, good wine, and beautiful coastlines and mountains. It was the idea that a liberal democratic Georgia, if successful, could help open up and transform the Southern Caucasus and the wider Black Sea region—thus creating a new arc of democratic reform and stability that could positively redraw the political and strategic map of Europe and Eurasia for the better.

How could we not support them? And how could I, as one of the early architects of the strategy of democratic enlargement, not try to help out? I was not the only one who was rethinking. A large part of what was referred to as the "mafia"—a loose collection of American and European think tanks, prodemocracy NGOs, journalists, and other veterans of the enlargement debate of the 1990s—now found itself gathering at conferences and workshops in Tbilisi and neighboring capitals debating how the West should respond. To many of us it seemed the logical follow-on project to the anchoring of Central and Eastern Europe to the West.

In the following years I wrote several articles and edited several books about Western strategy toward the wider Black Sea region. I helped spearhead a program at the German Marshall Fund of the United States bringing senior Americans and Europeans to Georgia to see the frozen conflicts in Abkhazia and South Ossetia firsthand. I got to know many of the key leadership figures in Georgia and what they thought—and feared. This work and these trips allowed me to better understand what made that country tick, what was really happening on the ground in Abkhazia and South Ossetia, as well as providing me, through my old connections with Washington and European governments, with a ringside seat on Western policy debates.

To be sure, this was Georgia and the Southern Caucasus, not Prague or Tallinn. It was rough-and-tumble, chaotic, and occasionally violent. Democratic roots were still shallow and nationalism ran deep. Hyperbole was ingrained in the local culture. U.S. ambassador John Tefft told first-time visitors that his first rule of Georgian politics was that everyone exaggerated by 25 percent—and sometimes more. Strategy sessions with the president and key advisors sometimes started around midnight and lasted until the wee hours of the morning.

There was a bit of a Wild West atmosphere as well as a cold war battle taking place between Georgia and Russia, complete with tit-for-tat bombings and assassinations. We called it wilder as opposed to wider Europe— the politically correct phrase Europeans often used to describe countries east of NATO and EU borders. The bar at the Tbilisi Marriott was like a scene out of a Rebecca West novel, teeming with Georgian officials, diplomats, and intelligence officials drinking and exchanging gossip until all hours of the morning.

Some will suggest that my involvement in Georgia and these issues makes me a partial observer of the events I describe in the pages that follow.

I believe this experience has given me firsthand insight into what happened and why. That is what I try to describe here. Fortune has provided me with a unique perspective on the events that led to this war and that make it a story worth telling. In any case, that is a judgment I leave for you, the reader, to decide yourself.

CHAPTER 1

THE DECISION

Georgian president Mikheil Saakashvili put down the phone. It was 2335 the night of August 7 in Tbilisi. He had just given the order for his armed forces to attack what his intelligence had reported to be a column of Russian forces moving from the small South Ossetian town of Java just south of the Russian-Georgian border toward the city of Tskhinvali, the capital of the small separatist enclave, as well as Russian forces coming through the Roki Tunnel on the Russian-Georgian border into Georgia. He had also ordered his armed forces to suppress the shelling by South Ossetian militia of Georgian villages in that province that were under the control of Georgian peacekeepers and police. That shelling had been taking place on and off for the previous week, but it had resumed and escalated that evening in spite of a unilateral ceasefire he had ordered. Georgian civilians and peacekeepers had been wounded and killed. He paused, picked up the phone again, and gave a third command: "Minimize civilian casualties."

Saakashvili had decided to go to war. It was a momentous decision, one that the EU's Independent International Fact-Finding Mission on the Conflict in Georgia (IIFFMCG), headed by Ambassador Heidi Tagliavini, would subsequently judge to be unjustifiable under international law. It would not only leave the future of Georgia hanging in the balance but would push Russia and the West to the brink of their biggest crisis since Communism's collapse twenty years earlier. The previous evening Georgia had intercepted cell phone conversations of South Ossetian border guards discussing the fact that Russian border guards had taken control of the Roki Tunnel just south of the Georgian-Russian border and that a Russian military column had passed through around 0400. Interior Minister Ivane "Vano" Merabishvili was in a late-night meeting when the news came through and immediately informed Saakashvili. How large a column had been involved was unclear. The Roki Tunnel is almost four kilometers long, and one of the border guards had claimed that "the tunnel is full."[1] Georgian intelligence had a source on the ground at the south end of the tunnel that claimed to have seen "150 pieces of armor," but the source was not a trained expert in military reconnaissance.

The intercepts also mentioned the name of the colonel who commanded the 693rd regiment of the Nineteenth division of the Russian Fifty-eighth army. That unit was not authorized to be in Georgia. Subsequent reports confirmed that elements of the 135th regiment were also there. Georgian intelligence estimated that a Russian infantry battalion may have been involved—i.e., about 550 men—but no one knew for sure.[2] Around the same time, Georgian peacekeepers observed Russian forces moving south along the bypass road from Java in the direction of Tskhinvali. Georgian peacekeeping commander Brigadier General Mamuka Kurashvili phoned his Russian counterpart and the overall commander of the peace-keeping forces, Major General Marat Kulakhmetov, to ask what those forces were doing, adding that there appeared to be heavy artillery. The Russian side promised to look into it and call back. They never did. It was another worrying sign that Moscow was up to something.[3]

Georgia had stepped up its reconnaissance efforts throughout the day as Tbilisi scrambled to figure out where these forces had gone and what they were up to. The Georgian military had many deficiencies, but Tbilisi had invested in long-distance reconnaissance capabilities, including thermal night vision equipment. Saakashvili's final order to go to war was triggered by several factors—the lack of any Ossetian or Russian response to his unilateral ceasefire, the renewed shelling of Georgian villages that evening, and the movement of Russian forces the previous evening, as well as fresh intelligence indicating that additional Russian forces were poised to move through the Roki Tunnel after dark. But the final straw was a Georgian reconnaissance unit's visual confirmation of a military column moving from Java toward Tskhinvali. Based on the numbers and type of equipment in the column—tanks, armored personnel carriers, and artillery—the Georgians concluded that these forces were neither South Ossetian nor North Caucasian "volunteers." It was the Russian army. It confirmed Saakashvili's suspicion that his country was being invaded by Moscow and triggered his late-night decision to fight back.

The Russian Fifty-eighth Army, Moscow's main military force in the Northern Caucasus, was known for its brutality in the Chechen wars. In the weeks prior to the invasion it had conducted major summer exercises called "Kavkaz 2008" in North Ossetia, north of the Georgian border. The official scenario for that exercise was the "detecting, blocking, and eliminating of terrorist groups" in the local mountainous terrain. The force included some 700 combat vehicles, fighter aircraft, and part of the Black Sea fleet. Such a force was hardly of great utility in fighting terrorists in the mountains, but it was ideal for a conventional invasion of a neighbor. In fact, this exercise was a trial run for the invasion about to take place. The exercise scenario involved Russian forces having to intervene in a fictitious breakaway former Soviet republic to protect Russian peacekeepers and citizens. It was de facto a war game to invade Georgia. Russian soldiers participating in the exercise had even been given briefing materials in advance that said, "Soldier, know your potential enemy!" The enemy those materials identified was Georgia.[4]

Following the completion of the exercises, many of the units lingered in place rather than returning to their home bases. A sizeable Russian force was gathered north of the Roki Tunnel. By the evening of August 5, nearly 12,000 soldiers,[5] along with their armor and artillery, were deployed and ready to strike Georgia. Three days earlier, on August 2, Nikolai Pankov, the Russian deputy minister of defense, and Anatoly Khrulyev, the deputy chief of intelligence and commander in chief of the Fifty-eighth Army, had visited South Ossetia to meet with the South Ossetian leadership as well as the commander of the Russian and North Ossetian peacekeeping forces—reportedly to finalize the plan of action for these units.

Moscow has officially claimed that its armed forces only entered Georgia on the afternoon of August 8 at 1400. That claim, however, is simply not credible. Exactly when regular Russian units began infiltrating across the border and how many had already entered South Ossetian territory illegally before the evening of August 7 is still unclear and is passionately disputed. Although both ends of the Roki Tunnel are on Georgian territory, Moscow controlled it and had repeatedly refused to allow international monitors to observe who was passing through. Moscow would claim that its forces moved through the tunnel only on the afternoon of August 8. Andrei Illiaronov, in an exhaustive study of Russia's war preparations, has argued that some 1,200 Russian soldiers along with medical and communication units were already in South Ossetia illegally by August 7, with another 12,000 troops poised "to be able to immediately cross the border to provide assistance to the peacekeepers in South Ossetia," as one official put it.[6] Subsequent sources and press reports during and after the war by journalists in South Ossetia also suggest that elements of the 135th and 693rd Regiments of the Fifty-eighth Army and the Twenty-second Special Forces Brigade as well as several tank units had already moved into South Ossetia between August 2 and the evening of August 7—and some of those units started fighting the Georgians early on August 8 when they entered Tskhinvali.[7]

This was in addition to the North Ossetian, Chechen, and Cossack "volunteers" who had been officially mobilized by Moscow and registered by Russian military authorities before they were sent across the border, where a number of them were assigned to the North Ossetian peacekeeping battalion starting on August 3.[8] They were, however, anything but peaceful. They were ideal for ethnic cleansing, which is what they would soon be used for. After the war was over, the Russian military paper *Krasnaya Zvezda* carried an article about a wounded Russian captain from the 135th Motorized Rifle Regiment who admitted that his battalion was already in South Ossetia on August 7 and was sent to Tskhinvali on August 8, where he was subsequently wounded in the fighting. As always, it is the cover-up that is most telling. After the article attracted too much attention, the text was first changed, then the officer was re-interviewed and suggested that his forces had only entered Georgia on August 8; finally he disappeared from public view.[9]

While Georgia had de facto lost control over large swaths of South Ossetia after the initial fighting in the early 1990s, this was still officially sovereign Georgian territory. Russia was officially allowed a limited contingent of "peacekeepers" on Georgian soil in the conflict zones of South Ossetia and Abkhazia in accordance with ceasefire agreements reached with the Organization for Security and Co-operation in Europe (OSCE) and the United

Nations in the early 1990s. However, the nature and equipment of these troops was required to be limited in accord with a peacekeeping mission. They were supposed to be part of a separate chain of command. Any rotation or reinforcement of such forces was supposed to be announced thirty days in advance. In reality, Moscow had long flouted these rules. These Russian troop reinforcements and movements were in violation of the existing agreements and therefore illegal.

Saakashvili had been receiving intelligence throughout the day on August 7 about Russian and other units gathering both north of the Roki Tunnel and around the Ugardanta military base outside of Java in South Ossetia. That base was supposed to have been disbanded years earlier, but Moscow had instead renovated it over the previous year, and it was now capable of holding and staging much larger forces. That, too, hardly seemed a coincidence. Already in mid-July, Georgian intelligence had received reports from friendly Western services of additional Russian fighter aircraft being moved to North Ossetia. On the morning of August 7, they received a report that on August 4 or 5 Moscow had pre-deployed additional military aircraft from the Ivanovo air base outside Moscow to the Mozdok air base in North Ossetia. That deployment included an airborne command plane capable of directing an air war against Georgia called the Russian A–50.[10] The Georgians were also receiving information that part of the Russian Black Sea fleet based in Sevastopol had left port several days earlier and was preparing for a major operation. It, too, had prepositioned itself for this invasion.

It was a chaotic day, and the Georgians were trying to comprehend exactly what was happening on their northern border—and why. The combination of ground forces gathering and airpower being moved into position looked increasingly ominous. The big question in Saakashvili's mind was whether the Russian forces gathering up north would remain there or would start to march south toward the city of Tskhinvali. And if they moved south, was their goal to take those villages and the territory Georgia controlled around Tskhinvali or much more? Was this just another attempt to pressure Saakashvili or was Russia actually preparing to invade Georgia? When Saakashvili tried to place a call to Russian president Dmitry Medvedev to discuss what was happening, he was turned down.

As the signs of Russian forces moving into South Ossetia multiplied, the Georgian president faced a choice fraught with peril—either to let it happen or to try to fight back. His Western allies had repeatedly urged him not to get into a fight with Russia—no matter what. But in the path of those Russian forces lay the Georgian villages in the Didi Liakhvi valley as well as the Tbilisi-supported alternative South Ossetian government in the village of Kurta. Those villages not only contained thousands of Georgian citizens that Tbilisi was pledged to protect, but Kurta also was the heart and soul of Georgia's own strategy to win over the hearts and minds of South Ossetians through "soft power." If Russian forces swept through those villages, it could lead to another wave of bloody ethnic cleansing and shatter Tbilisi's strategy for resolving the South Ossetian conflict peacefully and on its terms. Such an outcome, Saakashvili believed, would be such a political debacle that his government would not survive.

But Saakashvili also had bigger worries. He had always believed—and openly told visitors, including this author—that he did not think Moscow would ever make a military move just for South Ossetia. The tiny enclave was simply not worth it. If Moscow moved into South Ossetia, he assumed it would be a precursor for a broader assault with the goal of taking Tbilisi. South of Tskhinvali lay flat and open terrain from there to Tbilisi. So the question in his mind was: Would those Russian forces stop in the South Ossetian capital or simply continue on to the Georgian capital and go after him? It was hardly a secret that the Kremlin was trying to oust him. Kremlin pundits had hinted darkly on television about assassinating him.[11] Moscow had taken a variety of political and economic steps, both overt and covert, to try to destabilize his government. Putin had personally warned Saakashvili on more than one occasion that his pro-Western course would have consequences.

None of the threats had intimidated Saakashvili—up to this point. But he was jumpy. Georgian-Russian relations had been increasingly on the edge of conflict since the spring, when Moscow, in the wake of Kosovo independence in February and the NATO Bucharest summit, had increased the pressure by taking steps that amounted to a creeping annexation of the two separatist enclaves. Moscow had also been ramping up its own illegal military preparations, using the cover of its alleged peacekeeping role to illegally modernize infrastructure, deploy additional forces, and further arm separatist forces who were making preparations that would subsequently facilitate an invasion. Most of that effort had been focused in Abkhazia, where tension had intensified throughout the spring and summer. At times, Moscow even seemed to want to flaunt its breaking of the rules—for example, making no effort to hide from the Western media the illegal entry of Russian troops and armor into the separatist province in the early summer.

In Georgia's eyes, what the Russians were planning was obvious. Moscow was trying to de facto annex these two disputed enclaves bit by bit in slow motion—testing to see if the West would protest and daring Tbilisi to try to stop them. The Western policy response had been, as far as Georgia was concerned, limp and half-hearted. Tbilisi's allies urged restraint on both sides and repeatedly warned Saakashvili not to get into a fight with Russia but instead to rely on diplomacy to de-escalate the situation. But diplomacy was not working or stopping what Russia was doing on the ground to turn the status quo against Tbilisi. Georgia had tried its own secret diplomacy with Russia but failed to make any headway as well. In Tbilisi's view, diplomacy was failing and Moscow was consolidating a new partition of the country that would render nominal Georgian territorial integrity theoretical and meaningless. In doing so, it was breaking almost every rule in the book in full view of the international community. And it was simultaneously building its military option—its hammer to crush Georgia if Tbilisi dared to move to stop it.

August was known as the shooting season in the Southern Caucasus. It was something of a ritual for there to be final exchanges of artillery fire between South Ossetian and Georgian forces in late July or early August before the summer break settled in. The normal pattern during the previous summers had been that the South Ossetians would start shelling, the Georgians would retaliate, and then, after a day or two of exchanges, one side, usually but not always Georgia, would back down. One exception had been in 2004, when the Georgian side had in fact escalated and fought back, only to suffer significant casualties. It was a lesson that Tbilisi did not forget and it became much more cautious in subsequent years. In the summer of 2007, two Russian aircraft had bombed a Georgian radar site near the town of Tsitelubani on the border of the South Ossetian conflict zone. The missile failed to fully detonate, thus allowing Western experts to confirm its Russian origins in spite of Moscow's denials.

When the shooting began between South Ossetian and Georgian forces on July 29, 2008, many observers—both inside and outside Georgia itself—

initially dismissed it as more of the same. It soon became clear, however, that this summer's pattern of fighting was more worrying. When South Ossetian paramilitary forces opened fire on Georgian positions and villages on July 29, those barrages were more systematic and lethal than in previous summers. They lasted through the day and the evening and included 100 mm and 120 mm artillery—heavier weapons officially banned from the zone that had never been used previously in the conflict zone and were many times more powerful than any used before. These new weapons could have only been supplied to the South Ossetians through Russia. On August 4 the Russian peacekeeping commander, Major General Marat Kulakhmetov, confirmed that large-caliber artillery banned under the existing agreements had been used against Georgian villages. Although he refused to identify the perpetrators, the Georgians knew who was behind the attacks. They had intercepted phone calls showing that Russian and North Ossetian peace-keepers were collaborating with local South Ossetian militia to target Georgians and then hide the evidence.[12]

The use of heavier weapons predictably led to heavier casualties. An OSCE spot report from August 4 noted that the fighting since August 1 was the most serious since 2004. Between July 29 and August 7, six Georgian police officers, eleven peacekeepers, and fourteen civilians were wounded. Two Georgia peacekeepers were killed in action, and two later died of their wounds. Entire villages on both sides were essentially shut down, cut off, and in some cases destroyed. The Georgians fought back and inflicted their own casualties on the South Ossetian side. For example, six South Ossetian militiamen were killed in action the evening of August 1 (four by sniper fire) and thirteen were wounded (seven reportedly the result of sniper fire as well). Again, the Russian-led Joint Peacekeeping Force (JPKF) did little to try to stop such incidents even though they often involved attacks on Georgian peacekeepers nominally under the control of the Russian commander and for whose safety he was responsible.

The South Ossetian separatists were employing their own version of a tactic the world knows well from the Middle East, the use of human shields. In the Middle East, human shields are often used by Palestinian insurgents to protect themselves against Israeli attack, or to goad the Israelis into killing civilians, thus inviting international condemnation. In this case, however, South Ossetian forces used Russian and North Ossetian peacekeepers and their positions as shields to accomplish the same objective. They fired upon Georgian targets from positions adjacent to, behind, or even within a Russian peacekeeping post. In doing so, they were daring the Georgians to retaliate and run the risk of killing Russian soldiers—thus sparking a broader conflict with Moscow. It was another example of how the peacekeeping arrangements on the ground had become a farce.

It was difficult to believe that such attacks were not orchestrated with Moscow's support and blessing. The South Ossetian government, and in particular the chain of command on defense and security issues, was dominated by Russian intelligence officers. A dozen key members of the separatist government in Tskhinvali were Russian—including the prime minister and the defense and interior ministers, as well as the head of the national security council. The South Ossetian leader Eduard Koikoty had been installed by Moscow and the Kremlin had a direct line to his office in Tskhinvali. Russia's control over this leadership and what happened on the ground was near total—with the only question being exactly who in Moscow or elsewhere in Russia was actually calling the shots.[13]

On August 4, Georgian deputy foreign minister Grigol Vashadze got into his car and managed to sneak into the Georgian village of Nuli in South Ossetia. He found it nearly totally destroyed. He returned to Tbilisi and proposed taking the diplomatic corps to see for themselves what was happening. The next day, August 5, the Georgian government invited the entire diplomatic corps in Tbilisi to tour the region. The office of the European Union's special envoy to the region, Peter Semneby, reported back to Brussels that there was indeed evidence of mortar fire by the South Ossetians against Georgian positions but that both sides seemed to be jockeying to gain advantage. "At this stage," the EU report concluded, "it does not look that [sic] the sides are interested in a large-scale military conflict but a small local conflict with fatalities is highly likely." The view of the OSCE mission on the ground was more pessimistic and accurate. It sent in one report after another during that week that amounted to a diplomatic SOS—a distress signal warning that the situation on the ground was becoming dangerous. But no one was paying attention. The attention of the world was focused on the opening of the Olympics in Beijing on August 7—or on the approaching summer holidays.

It was not just the intensity of the shooting, however, that gave Tbilisi cause for alarm. Koikoty's separatist government had taken a series of steps that suggested they were putting South Ossetia on a war footing. On August 2 South Ossetia had announced an evacuation of women and children from the South Ossetian capital. In the run-up to the outbreak of hostilities, the overwhelming majority of the population living on what was to become the battlefield were evacuated to North Ossetia. The media coverage on state-run South Ossetian and Russian TV also become increasingly belligerent over the course of the week, suggesting an impending conflict with Georgia. Speaking to the Russian and local media on the morning of August 7, Koikoty issued a warning that his forces would "clean out" local Georgian forces and villages if the Georgian forces did not withdraw.[14] Nearly fifty Russian journalists representing mainstream TV, radio, and newspapers also arrived in Tskhinvali between August 2 and 6.[15] This was not the norm.

Clearly something was up. And it was all happening while much of the Georgian leadership, thinking the worst of the crisis of the spring and summer had passed, had left the country on vacation. The Georgian defense minister was out of the country, and his two key deputies were preparing to go on leave as well. Georgia's armed forces were at their lowest level of readiness because commanders had finally been allowed to grant units leave after months of mobilization. Saakashvili himself had gone off to a "fat farm" in Italy to fight a weight problem and enjoy a short holiday with his family before heading to Beijing for the opening of the Olympics. Sitting in his hotel room in Italy, his alarm was sparked as he was channel surfing and started watching Russian TV coverage of events in South Ossetia. He was taken aback by the belligerence of the Russian media and became suspicious. He rushed back to Tbilisi in early August to take charge of the situation.

It was not unprecedented for Moscow to use Abkhaz or South Ossetian separatists as pawns to keep Tbilisi off balance. That was a central part of the Russian strategy to keep Georgia guessing and to constantly remind the outside world how unstable this country was, thus undercutting its desire to be embraced by the West. It was also designed to goad or provoke Tbilisi into taking military action that would lead to violence on the ground and reinforce Saakashvili's image as an impetuous, trigger-happy leader. Throughout the spring and summer, tension had been focused on Abkhazia—where Moscow and Georgia had come to the brink of war—with the Russian media suggesting on more than one occasion that war was imminent. But the crisis had seemed to pass in mid-July.

Sitting in his chancellery on August 7, Saakashvili realized that he had relaxed Georgia's guard too soon. He was now in a quandary, confronting a decision he both feared yet had anticipated he might face one day. The conflicts in Abkhazia and South Ossetia were a Damocles' sword hanging above his head. While many well-meaning advisors and Westerners had suggested he downplay the importance of the frozen conflicts and blame their de facto loss on his predecessors, he believed passionately in Georgia's territorial integrity and had made the recovery of these separatist provinces a key part of his political manifesto. He did not believe he could survive as president of Georgia if he failed to defend the Georgian citizens in those areas he still controlled or if he lost these provinces once and for all. Living with the status quo was bad enough. But since the beginning of the year, Moscow had been systematically turning the status quo against him. Saakashvili had tried to get his Western allies to push back against Moscow and to become more involved on the ground to halt that dynamic—but without success.

Perhaps better than anyone else, Saakashvili knew how much Moscow, and Vladimir Putin in particular, hated him and what he represented in the region. After all, he had been on the receiving end of a string of increasingly ominous and personal threats from Russia and from Putin personally about what Moscow would do to him and to Georgia if he did not change course. While he was accustomed to Moscow's rough tactics, he was nevertheless taken aback by what he now saw unfolding before his eyes. There was a big difference between using South Ossetian separatist forces to shell Georgian villages and peacekeepers and the infiltration and a possible invasion of his country by the Russian army. Had Putin finally decided to make good on his threat of regime change—and was Russia preparing to march on Tbilisi with the goal of toppling his government? Or was this precisely the kind of trap his Western friends and allies had repeatedly warned him to avoid?

Saakashvili had few illusions about the West's coming to Georgia's assistance militarily if he got into a fight with the Russians. No one knew better than he did how often and how clearly Washington had warned him the U.S. cavalry would not be coming over the hill to save him. Speculation over whether Washington had given Tbilisi some kind of green light misses the point. No senior Georgian official has actually ever suggested that Washington did so. On the contrary, they all admit that warnings had been given repeatedly by senior American and European officials. But they also point out that Tbilisi had warned in return that it, too, had red lines and that if Moscow crossed them, no Georgian government could simply stand by and passively watch the country be dismembered.

The problem was a different one. The two sides were talking past each other. The West's bottom line was for Tbilisi not to get into a fight with Russia—period. Georgia's was that it could not stand back and lose the provinces without doing something. They were not the same thing. Even though he only controlled a small sliver of Abkhaz territory and less than half of South Ossetia, Saakashvili had repeatedly told his American and European counterparts that Abkhazia and South Ossetia were existential issues for him and that there could come a point where he would have to act in order to avoid losing them once and for all. This was the part of the Georgian message that the West did not want to hear or take into account. Its response was always the same: don't get into a fight you can only lose. That was the gap between Georgia and the West that Moscow was now exposing and exploiting—and where it was laying its trap.

The moment of decision had arrived, and the Georgian leader made his choice. He went against that advice and decided that the threat to Georgian citizens in South Ossetia and to his country's territorial integrity as well as his political survival as president required him to try to fight against what he saw playing out in front of him. There was little doubt in his mind—based on the intelligence he had on that fateful evening as well as his years of dealing with Moscow—that Russia was invading his country. Rather than run the risk that the Russians and their separatist allies would overrun Georgian villages and outposts under his control and possibly march on Tbilisi, Saakashvili opted to preempt what he thought was Russia's impending move. He believed his oath as president to defend his citizens and his country's territorial integrity required him to do nothing less.

That decision was made neither in isolation nor without consultation. While often seen as an autocrat, Saakashvili had his own way of reaching out to people and a loose style of collective decision making. The Georgian president had been talking with his national security team throughout the day. At 1300 he convened a meeting of the Georgian National Security Council (NSC) to discuss the rapidly deteriorating situation. In attendance were Interior Minister Vano Merabishvili, Defense Minister David Kezerashvili, head of the presidential administration Zurab Adeishvili, Tbilisi mayor Gigi Ugulava, and National Security Council secretary Alexander Lomaia. Several of Saakashvili's key lieutenants were out of the country on vacation, such as chairman of the parliament David Bakradze, deputy head of the parliament's Committee of Security and Defense Nick Rurua, and Deputy Foreign Minister Giga Bokeria. Foreign Minister Ekaterine Tkeshelashvili and intelligence chief Gela Bezhuashvili were absent as well.

The meeting was held at a presidential guest house in Tseravani, a town located halfway between Tbilisi and Gori, where Saakashvili had been visiting wounded Georgian police and peacekeepers in the hospital. These men had sat around the table and debated many times what they should or should not do if Russia ever moved against their country militarily. Now it was for real. The meeting lasted for one hour. Interior Minister Merabishvili started by briefing on the previous evening's intelligence intercepts of Russian forces taking control of and then moving forces through the Roki Tunnel. No one knew for sure how many Russian forces might have entered, but the Georgian estimate was a battalion.[16]

Saakashvili asked the group whether they thought the combination of these new factors—the use of heavier weaponry in the conflict zone, the buildup of Russian ground and airpower, reports of Russian forces already deployed in South Ossetia, the inflow of North Caucasian "volunteers," and the news of Russian troops taking control of and coming through the Roki Tunnel the previous evening—constituted Moscow's crossing a new red line in its efforts to intimidate and threaten Georgia. Was Tbilisi now confronted with a qualitatively different situation than in the past? he asked. At what point did a sovereign state have to act to defend itself?

Every council member in the room agreed that Russia had crossed that red line and that Georgia faced a qualitatively new situation. They all believed Georgia was being invaded in a kind of slow-motion, incremental way. The question was what to do about it. At the end of the meeting, Defense Minister Kezerashvili received a phone call and turned pale. He announced to the group that another Georgian peacekeeper had been killed. Saakashvili gave the order to deploy Georgian troops to the edge of the conflict zone in case they were needed—and at 1430 the Ministry of Defense issued a public mobilization order. Around 1800 those forces were ordered to deploy to the edge of South Ossetia and the conflict zone.

But Moscow had timed the invasion well. Georgia was unprepared for a major operation in South Ossetia. In spite of the mobilization of the Georgian army that spring and the concern over a possible face-off with Russia, Tbilisi's attention had been almost entirely focused on Abkhazia. For reasons we will explore later, there were no up-to-date contingency plans for the Georgian army to fight in South Ossetia. After having been on high alert since the spring, many Georgian military units had been allowed to drop their readiness level and soldiers had been released to work their fields before the fall harvest or else to take summer holidays. Tbilisi's armed forces were actually at their lowest level of readiness that first week of August. Deputy Defense Minister Batu Kutelia was leaving on vacation with his water skis in the back of his car when he received a phone call ordering him to head to Gori and plan for war. Plans for the operation had to be drawn up within twenty-four hours. When the war broke out, a significant portion of Tbilisi's modest tank force was in the shop for a long-planned upgrade and was unavailable for the fight.

Georgia's armed forces were also in the wrong place for the fight. The elite First Brigade was normally headquartered in Gori—some fifteen miles from the South Ossetian capital of Tskhinvali—but it was now deployed in Iraq. It would be called back after hostilities started but too late to play a major role in the war. Georgia's Fourth Infantry Brigade was in predeployment training for Iraq. Washington had initially asked for Georgia's Second Brigade, deployed in Senaki near the border of Abkhazia, but Tbilisi had refused given the role that brigade played in Georgia's own defense plans and because of growing tensions in that area. The two sides had settled on the Fourth as a compromise.

On the evening of August 6 that brigade's commander, Major Grigori Kalandadze, was at a *supra*—a traditional Georgian feast bringing together friends and family around a table loaded with food and wine complete with toasts, heavy drinking, and dancing into the wee hours of the morning, often accompanied by a hangover the next day.[17] The next day Kalandadze was ordered to pull his brigade out of its U.S.-led pre-deployment training for Iraq and move to Gori to prepare to fight the Russians. In less than twelve hours he had to reorganize his brigade for a possible operation in South Ossetia: call back soldiers and commanders who were or had been on leave; replace his soldiers' newly purchased American M4 carbines, for which ammunition was still scarce, with older Russian-made Kalashnikovs, for which ammunition was plentiful; and then move his brigade to Gori by road and rail. Three days later, Kalandadze was wounded, two of his battalion commanders were dead, and his Fourth Brigade was withdrawing from Tskhinvali in the face of a fierce onslaught of Russian armor and air power. However one assesses the Georgian military's performance, this was not a country or an army prepared for an offensive military operation in South Ossetia, as Moscow's propaganda would later claim.

In parallel to convening his NSC, Saakashvili initiated a last-ditch diplomatic mission to extend an olive branch that could still prevent a war. On August 7, he dispatched another key aide, special envoy and minister for reintegration Temuri Yakobashvili, to Tskhinvali to try to establish direct contact on the ground with both Russian and South Ossetian authorities to head off what was starting to look like a looming conflict. Yakobashvili now found himself in a car headed to a potential war zone in a last-ditch effort to prevent an outbreak of hostilities. His mission was to get in touch with either senior Russian or local South Ossetian authorities, get a sense of what was happening on the ground, see if there was a way to de-escalate the situation, and to report back as soon as possible.

Yakobashvili had already been in touch with his Russian and South Ossetian counterparts. The South Ossetian authorities flat out refused to meet with him. His Russian Foreign Ministry counterpart, Yuri Popov, had initially agreed to meet him in Tskhinvali. But when he called to finalize a meeting place, Popov told him he was stranded in nearby Gori with a flat tire and unable to come. When Yakobashvili asked whether he had a spare, he was told that was flat, too. The Russian hardly seemed in a hurry or keen to discuss ways to de-escalate the crisis. Yakobashvili headed to the

South Ossetian capital nevertheless. The one Russian who did agree to meet him was Major General Kulakhmetov, the head of the JPKF. In that position, Kulakhmetov had overall command of the Russian, Georgian, and Ossetian units who were supposed to work together to maintain peace on the ground. Western visitors as well as the Georgians had generally found him to be an honest professional.

Yakobashvili was met at the administrative border with South Ossetia by Russian peacekeepers who escorted him to the headquarters of the Joint Peacekeeping Force on the northern side of Tskhinvali. The JPKF had two headquarters—one referred to as "Nizhniy Gorodok" in the northern part of Tskhinvali where the commander had his office and a second one at "Verkhniy Gorodok" in the southwestern part of town. Yakobashvili was headed to the main headquarters at Nizhniy Gorodok. At the border crossing into Tskhinvali, there had stood until recently a huge billboard of Putin. Although this was ostensibly sovereign Georgian territory, the locals had put up this large picture with the slogan "Putin—Our President" within sight of the Georgian checkpoint. It was a less than subtle way of signaling that while Georgia's territorial integrity might still exist on paper, there was little doubt who really ran the place. The poster was taken down after Medvedev succeeded Putin as Russian President.

As he entered Tskhinvali, Yakobashvili was struck by how deserted the streets were. It looked like a ghost town, he thought to himself. An estimated 3,000 to 4,000 people were left in the city after the evacuation conducted by the South Ossetians.[18] Yakobashvili entered the main headquarters and sat down with the general *à deux* in his private office. Kulakhmetov turned on a scrambling device to ensure that no one could listen to their conversation. The two men openly discussed the deteriorating situation. According to Yakobashvili, Kulakhmetov admitted that some of the attacks on Georgian forces were taking place from positions adjacent to or even within his positions—and that the South Ossetians were using the Russian peacekeepers as human shields. He said that there was nothing he could do about it as he could no longer control the South Ossetian forces.

Yakobashvili was taken aback. What was the general trying to tell him? Was he saying that he had simply lost control of the situation, including the forces ostensibly under his command, or that such actions were being directed by a higher Russian authority? It was, in either case, bad news. Yakobashvili was convinced that the Russian general was trying to keep the situation from spinning out of control. But it was also clear that Kulakhmetov was no longer calling the shots on the ground. Before leaving, he asked the general for his advice on how to keep the situation from deteriorating further. Kulakhmetov responded that the only way out was for the Georgian side to declare a unilateral ceasefire—"and to keep it as long as you can." He suggested that the ceasefire be for at least a day and preferably longer. Yakobashvili responded: "I can't promise but I will try. Let me report back to my boss and we will make a decision."

Saakashvili was his usual impatient self. During the NSC meeting, he had tried to call Yakobashvili three times on his cell phone while the latter was in Tskhinvali. After Yakobashvili left the South Ossetian capital, he immediately phoned the Georgian president to brief him on his discussions. Saakashvili promptly agreed to the idea of a ceasefire. As soon as he arrived back in Tbilisi, Yakobashvili gave a press conference and announced the ceasefire at 1840. It was the only way the Georgians had to communicate their offer to the South Ossetians, who were rejecting all attempts at communication, let alone mediation. Saakashvili himself reaffirmed Georgia's ceasefire in his own press conference a half hour later. At the same time, the Georgian forces were deploying to the edge of the conflict zone, waiting.

Around 2100 Yakobashvili went to visit Saakashvili in the chancellery. Saakashvili wanted to again go over all the details of his trip to Tskhinvali that afternoon. He was still trying to discern Russian motives. "You understand how much it matters," he told Yakobashvili. "Every detail matters." The president grilled Yakobashvili on the mood and disposition of his interlocutors, asking whether he thought they were lying or telling the truth. He was trying to avoid a confrontation with Russia and looking for a way to back down—hoping that if the ceasefire held, the fighting could then be blamed on the local South Ossetians. But the big question was whether the ceasefire *would* hold—and what *were* those additional Russian forces now on Georgian territory going to do? And if they moved, were they headed to Tskhinvali—or Tbilisi?

The telephone in the chancellery rang again shortly after 2030. It was Minister of Interior Merabishvili calling to say that the shelling of Georgian villages had resumed. "Do not respond," Saakashvili told him. Shortly after 2230 Defense Minister Kezerashvili called to say that additional Georgian villages were again being shelled, that the Georgian peacekeeping positions had been attacked, and that there were Georgian soldiers killed and wounded. Unless Georgian forces were allowed to return fire, he told the president, they could not evacuate the wounded, and there would in all likelihood be further deaths. Saakashvili took a deep breath and again ordered, "Do not respond."

Around 2330 the phone rang again. This time, according to Yakobashvili, Saakashvili turned pale. Not only were there reports of renewed shelling against a number of Georgian villages and positions, but Tbilisi also had intelligence reports from earlier in the day that additional Russian forces had moved into the Roki Tunnel and had orders to cross over that evening. And Georgian reconnaissance scouts were reporting a sighting of what they believed was a Russian army column moving from Java south toward Tskhinvali. The Georgians suspected that these were the Russian forces that had come through the Roki Tunnel the previous evening and headed to the Russian base outside of Java. There was no longer any doubt in Saakashvili's mind that an invasion was coming. He phoned Georgian chief of staff Zaza Gogava and gave two orders: stop the Russian columns heading toward Tskhinvali and coming through the Roki Tunnel, and suppress the Ossetian shelling of Georgian positions and villages. After hanging up, he paused, then picked up the phone again and added a third order: "Minimize civilian casualties." It was 2335.[19]

Saakashvili then looked at Yakobashvili and said, "It has started. Do you think we will end up as Israelis or Palestinians?" It summed up his hope that little Georgia could somehow prevail in a David versus Goliath fight with Russia—and that if it failed, his country would be partitioned and subjugated as it had been in the early 1920s. At 0144 a new intelligence report arrived in the president's office claiming that the first units of the Fifty-eighth Army had already been sighted entering Tskhinvali.[20] It was an unnerving piece of intelligence to receive at that hour as the battle for the South Ossetian capital was beginning. It reinforced the Georgian conviction that a larger Russian invasion was already in the works.

To this day, controversy swirls around Saakashvili's decision to fight. While many Western countries subsequently expressed their solidarity with

Georgia, not a single country in the West has defended the Georgian leader's decision to go to war. Even Georgia's closest ally, the United States, while calling the Russian invasion "premeditated," has also termed his decision to stand and fight a "mistake."[21] Many see it as proof of the Georgian president's impulsive or hot-headed nature, and an indication of why the West was right to be careful in embracing him lest he pull it too into a conflict with Moscow. Moscow of course claims that Georgia committed an act of military aggression and attempted genocide against South Ossetia to which it responded in defense of both Russian peacekeepers and citizens there.[22]

Why did Saakashvili do it? A close look at the record of the Georgian decision-making process that day leads to several key conclusions. First, there was little doubt in his mind when Saakashvili made the decision to go to war that Russian forces were entering his country. Moscow had been engaged in a significant military build-up; his intelligence was telling him that those forces were crossing the border, and thousands of Georgian citizens in villages in South Ossetia were in potential danger. That sense of impending danger was reinforced by his conviction that a confrontation with Moscow had been looming for some time and was increasingly inevitable. While Georgia was caught tactically by surprise on that crucial day, a Russian invasion was not unexpected. On the contrary, the conviction that a potential fight was brewing was a mind-set reinforced by years of a de facto cold war between Moscow and Tbilisi, Russian efforts to destabilize the Georgian government, Saakashvili's conversations with both Putin and Medvedev, and the creeping annexation the Georgian president saw taking place in front of his eyes since the spring. The August war is inconceivable without the prehistory of Russian pressure, violations of Georgian sovereignty, provocations, and threats, all of which had left the Georgian leadership very much on edge.

The ferocity of the shelling of Georgian villages and positions in the first week of August did mark an escalation over previous years and was the worst fighting since a serious outbreak in 2004. South Ossetian shelling was accompanied by rhetoric and actions that suggested Tskhinvali was going on a war footing. For months Georgian intelligence had observed Moscow illegally moving in additional equipment and creating new infrastructure in the conflict zones, stepping up reconnaissance, and taking other steps that suggested preparations for a confrontation. While Russian military exercises had taken place north of the border for several years, this year's maneuvers were actually war games for an intervention scenario involving Georgia. Intelligence reports of the pre-deployment of Russian air power to bases from which they could mount an air war against Georgia also contributed to a growing sense of siege. Reports of Russian forces taking control of the Roki Tunnel and of irregulars and then actual Russian forces moving through the tunnel and the subsequent sighting of what was believed to be a Russian column coming down from Java all pointed to a looming attack.

To be sure, those reports were not definitive, and the day was chaotic. The fog of war was already setting in. Georgian intelligence was certainly not as good as one might have wished. Exactly what combination of Russian, North Ossetian, Chechen, and other troops were involved was not always clear—and is not to this day. What was clear was that these movements were a violation of existing accords and of Georgian sovereignty. They were threatening to Georgian villages and positions in South Ossetia and possibly to the Georgian government itself, given past Russian calls for regime change. Tbilisi's growing sense of siege was reinforced by the fact that neither Moscow nor South Ossetia made any effort to respond to Saakashvili's ceasefire or to his sending an envoy to meet with senior Russian or South Ossetian officials. There was no evidence that Moscow wanted to calm the situation.

On the contrary, Saakashvili was cornered by a Russia that seemed intent on escalating the pressure on Tbilisi by creating new facts on the ground. Moscow was delivering a de facto ultimatum. He could either acquiesce to the encroachment of Russian power and abandon and lose the separatist provinces once and for all or he could fight back in a hopeless battle to try to defend Georgian citizens and positions there with the likelihood that he would be crushed—but with some hope that a show of military force might lead the Russians to halt their plans or mobilize the West to intervene diplomatically before Moscow could crush him. That was the choice he thought he faced on that fateful evening of August 7.

It was an agonizing choice. Russia could obviously crush Georgia in any war if it chose to. But Saakashvili had pledged to defend his country's citizens and uphold its territorial integrity. As mentioned earlier, he did not believe he could survive politically at home if he did nothing to try to defend the thousands of Georgian citizens in South Ossetia that were in danger. He also feared that he was being invaded in slow motion with the goal being not "just" South Ossetia but his government's demise and the crushing of Georgia's democratic experiment. He made his choice to fight back. His calculation was to buy time and hope that the international community, above all the United States and Europe, would wake up and intervene to save his country. One can still consider that decision a mistake. But why he did it is not a mystery.

To this day controversy surrounds several key issues. First and foremost among them is the question of Georgia's war aims. Controversy centers on the remarks of Georgian brigadier general Mamuka Kurashvili, commander of the Georgian peacekeeping contingent in South Ossetia. He made headlines when he suggested late in the evening of August 7 that Tbilisi's goal was "to restore constitutional order in the whole region." That statement suggested that Georgia's goal was in essence to reconquer South Ossetia. But those were the remarks of a general in the field who misspoke when he found himself with a microphone in his face. The statement was not only unauthorized but at the time Kurashvili was not yet fully briefed about the key thinking in Tbilisi or the Georgian defense planning that had started the day before. His statement was nevertheless a public relations disaster. His remarks echoed around the world and were read with horror on the BlackBerrys and computer screens of Georgia's friends and allies.

Saakashvili's real objectives were reflected in the actual orders he gave. They were not "to conquer" South Ossetia. Georgian forces were ordered to fight a limited defensive engagement around Tskhinvali to protect threatened Georgian villages and to try to intercept Russian forces entering form the north. Had their goal been the former, they would have needed a different operational plan than the one they employed. The Georgian strategy—and critics might say the illusion—was to defend their citizens and to hope that this show of force and the willingness to fight back might deter further escalation.

An illustration of what Georgia's military aims were in reality can be seen in the armed forces' focus on the Gupta bridge. The bridge is south of the city of Java and north of the first Georgian enclave. Just south of it the key bypass roads to and around Tskhinvali start. If Georgia's plan was to conquer all of South Ossetia, taking and holding that bridge would have been essential to allow the passage of Georgian forces to the north to occupy the region. However, the top goal in Georgia's operational military plan was to destroy the Gupta bridge—precisely because they were fighting a defensive operation with the objective of protecting the Georgian enclaves north of Tskhinvali and because their goal was to prevent the flow of Russian forces from Java to Tskhinvali. That bridge was attacked three times by the Georgians in an effort to take it out. Their failure to fully destroy it was key in determining the course of the battle. The Russians managed to repair it in a few hours on August 8, and soon Russian forces started to pour in from the north across the bridge in the direction of Tskhinvali.[23]

These limited war aims were also reflected in Georgian diplomacy. Soon after the war broke out, U.S. secretary of state Condoleezza Rice pushed for a three-point ceasefire package. The plan called for an immediate ceasefire, the withdrawal of Russia and Georgian forces to the August 6 status quo, and a new international peacekeeping force to be deployed in South Ossetia along with new elections there. It was at a time when Georgian forces briefly held their ground and largely occupied Tskhinvali. That plan was the focal point of talks between Rice and Russian foreign minister Sergei Lavrov. Saakashvili agreed to the essence of the package but refused to allow the return of the Koikoty government and insisted on new elections to decide who would govern the region. That idea was quickly rendered obsolete as Moscow escalated its military campaign, and it became obvious that Russia's own war aims were broader and more ambitious. But it also shows that Saakashvili's political and military objectives were limited to defending the Georgian enclaves and positions around the South Ossetian capital.

The drive by Georgian forces on Tskhinvali was motivated as much by tactical military objectives as by political objectives. South Ossetian artillery and forces were embedded in the city. They were targeted under Saakashvili's order to suppress fire against such positions. Going through Tskhinvali was also the shortest route to get to the vulnerable Georgian villages and enclaves north of the city. Saakashvili had ordered his forces to create corridors to evacuate citizens if necessary. Georgian forces undoubtedly considered

Tskhinvali a target of psychological value and enjoyed temporarily liberating the city they considered the capital of a hostile separatist government. Local Gori officials reportedly had plans for a victory parade in Tskhinvali and are alleged to have loaded two trucks full of lecterns, red carpets, and Georgian and South Ossetian flags for the celebration they hoped would take place.

None of this changes the bottom line that Georgia walked into a war it was not prepared for and could not win and that its own war goals were limited both politically and militarily. One reason the Georgian armed forces did not perform very well is that they were not planning to fight there—and most certainly not against the Russian army. The hasty and haphazard way in which the military pulled together a last-minute operational plan is perhaps the most solid evidence that this was the opposite of a long planned Georgian move to conquer South Ossetia.

One paradox of Georgia's drive to join NATO is that while such cooperation helped produce a more modern military, Alliance doctrine compelled Tbilisi to downgrade a possible Russian threat, adopt Alliance priorities for counter-terror and peacekeeping operations instead, and deflect money and attention away from territorial defense capabilities. Georgia did so to boost its chance of getting close to NATO. The irony is that Georgia ended up neither obtaining the close relationship it sought with NATO nor being militarily prepared to fight the adversary it had to confront in August 2008.

Russia's war aims and rationale are far more murky. Initially Moscow's official casus belli for the invasion was to prevent a possible Georgian "genocide" against South Ossetians. Russian and Ossetian separatist leaders claimed that some 2,000 Ossetians in Tskhinvali had been slaughtered during the opening hours of the war. [24] Those claims helped spark subsequent ethnic cleansing and reprisal killings against Georgian civilians. [25] However, they turned out to be false, as the EU's Tagliavini Report also subsequently confirmed. As of December 2008, the investigative committee of the Russian Federation's Prosecutor's Office listed some 162 dead for South Ossetia as a whole. The Russian NGO Memorial has come up with a comparable figure but has emphasized that there is no credible or comprehensive list available. The South Ossetians claim that over 350 of their citizens died, but that list does not differentiate between combatants and civilians, and some persons on the list appear to have died of other causes or at other times. The official

Georgian casualty figure from the war is 412 with 184 of those being military and police. Russia has claimed that 67 of its soldiers died.[26]

Another official war aim of Moscow was the defense of Russian citizens in South Ossetia. Without in any way minimizing the tragedy of the loss of life in this war, one should not forget that Russian citizens in South Ossetia were essentially a diaspora that Moscow itself had created with its dramatic expansion in the granting of Russian passports. Having handed out thousands of passports to individuals living on what it still recognized as Georgian territory, Moscow would now claim the right to defend its newly minted "citizens." As the EU's Tagliavini Report would conclude, Moscow's so-called passportization policy was actually illegal and constituted an open challenge to Georgian sovereignty and intereference in Georgia's internal affairs.

As more than one observer would point out, that doctrine was reminiscent of what Nazi Germany had done in the Sudetenland in the late 1930s, using the German diaspora to agitate in favor of unification with Germany and then justifying the dismemberment of Czechoslovakia with the need to protect ethnic Germans suffering persecution in Prague. The defense of ethnic citizens beyond one's borders also echoed some of Slobodan Milošević's cynical justifications for his wars in the Balkans. As Swedish foreign minister Carl Bildt put it in an official statement at the time:

> No state has a right to intervene militarily in the territory of another state simply because there are individuals there with a passport issued by that state or who are nationals of that state. Attempts to apply such a doctrine have plunged Europe into war in the past—and that is why it is so important that this doctrine is emphatically dismissed. The same doctrine can be equally dangerous in other situations. We did not accept military intervention by Milošević's Serbia in other former Yugoslav states on the grounds of protecting Serbian passport holders. And we have reason to remember how Hitler used this very doctrine little more than half a century ago to undermine and attack substantial parts of central Europe.[27]

But the third and perhaps politically most potent part of Moscow's justification for its military move—and one that Russian president Medvedev personally emphasized in his conversations with President Bush and other Western leaders—was the death of Russian peacekeepers. That claim had a key impact in Western capitals in reinforcing the sense that Saakashvili had made a foolish move and that Russia had a legitimate right to respond. The EU's Tagliavini Report also condemned Georgia for its attacks on Russian peacekeepers. The Russian Ministry of Defense has reported that two peacekeepers were killed early on the morning of August 8 and that a total of fifteen Russian peacekeepers were killed and another forty-nine wounded in action during this conflict. There are, however, several questions surrounding this story, too.

The reality is that these peacekeeping forces had long ceased to be neutral or to be peacekeepers in any traditional sense. They did not prevent South Ossetian shelling of Georgian villages or peacekeepers—often within view or from their very own positions. They sometimes sheltered South Ossetian militias conducting those barrages and worked with them in other ways. Russian peacekeepers were no longer the arm of an international community seeking to maintain peace. They, too, had become an extension of Russia's own imperialist policy as opposed to the objectives of the international community they were supposed to serve. The division between friend, foe, and neutral peacekeeper had become blurred on the ground during peacetime—and thus quickly became blurred in battle as well.

Tbilisi was aware of the risks of killing Russian peacekeepers—and took precautions to avoid such casualties. Prior to launching the assault on the evening of August 7, Kurashvili phoned Kulakhmetov to tell him that Russian peacekeeping positions would not be attacked so long as they stayed neutral. Georgian artillery target lists were constructed to avoid peacekeeping positions, and Georgian forces were issued orders not to fire on Russian peacekeepers unless fired upon first. Peacekeepers were stationed at some fourteen checkpoints in the Tskhinvali region. At many of those positions Russian and Georgian peacekeepers remained co-located during the battle until the Georgians withdrew. After Georgia's initial artillery barrage of Tskhinvali during the night of August 7, a Russian peacekeeping command's spokesperson stated that no Russian peacekeepers had been killed at that point in time.

The first Russian peacekeepers were killed during initial exchanges that took place on the ground around 0600 on August 8.[28] But it is also clear that many Russian peacekeepers entered the battle as combatants as soon as the fighting commenced. This then made them legitimate military targets under international law. Who fired on whom first is thus an important issue. When

Kurashvili called Kulakhmetov on August 7 to tell him that Georgians would not target Russian peacekeepers if they stayed neutral, the Russian general's response was "that is not how it works."[29] Shortly after the Georgian artillery barrage had commenced during the evening of August 7, the Georgians suspected that the Russian peacekeepers were assisting the South Ossetians direct counter fire against them. Kurashvili phoned Kulakhmetov again, demanding to know whether Russian peacekeepers were helping the South Ossetians target Georgian positions. Kulakhmetov responded, "Of course they are giving [coordinates]. Why did you think that we would not? You are pounding us here and you think that we should do nothing about this [****]?"[30]

When special forces of the Georgian Interior Ministry moved into southern Tskhinvali around 0600 on the morning of August 8, they encountered heavy fire from the southern Russian peacekeeping headquarters, aptly called Verkhniy Gorodok, City Heights, because it was located on a hill and was ideal for observing and targeting advancing Georgian forces. The roof of the building was being used to target approaching Georgian forces with artillery. Claims on the Georgian side that the Russians opened fire first are buttressed by a blog by a Russian journalist who was in Tskhinvali during the war. He interviewed two doctors who were in Verkhniy Gorodok when the war broke out and who explained how at 0400 they were given arms and orders to shoot at any approaching Georgian forces.[31]

And they did. Once fired upon, the Georgians returned fire—as they were in principle entitled to do. In the subsequent exchange, the initial Russian peacekeepers as well as South Ossetians were apparently killed. One of those who died was a South Ossetian lieutenant from an artillery intelligence unit. His obituary, however, confirms that he died while directing artillery fire against Georgian forces.[32] The Georgian side claims that Russian peacekeepers were also targeting Georgian forces, working side-by-side with the South Ossetians. This rebuts the argument that Russia's initial military action was in response to the deaths of Russian peacekeepers simply fulfilling their peacekeeping mission. Russian press sources also confirm that key elements of the South Ossetian leadership had sought refuge at the main Russian peacekeeping compound headquarters at Nizhniy Gorodok after hostilities broke out and later conducted joint military operations against Georgian forces from there.

That made the main peacekeeping headquarters a legitimate military target under international law as well. In reality the distinction between peacekeeper and non-peacekeeper had become almost meaningless on the ground as Russian peacekeepers joined other Russian and South Ossetian forces to fight the Georgians. In an interview with the Russian press, Anatoly Barankevich, the head of the South Ossetian National Security Council, actually explained how the South Ossetian regime tried to organize its own defense while hiding in the Russian peacekeeping headquarters and awaiting Russian reinforcements. He also describes how he and others decided to secure the entrances to the JPKF headquarters as well as launch several ambushes on Georgian police and military forces passing by.[33] In spite of such attacks, Georgian forces never disobeyed their order not to fire on the JPKF headquarters. There are also other examples of Georgian forces holding fire when running into Russian peacekeeping units—only to be fired on themselves.

Equally disturbing is the fact that Russian diplomats appear to have claimed that Russian peacekeepers had been killed before any of them possibly could have. Deputy Foreign Minister Grigol Vashadze was the key Georgian contact with the Russian Foreign Ministry, having lived in Russia for many years and even holding a Russian passport. At 0200 on August 8 Vashadze received a phone call from the Russian deputy foreign minister, Grigory Karasin. According to Vashadze, Karasin claimed that Georgia's artillery shelling had killed Russian peacekeepers and "the matter is now in the hands of the General Staff." One hour later the Russian ambassador to Georgia, Vyacheslav Kovalenko, arrived at the Ministry to lodge an official protest as well. However, the Russian defense ministry spokesperson subsequently told Western reporters that the first Russian peacekeepers were killed after 0600 as Georgian forces moved into southern Tskhinvali. It is an additional piece of evidence that suggests that the war—including its rationale—may have been preplanned.

A final accusation against Tbilisi is that the initial Georgian artillery attack on Tskhinvali was indiscriminate. This is also a major point of criticism in the EU's Tagliavini Report. A small OSCE mission team was in Tskhinvali the evening war broke out. Although they sought shelter in a basement after the shelling started, they were above ground until midnight. They subsequently reported that they could not confirm the Georgian claims of significant South Ossetian shelling of Georgian villages, which was a key part of the reason Saakashvili launched his offensive. That has given rise to the accusation that Georgia exaggerated the extent of these shellings as a pretense to launch its own offensive. Those doubts attracted international attention when they were reported in the *New York Times*. That story also suggested that some villages Tbilisi had claimed were shelled had not in fact been attacked.[34] Since then, however, South Ossetian shelling of many Georgian villages that evening has been documented by refugees who fled such shelling as well as by Georgian seismic monitoring records from the area north of Tskhinvali.[35] But the full extent of who shelled whom and where remains one of many contested issues surrounding the origins of the war.

The Georgians did launch a three-pronged artillery attack on the evening of August 7, and areas of Tskhinvali were among their targets. Most of the Georgian artillery fire against Tskhinvali was directed at South Ossetian artillery located on the high ground east and west of the city. In the center of the city, the Georgians targeted buildings believed to be military targets as well as locations of South Ossetian artillery firing at them, but they claim that such targets were limited.[36] Georgia claims it did not launch a massive attack against civilian targets in Tskhinvali using the controversial GRAD system with cluster munitions. Other sources, including the OSCE, have concluded otherwise. The Georgians used primarily howitzers and self-propelled artillery. Some of the systems used were old but had been upgraded with modern battle management systems that should have ensured accuracy. However, the extent to which the Georgians had been properly trained in the use of these systems is not clear as they were in the process of being upgraded. Both OSCE and other observers confirmed that the shelling of Tskhinvali on that evening was massive—and was accordingly singled out for criticism in the EU's Tagliavini Report. The Georgians did use the GRAD system to target Russian forces approaching Tskhinvali on the bypass roads as well as against specific military targets adjacent to Tskhinvali, including Verkhniy Gorodok, where Russian peacekeepers kept their supplies.[37]

The allegation that Tbilisi's artillery attacks against Tskhinvali using cluster munitions led to massive loss of civilian life does not hold up, however. The Georgians appear to have initially occupied large parts of the South Ossetian capital with the city largely intact—as TV footage of Georgian troops moving in on the morning of August 8 suggests. A subsequent UN study using satellite photography also confirms modest damage at that point.[38] But the Russians subsequently unleashed a withering counterattack using their own GRAD artillery as well as massive airpower. Exactly how much of the damage to Tskhinvali was the result of the initial Georgian assault as opposed to subsequent Russian bombings, artillery counterattacks, or subsequent house-to-house fighting may never be known.

This is not to say that the Georgian military performance was perfect; far from it. As their military fortunes declined, the Georgians employed whatever capabilities they still had in whatever way they could in a desperate effort to avoid being decimated or crushed. Many people consider the shelling of any city or the use of cluster munitions under any circumstances to be wrong and reprehensible. Allegations by South Ossetian refugees of misconduct and atrocities by the Georgian armed forces certainly deserve to be investigated. But clearly most of the atrocities in this war were perpetrated during the mass ethnic cleansing of Georgian villages by South Ossetian militia with the support of North Caucasian irregulars as part of a conscious policy pursued to create a larger and more ethnically homogenous South Ossetia. That policy was tolerated and often executed with the tacit support of the Russian army.[39]

There's also no evidence that Saakashvili was given a green light or encouragement from the United States to act militarily. On the contrary, the record of U.S. warnings not to do so is clear and consistent. The United States knew, of course, that Tbilisi was engaged in contingency planning. Like other allies, they watched the Georgian buildup and heard the talk in Tbilisi about a possible military option. Various American officials were on occasion informally shown maps of such contingency plans, including by Saakashvili himself, laying out how Georgian forces might move militarily.

Sometimes Georgians pushed to see whether Washington's "no" was definitive. Surely Washington would understand if ethnic Georgians were being killed and they had to intervene to save lives? they would ask. Might not Washington still be compelled to come to Tbilisi's rescue at least diplomatically or politically? After all, the Bush Administration was firmly and publicly committed to Georgia. It was the number one American ally in the region. Other Georgians believed they might never have a more supportive administration in Washington and that perhaps the time to act was while Bush was still in office. Might the United States, in spite of its repeated warnings not to act, support them if they succeeded in scoring a quick victory and create a fait accompli on the ground? What if it was done quickly, in a matter of two or three days, and victory was clear?

But from President Bush down, the American message to Georgia was "don't do it." Bush himself delivered that message personally to the Georgian leadership during his visit to Tbilisi in the spring of 2005. A succession of American officials, advisors, and friends—including this author—spent hours with Georgian officials trying to convince them of the folly of such a move. On those occasions where it became clear that that message might not have been fully understood, American officials went back to make sure it was. As President Saakashvili subsequently testified, he did not seek the approval of any foreign government to defend Georgian citizens or the Georgian state. On that crucial day the Georgian president did not speak to a single senior American official. He did not have to. He knew what the American position was. He had heard it many times, most recently from Secretary of State Rice in mid-July.

The problem with Western policy was not some mythical green light for a military adventure. It was the underestimation of Russian determination to punish Georgia, the failure to recognize how Kosovo and the NATO Bucharest summit had provided the opportunity to do so, and the failure to intervene diplomatically in Moscow to halt the escalation or to engage sufficiently on the ground in ways that could have stabilized the situation. Warnings to Georgia not to do anything stupid were not matched with a sufficiently effective diplomatic strategy to defuse the trap Moscow was setting. The steps taken were too little and too late to halt the march to war.

The possibility of Russian aggression and the question of what Georgia should do if Moscow attacked were hardly top secret. At times it seemed a favorite topic of discussion in Tbilisi's talkative political class. It was debated with gusto in offices—and at Georgian *supras* over large quantities of wine or in discussions that rambled on into the wee hours of the morning, more often than not concluding in the bar at the Tbilisi Marriott Hotel. Was it better to attempt yet more last-minute confidence-building measures or to purchase Stingers on the black market? When was the ideal time of the year to move if one had to, Georgians sometimes debated among themselves. Was it the New Year when Russians were likely to be drunk, or the summer when

everyone was on vacation? Americans would urge their Georgian counterparts not to do anything stupid, not to walk into a Russian trap—and the
Georgians would passionately recall how their forefathers had not fought
the Bolsheviks in 1921 and had lost their independence for the next seventy
years. They would with great emotion explain how no Georgian leader could
afford to lose the separatist provinces without a fight. An argument would
ensue over whether it was better to fight a hopeless battle and die a patriot
or simply abandon the territories if and when Moscow moved.

More than one Westerner tried to ring the alarm bell. One of the first
was Richard C. Holbrooke, who as early as the fall of 2006 warned in an
editorial in the *Washington Post* that with the United States preoccupied in
the Middle East, Moscow was going all out to undermine and get rid of
Saakashvili.[40] Other voices would make the same argument on both sides of
the Atlantic as the crisis slowly built in 2007 and early 2008.[41] In the nine
months running up to the war, I also wrote or coauthored no fewer than
three columns warning the West that it was sleepwalking into a war, that we
needed to embrace the Georgians more closely to reassure them, and to become directly involved on the ground if we were to head it off. The last of
those columns, dated July 15, started with the sentence: "There is war in the
air between Georgia and Russia."[42]

On August 7 what had once been the topic of theoretical debate in
bars, cafés, and chancelleries became a chilling reality. Georgia on August
7 was like the kid on the playground was has been taunted, picked on, and
bullied for a long time until he finally snaps and punches back even though
the person he is punching is considerably larger and stronger and there is
little doubt that he will be drubbed in return. Based on the intelligence he
had, Saakashvili believed that Russian tanks were rolling toward him—at
a minimum against Georgian positions in South Ossetia and maybe even toward Tbilisi. The Georgian decision to use force was made at the last second by a leader who felt cornered, feared he was about to lose a significant
part of his country, felt his own political survival was on the line, and concluded he had no alternative but to fight. He hoped against hope that
Moscow might back down when Tbilisi fought back and blame it on the
local separatists. He also hoped for rapid Western, and above all American,
diplomatic intervention. He was wrong on the first count. While the second

eventually occurred, it was very late in the game. His government was on the edge of crumbling, and Georgia's future hung in the balance.

What should the Georgian president have done? Many in the West have suggested Saakashvili should have simply hung back and waited for the Russians to make their move, absorb the consequences—thus demonstrating to the world that Moscow was the aggressor—and then wait for the West to intervene. He was not willing to do that because he considered it an abdication of his responsibility to protect his citizens in South Ossetia, because he doubted that the West would come in time even under those circumstances, and because he did not believe he could survive politically if he did. This is not to say that he was right to act as he did—knowing that his armed forces could never stand up to the Russian army and that the U.S. cavalry would not be coming over the hill. It is simply to point out that not acting also had risks and consequences. On the evening of August 7 the ambiguity about Georgia's future territorial integrity, the make-believe nature of Russia's role as peacekeeper, the marginalization of the UN and OSCE missions, and the lack of political will and interest from the West came together with a Russian agenda and a cornered Georgian leader to produce this war.

Sitting in his office one evening six months after the war, I asked President Saakashvili what he believed would have happened if he had followed that advice, had not acted on that fateful evening of August 7, and had instead waited for the rest of the world to see who was to blame and to respond and come to his defense. His answer was clear: he did not believe that he would have survived as president of Georgia because the Georgian people never would have forgiven a president who simply stood by and accepted the loss of South Ossetia and Abkhazia without trying to stop it. He doubted that Georgia today would exist as a sovereign country because he was also convinced then that the real Russian target was not control of the separatist provinces but the discrediting and the downfall of his government and the destruction of Georgia's pro-Western course.

One can still consider what he did a mistake, but the motivations behind President Saakashvili's fateful decision of August 7 are not a great mystery. Perhaps the real question that should be posed is how and why Tbilisi ended up facing the choice between a hopeless David-versus-Goliath fight against Moscow and capitulation in face of a Russian strategy of creeping annexation, rollback, and possible regime change. Why was this crisis allowed to reach this stage in the first place? Why wasn't it nipped in the bud? Where were the West and those institutions and mechanisms created and designed to ensure that such conflicts and war would not occur? To understand that, we need to first go back and examine the origins of this conflict and the run-up to the events of that fateful day.

CHAPTER 2

FROM COLD TO HOT WAR IN THE CAUCASUS

I n the summer of 2008, even as the situation in Georgia threatened to spin out of control, the average American or European reader could be forgiven if they had a hard time finding the separatist provinces of Abkhazia and South Ossetia on a map. One is tempted to recall Neville Chamberlain's famous words in the 1930s about Czechoslovakia and the danger of a war in "a far away country between people of whom we know nothing." These conflicts between Georgians on the one hand and Abkhaz and South Ossetians on the other certainly had their own fascinating and complicated local histories, grievances, and dynamics. After even a short trip to the Southern Caucasus, a visitor might conclude that this region—located at the intersection of the Russian, Persian, and Ottoman empires—had perhaps a bit too much history for its own good.

What made these conflicts so explosive, however, was less this history than how these conflicts and disputes were being manipulated by an outside power, namely Russia, and how they became pawns in a broader geopolitical struggle between Moscow and Tbilisi. That Russo-Georgian struggle had started long before August 7. The two countries had been involved in a kind of covert cold war for years. That war went hot on that fateful night in early August 2008. The issue that sparked it was not the aspirations of South Ossetia or Abkhazia for greater autonomy or independence— although those aspirations were real. This war started and was fought over the future strategic direction of Georgia and the Southern Caucasus as a whole. Simply put, it was about Georgia trying to go West and Russia's determination to stop it.

A brash and brilliant pro-Western leader of the Rose Revolution in November 2003, Saakashvili made no secret of his desire to liberate his country from Russian domination and to take it West—first into NATO and eventually the European Union. Moscow was equally clear about its desire to stop him. In that struggle, the conflicts in Abkhazia and South Ossetia were hijacked as part of a strategy to undercut Tbilisi's Western aspirations. They became the flash point that would spark this war.

The long and mixed history of Russo-Georgian relations helps explain what drove this disagreement into actual armed conflict on the evening of August 7. Georgia occupied a special place and Georgians played a special role during the Russian and Soviet empires. Georgia was first incorporated into the Russian Empire during the first half of the eighteenth century as the orthodox southern outpost of a Russia competing with the Turks and Persians for influence in the region. An independent Georgian republic had emerged briefly after World War I but was crushed by the Bolsheviks in 1921. The decision by the government in Tbilisi then not to fight for their independence left a legacy that would shape Saakashvili's decision in August 2008. It had taken Georgia seventy years to regain its independence and many Georgians were not about to give it up a second time without a fight.

When the Bolsheviks reacquired the Southern Caucasus after their brief flirt with independence after the end of the World War I, they created the borders and ethno-political units in the Northern and Southern Caucasus we know today. But the exact shape of those borders evolved over time and took different forms on the northern and southern sides of the Caucasus mountains. By 1921, Moscow had essentially reacquired early all of the territory once held by the czars. The initial idea was to create a single entity covering both the Northern and Southern Caucasus and in December 1922 the Transcaucasus Soviet Federative Socialist Republic was officially created, with its capital in Tbilisi. In 1936, however, the three South Caucasus republics were made separate union republics. In Georgia, three regions were given special status: Abkhazia as a separate socialist republic unified by treaty with Georgia; Adjara as an autonomous republic; and South Ossetia as an autonomous province.

To this day there is a debate over whether Soviet leaders drew their boundary lines as part of a grand strategy of divide and rule or whether they were driven by the pseudo-Marxist ideas of the young Joseph Stalin, who was Commissar for Nationalities at the time, and who developed his own views on the differences between "nations" and "peoples" as the basis for which group deserved what status. Such borders were not always that meaningful in the highly centralized USSR, where the center controlled nearly everything. But they did lead to a kind of Soviet affirmative action policy where local ethnic elites were given preferences and were able to build their own power bases. Decades later those elites would to turn to nationalism to preserve their power as the pillars of Soviet rule started to crumble and independence movements took hold.

During Soviet times Georgia, with its beautiful combination of mountains and beaches, temperate climate, and delicious cuisine, had become a favorite playground for Russian and Soviet elites to vacation. But Georgians, too, came to play a prominent role in Soviet history, producing a long list of personalities in the arts, the military, and politics. At the top of that list are some of the worst despots in Soviet history—most famously Joseph Stalin and his secret police chief, Laurenti Beria—but also figures like Eduard Shevardnadze, who would play a key role in ending the Cold War. When the Baltic states and Georgia spearheaded the drive for national independence and the breakup of the USSR in the late 1980s, those aspirations elicited a special sense of betrayal and loss in Moscow. While Moscow was loath to admit to the secret protocols of the Molotov-Ribbentrop Pact, many Russians would privately admit that the Baltic states had been illegally annexed and had a right to independence. But losing Georgia was much harder for many Russians to accept because the historical ties with Tbilisi went far deeper.

Many senior Russian officials had family ties to the region, and Georgians to this day constitute a major diaspora in Russia. Many Russians felt they were "losing" not only a part of the former Russian (as opposed to So- viet) Empire but a nation that had played a key role in shaping their own his- tory. Russian conservatives and nationalists sought actively to undermine Georgia's drive for independence in the early 1990s by, among other things, assisting the Abkhaz and Ossetian separatist movements. Russian intelli- gence and military officials—with varying degrees of official knowledge and support—armed, advised, and at times even fought with these separatist movements in the early 1990s as part of an effort to discredit Georgian in- dependence and reign in Tbilisi.

Many nationalistic Russians also harbored a special hatred for Eduard Shevardnadze, who had returned to his native Georgia in the early 1990s. They blamed Shevardnadze, who had been Soviet foreign minister under Mikhail Gorbachev, for dismantling Moscow's empire in Eastern Europe and ostensibly capitulating to the West in ending the Cold War. Shevard- nadze had survived several assassination attempts in Georgia that everyone suspected were directed from Moscow. And in the late 1990s Russia had al- ready threatened to directly intervene in Georgia again, ostensibly in hot pursuit of Chechen rebels seeking refuge in the Pankisi Gorge on Georgian territory. This fight between Russia and Georgia was not only strategic but often personal.

Enter Mikheil Saakashvili, who was another large Georgian personal- ity with aspirations of changing his country and the region. The Kremlin would come to despise him even more than Shevardnadze. He did not look north to Russia and Moscow but to the West for inspiration. He saw his role models as historical figures such as the Turkish leader Kemal Atatürk, Finnish marshal Carl Gustaf Mannerheim, and the Georgian king David the Builder. Atatürk symbolized top-down Westernization and democratization. Mannerheim had been the wartime leader of a country that fought the Red Army to a draw in the bloody Winter War of 1939–40. And David the Builder was a legendary Georgian king who was able to defeat separatist forces and reunite Georgia. Flamboyant, brash, and at times autocratic, Saakashvili was determined to paint on a larger historical canvas. Inspired by the success of NATO enlargement in the 1990s, he wanted Georgia to fol- low in the footsteps of the Baltic states as former parts of the Soviet empire that became reformist democratic tigers overcoming the odds to join the

West. He was a swashbuckling figure in a region that had produced a disproportionate share of bigger-than-life personalities.[1]

There was another component to the conflict between Tbilisi and Moscow that gave it an edge. The Rose Revolution was driven by a younger generation of Georgian leaders who wanted true independence. They no longer wanted to live in a semi-failed state. They wanted to pull themselves once and for all out of Moscow's sphere of influence, which they felt was holding Georgia back. They wanted to break what they considered to be Georgia's quasi-colonial relationship with Russia. They no longer wanted to play the game where nominal sovereignty masked the reality of Russia still exerting de facto control through its figures in the cabinet, links through intelligence and security officials, as well as corruption and organized crime. That is inter alia why they placed so much emphasis on building a strong Georgian state capable of defending itself and pushed to resolve the territorial disputes, as they understood these were preconditions to gaining that independence.

But Saakashvili's dream was to transform not just Georgia but the region as a whole. Working with Azerbaijan, he wanted to make Tbilisi an essential part of a new independent energy corridor bringing Azeri and eventually Central Asian energy resources to the West, bypassing Russia. The development of these resources and the export routes to deliver them to the outside world would go a long way in determining whether a small state like Georgia could secure its sovereignty and independence.[2] It was all part of a larger plan to anchor this region to the West. Saakashvili was set on a crash course to turn Georgia from a semi-failed state into a reform tiger that could become the catalyst for creating a democratic pro-Western corridor in the Southern Caucasus between an unstable Russia to the north and a radicalizing wider Middle East to the south. It was a breathtaking vision and one Moscow despised.

The United States occupied a key role in that Georgian vision. Saakashvili had studied law at Columbia and George Washington University in the United States and had become a big fan of the country. American power, principle, and diplomacy were essential in his eyes if he was to ever succeed. Visiting his office you were as likely to see a biography of Kennedy or Jefferson as Atatürk or Stalin on his bookshelf. American NGOs had been major supporters of Georgian civil society and their support was a key factor in enabling the Rose Revolution. The U.S. government, for its part, had a more mixed relationship with Georgia. Washington had enjoyed good relations with Eduard Shevardnadze, Saakashvili's predecessor, and a key partner from the days of German unification. The U.S. ambassador in Tbilisi, Richard Miles, had famously sent in a cable before going to bed on the eve of the Rose Revolution in November 2003 predicting Saakashvili's failure—only to wake up to find he had become the leader of the country overnight.

But Washington made up for its initial hesitation. Saakashvili soon became a poster child for the Bush Administration's "freedom agenda" and democracy promotion efforts. A whole cadre of Georgians who had been studying overseas or working in civil society now joined his reform team, led by the trio of President Saakashvili, Prime Minister Zurab Zhvania, and the parliamentary leader Nino Burjanadze. American money, advisors, and friends poured into Georgia to assist in this attempt to remake the country. Georgia became a major beneficiary of U.S. aid and economic assistance programs. Saakashvili's clampdown on petty corruption boosted his popularity at home, and his tough economic reforms made Georgia one of the biggest recipients of foreign capital and fastest-growing economies in Europe or Eurasia.

At a time when the U.S. image around the world was plummeting in the wake of the Iraq war, Georgia was one of the most pro-American countries in the world. Tbilisi understood that American power and support were essential to balance Russia and to join NATO. Saakashvili was feted in Washington like a rock star and enjoyed powerful friendships on both sides of the political aisle with figures ranging from John McCain to George Soros and Richard Holbrooke. In January 2005, Senators Hillary Clinton and John McCain jointly nominated him for the Nobel Peace Prize. When President Bush visited Tbilisi in the spring of 2006, he received a hero's welcome as over 100,000 Georgians turned out to cheer him in Freedom Square—with the Georgians subsequently naming the boulevard to the airport after him.

Georgia never inspired the same enthusiasm in or had the same close relationship with Europe. While countries like Germany and France had historic cultural links to Georgia, they were cautious about Georgia and its aspirations. The roots of what we today consider Western civilization can arguably be traced back to these ancient Christian civilizations around the Black Sea. But these countries had disappeared from the Western consciousness in the twentieth century as they disappeared into the Soviet Union. Even after they reappeared, many Europeans were not even sure a country like Georgia, nestled next to Turkey on the eastern edge of the Black Sea, was part of Europe. Enlargement fatigue was already setting in across Western Europe and a new expansion into the Southern Caucasus seemed a high-risk proposition. Saakashvili's embrace of Bush and his Euro-skepticism did not help either. It was not uncommon to hear senior European officials remark that Saakashvili was an American-backed hothead who spelled trouble.

My own entrée into Georgian politics actually resulted from Tbilisi's desire to find this better connection with Europe. Though American, I was seen as pro-European. My background in EU and NATO enlargement was considered important. The late Zurab Zhvania had reached out to me and asked me to serve as an informal advisor. Zhvania was prime minister at the time and the yin to Saakashvili's yang in Tbilisi. The Georgians knew that Saakashvili came across well in the United States but rubbed many Europeans the wrong way. And while Georgia needed American support, its real goal was to come closer to Europe. And that required a different strategy and approach.

Zhvania was a different kind of political personality, one much better equipped to connect with European leaders as well as with Moscow. He intended to become Georgia's face to Europe and to establish a better balance in Tbilisi's Western ties. In the fall of 2004, I spent a weekend with him up at a villa complex in the mountains outside of Borjomi, an old czarist spa. I arrived for dinner—held at Stalin's former villa—and was informed that our working session would start around midnight and go until 0300 or 0400. A small team of us brainstormed about how to better connect Georgia with Europe—with Saakashvili checking in every twenty minutes or so to toss in his own ideas. I saw up close how the two leaders worked together and complemented each other. We left the next day having no illusion that it was going to easy but also sensing that a plan was starting to come together. Zhvania's untimely and mysterious death in February 2005 sidetracked those efforts. I have often wondered whether history might have unfolded differently had he lived and been able to pursue his plans. Irrespective of whether his death was instigated by Moscow or not, Georgia had lost the person in the senior leadership who could best communicate with both Europe and Russia and who often provided a balance to Saakashvili's strong personality.

Georgia's Achilles' heel was the frozen conflicts of Abkhazia and South Ossetia. These conflicts, too, had their own distinct histories and dynamics, and the relations between Georgia and on the hand and these separatist provinces on the other are as complicated as those between Georgia and Russia. In Western discourse, the Abkhaz and South Ossetian issues were often mentioned in the same sentence, like Siamese twins. But that obfuscated a more complex reality. They were different ethnic groups with their own histories of how they had migrated to the region. Both had enjoyed degrees of autonomy during Soviet times, although the exact nature of that status had evolved, especially in the Abkhaz case. But they faced a common dilemma with the weakening and eventual collapse of the Soviet center under Gorbachev's perestroika. In the waning years of the USSR, the local minority elites in both Sukhumi and Tskhinvali feared a loss of their power and privileges in a newly independent Georgia, especially when confronted with the rise of a Georgian national movement with its own xenophobic side.

Georgian leaders, in turn, were so enthralled with their new national freedom that they proved unwilling or unable to propose the kind of enlightened extensive autonomy that might have assuaged those fears. They were worried that these minorities were or could become fifth columns that Moscow would use to undermine their fragile independence.[3] This paved the way for wars in both provinces in the early 1990s. Georgia was then led by Zviad Gamsakhurdia, mainly known in the West as a scholar and dissident. But he was also a fiery Georgian nationalist who rode to power on a wave of chauvinist passion and calls for a "Georgia for the Georgians." The dark side of that vision was a desire to settle scores with the Abkhaz and Ossetian leaders who were seen as having benefited from a past Kremlin policy of divide and rule. When Gamsakhurdia moved to curtail these rights and autonomies, he lit a powder keg.

The spark that first set off the violence occurred in South Ossetia in 1990 when the local Ossetian district administration declared a separate republic within the Soviet Union, and moved to unite with the republic of North Ossetia across the mountains. South Ossetia was about two-thirds Ossetian and one-third Georgian at the time. In response to this move, Gamsakhurdia declared the South Ossetians were "agents of the Kremlin" and part of a Russian plot to dismember Georgia. Tbilisi revoked South Ossetia's autonomous status and sent in troops. The poorly trained Georgian forces, however, met with fierce resistance from the South Ossetian militia supported by elements of the Russian army and irregulars from North Ossetia. In July 1992 a cease-fire agreement halted hostilities and initiated final status talks. That war had produced several thousand casualties and some 10,000 refugees, who fled both north into Russia and south into Georgia proper.

The war in Abkhazia started later but ended with an outcome even more disastrous for Georgia. In Abkhazia, the Abkhaz themselves were a minority of some 20 percent of the population with the Georgian population numbering nearly 50 percent. Yet a similar dynamic took hold. To Abkhaz political and intellectual leaders, Georgia's exit from the USSR threatened to diminish their influence in Sukhumi. The coming to power of Gamsakhurdia fueled their fears of marginalization and discrimination. When Gamsakhurdia ran into problems back home over his increasingly autocratic and irrational rule, the Abkhaz moved to take advantage of their chance and push for independence, too.

In January 1992, a military council in Tbilisi deposed Gamsakhurdia, who fled into exile, and instead invited Eduard Shevardnadze back to form a new government. Shevardnadze initially returned as chairman of the council and then was subsequently elected president in 1995. While he did his best to unite the quarreling Georgian factions as well as negotiate settlements with the Abkhaz and South Ossetians, he was not in full control of the situation. In the summer of 1992 the Georgian defense minister launched an unauthorized attack in Abkhazia. Georgian troops and paramilitary forces marched into the separatist province and initially succeeded in capturing the capital of Sukhumi, but they could not sustain their positions. Russian military commanders came to the assistance of the Abkhaz as did several North Caucasus leaders.

By the end of 1993, the Abkhaz, with the help of Russian forces as well as North Caucasian irregulars, pushed back the ill-prepared Georgian forces. The final Georgian defeat came when Shevardnadze, seeking to end the war, agreed to withdraw Georgian troops and heavy artillery from Sukhumi in return for a ceasefire. The Abkhaz immediately violated the truce and over-ran the remaining Georgian positions, pushing the Georgian forces back to the Inguri River dividing Abkhazia and Georgia proper—where they remained until August 2008. That defeat was also accompanied by the expulsion of some 230,000 Georgians. It was similar to the ethnic cleansing taking place in the former Yugoslavia, where war had also broken out in 1991.

The Abkhaz's actions could not have been carried out without the support of elements of the Russian military. Russia's involvement was exposed when an unmarked fighter was shot down and its pilot turned out to be a Russian air force officer in uniform. That expulsion of Georgians was not a spontaneous act of revenge, but a deliberate government campaign and strategy aided by, if not directed by, an outside power—Russia. A security zone was established at the end of the war that ran along the eastern edge of Abkhazia, historically populated by the Georgians, but now largely depopulated. It extended twelve kilometers on both sides of the border into what was now called Georgia proper and was complemented by another twelve-kilometer zone on both sides where heavy weapons were also restricted.

The wounds of this war ran deep. Terrible atrocities had been committed on both sides in brutal fighting that at times involved house-to-house combat. The Georgians were no saints, having committed atrocities, sacked Sukhumi, and destroyed prized Abkhaz national treasures. Even as they fled, they, too, had conducted a brutal scorched-earth policy. Neal Ascherson, a well-known British foreign correspondent and the author of *Black Sea,* the best-known English-language book of history and reportage on the region, described how much of Abkhazia's heritage had been destroyed when he visited Sukhumi some nine months after the fighting had ended. The Abkhaz, he wrote, had indeed finally become "masters in their own house"—but it was a house that was roofless and in which they wandered lonely through the empty rooms. The crown jewels of this small but proud population—

the National Museum and States Archives—had been destroyed by Georgian forces, leaving Abkhaz history in ashes.[4]

A visit to Sukhumi or Tskhinvali a decade later was still quite an experience. In 2005, I was part of a small team that began organizing study tours to Georgia and the frozen conflicts in Abkhazia and South Ossetia on behalf of the German Marshall Fund of the United States. The purpose of these trips was to allow Western policymakers, think-tankers, and journalists to gain a firsthand exposure to these conflicts. I remember my first trip to Abkhazia, flying by UN helicopter to Sukhumi (diverting over the Black Sea waters so as not to run the risk of being shot at) and landing at what had once been a major airport. We could see palm trees and the beautiful black beaches as we got ready to touch down. We then entered a deserted and slightly tawdry terminal. On the way into town, traffic to the airport was so sparse that we had to shoo cows off a largely deserted road.

The pre-war population of Abkhazia had been some 500,000 but had been reduced to 200,000 after the war. Sukhumi was only partially inhabited—a consequence of ethnic cleansing and de-population—and still bore the scars of war. There were simply no people to replace the Georgians and others who had been expelled or left. Trees grew from the centers of roofless, burnt-out homes. There was a disproportionate number of BMWs and Mercedes with smoked windows and burly bodyguards, a sign that some trades, most likely illegal, were flourishing. The so-called Abkhaz Foreign Ministry was a sleepy little building where we initially had to find someone to unlock the door and let us in. Carl Bildt, a veteran of the Balkan wars who was soon to become Swedish foreign minister, headed the delegation. Asked by our Abkhaz hosts about his impression, he responded, "A bit like the Balkans, perhaps a bit worse." They grimaced.

South Ossetia was even more artificial. It was even smaller and poorer than Abkhazia. It had a population of around 100,000 when the USSR collapsed. But some experts believed that number was down to 60,000 by the summer of 2008. Like so much else in the Caucasus, precise numbers were hard to come by and were highly politicized, passionately debated, and manipulated by different sides to try to make their case. Economically, the mountain ranges to the north meant that trade and commerce were oriented south toward Tbilisi. Apart from agriculture, the city's economic lifeline consisted largely of smuggling contraband via the road north to the Roki Tunnel and Russia. An OSCE official suggested to me that if one placed a normal customs post at the Roki Tunnel to control the smuggling, the province's revenues would dry up and it might be forced to sue for peace.

The one advantage South Ossetia had was that the war of the early 1990s had not left quite the same deep scars as in Abkhazia. In contrast, Abkhaz, Georgians, and Ossetians still lived together in South Ossetia in spite of all the troubles. Tskhinvali had never been a multiethnic city like Sarajevo. But Ossetian and Georgian villages were intertwined in what seemed to be a checkerboard manner across hills and valleys. These communities continued to coexist and still had a fairly high rate of interaction and intermarriage. Moreover, the administrative borders between South Ossetia and Georgia proper were porous and more easily crossed. The local South Ossetian population could and often did drive to Gori for medical treatment or even to Tbilisi for dinner.

This in no way precluded local rivalry and feuds. Indeed, often when fighting broke out, it was not easy to tell whether it was part of a bigger geopolitical struggle or some local Hatfield-McCoy-like feud that often went back decades if not centuries. The official conflict zone in South Ossetia consisted of maybe half of the district—essentially a circle with the center in Tskhinvali and a radius of fifteen kilometers. At least half of that conflict zone was also controlled by Georgia—one enclave to the north and east of Tskhinvali as well as the territory south of the city toward Gori. It was hardly a viable entity. It seemed so artificial that many people suspected Russia was holding South Ossetia as a pawn in a larger game—a pawn it might sacrifice depending on what it could get in return.

Russia's influence and leverage on the ground in Abkhazia and South Ossetia were further amplified by the set of monitoring and peacekeeping arrangements put in place in the early 1990s at the end of these wars—and blessed and tolerated by the international community ever since. It was the equivalent of original sin in these conflicts and would come back to haunt the West in the summer of 2008. A cardinal principle of effective conflict resolution and peacekeeping is that a peacekeeping force must be neutral and must enjoy the trust of both sides. This principle was discarded in the Georgian case. While it was prepared to help broker a ceasefire through the auspices of the OSCE or the United Nations, the West was not prepared to put its own peacekeeping forces on the ground in a distant country that was part of the former Soviet Union. What Secretary of State James Baker had famously said in the early 1990s about the break-up of the former Yugoslavia—that he had no dog in that Balkan fight—seemed doubly true when it came to Georgia and the Southern Caucasus.

Instead, Washington and its allies in the West decided to take a gamble. It hoped that the new Russia of Boris Yeltsin and Foreign Minister Andrei Kozyrev would be different and that it would behave in a post-imperialist fashion. There seemed to be little alternative at the time. In two separate sets of arrangements with the United Nations and the OSCE respectively, the West sanctioned Russia to be the main peacekeeping force on the ground in both Abkhazia and South Ossetia. Russia was allowed 3,000 peacekeepers in Abkhazia—with no Georgian participation of any kind. In South Ossetia a Joint Peacekeeping Force was formed with a battalion of Russian, North Ossetian, and Georgian forces under Russian command. Those arrangements were supported by the West, and their mandate was renewed every year for the next decade and a half.

That gamble never paid off. On the contrary, the design flaws in these arrangements became dangerous and destabilizing over time. They ended up being a key contributing factor in the war in the summer of 2008. Georgia was locked into an asymmetrical battle with Russia in which it never had a chance to get a fair deal. The fox was in essence guarding the chicken coop. As Russia drifted in a more nationalist direction, it exploited its asymmetric position in an increasingly predatory fashion. What was supposed to be a neutral peacekeeping force became an imperialist and eventually an invading force. The West tolerated this situation and often turned a blind eye, believing that this was the best of a set of bad options and that a UN observer mission in Abkhazia and an OSCE mission in South Ossetia was better than nothing—and could at least guarantee some element of transparency and act as a partial brake on any potential Russian aggression.

For Georgia, this arrangement created an increasingly disadvantageous and at times surreal situation. The separatist leadership of Abkhazia and South Ossetia demanded full independence—period. Georgia countered by offering far-reaching autonomy in some loose confederation. Russia had mandates from the international community to both maintain the ceasefire as well as to promote a reconciliation and negotiation process to resolve the conflicts. Yet, it clearly had little interest in actually doing so. And these mandates provided an international cover under which Moscow had a more or less free hand. Tbilisi was locked into a three-sided diplomatic format in which the ostensible mediator was openly allied with one of the parties in the conflict. Russian troops on the ground were peacekeepers in name only.

As Russian policy toward Georgia hardened, these troops were increasingly in league with the local separatist rulers and militias in preventing any steps toward opening up the regions and instead helped pursue policies that could cement the separation of the provinces from Georgia. When Georgia went to the UN or the OSCE to ask it to investigate incidents or to request a broader international presence to provide some balance on the ground, they again ran up against Moscow, which used its veto right to block such moves. Georgia was trapped in a system where all roads seemingly led to Moscow, which was determined to keep it that way.

Mikheil Saakashvili inherited this situation when he became president of Georgia after the Rose Revolution. He was determined to break with the past in two fundamental ways. The first was his aspiration to Westernize his country. He had watched how Central and Eastern Europe and, more importantly, the Baltic states, had defied the odds and managed to anchor themselves to the West through NATO and EU membership. He wanted to emulate the Baltic states and turn Georgia into a reformist tiger that could recast the way in which it was seen by the West and be embraced as part of an enlarging Western community. Although Georgia was bankrupt and teetering on being a failed state when he took power, the leaders of the Rose Revolution initially succeeded in implementing far-reaching reforms that turned the country around and made it one of the most successful transition economies in a matter of a few years.

Between 2005 and 2008, Georgia enjoyed real growth in its gross domestic product (GDP) of 8.5 percent or higher. Nominal GDP more than tripled during this period, and per capita income went up almost 150 percent. Tax revenue collection went up some 400 percent, foreign currency grew almost eightfold, and public debt was cut. Corruption was brought down from very high levels to one of the lowest in Central and Eastern Europe.[5] Georgian troops signed up for U.S. and NATO missions in the Balkans and Iraq. The goal of aligning Georgia with and eventually bringing it into NATO, and perhaps farther down the road into the European Union, was still clearly a long shot. But it was no longer mission impossible.

These aspirations to "go West" put Georgia on a collision course with Moscow. Following the collapse of Communism and the USSR in 1989 and 1991 respectively, the West had embraced the goal of creating a Europe that was whole, free, and at peace. A core principle of that undertaking, enshrined in the Charter of Paris and reaffirmed almost a decade later in the OSCE's Charter for European Security, signed at Istanbul in 1999, was the right of equal security and the ability of countries to choose their own security policy, including their Alliance affiliation. It was supposed to be part of the foundation of a post–Cold War Europe without dividing lines or spheres of influence. NATO and EU enlargement were initially conceived as part of this vision of reunifying Europe and overcoming the old Cold War divide. It was part of an effort to reinvent NATO for a new era and anchor Central and Eastern Europe to the West while in parallel reaching out, embracing, and deepening cooperation with Russia.

Moscow eventually acquiesced to NATO enlargement to Central and Eastern Europe, and the Alliance took its first steps toward building a parallel NATO-Russia relationship. But it was not easy. President Yeltsin publicly opposed NATO enlargement although in private he would admit he did not consider the Alliance a threat and even expressed his understanding of the Central and Eastern European impulse to go West. After all, he wanted Russia to go West, too. He often overruled advisors who urged him to take a tougher stance on the issue. His real worry often seemed to be that the NATO enlargement issue would be used against him at home by his domestic opponents—both the nationalist right and the Communist left. Yeltsin was open to a compromise in which NATO enlargement would go forward with appropriate assurances that the Alliance would not engage in major military buildup on the soil of new members and would deepen relations with Moscow at the same time.

That was the political understanding that underpinned NATO's first round of enlargement and the NATO-Russia Founding Act in 1997. The same key principles were reaffirmed at the OSCE summit in Istanbul in

1999, when member states—including Russia—signed a new and updated charter. I was involved in the initial drafting and subsequent negotiation of this document, which affirmed "the inherent right of each and every participating state to be free to choose or change its security arrangements, including treaties of alliance, as they evolve" as well as rejecting any claim to "spheres of influence" by any OSCE member state.[6] When it came to the second round of NATO enlargement launched at the Prague summit in 2002, Moscow actually put up less political resistance than it had for the first round even though NATO was entering post-Soviet space by admitting the three Baltic states. The Alliance offered to deepen its cooperation with Moscow prior to the admission of this second round by creating a new NATO-Russia Council, or NRC, where Moscow would sit as an equal among Alliance members. That new council was inaugurated shortly after the Prague summit. Symbolically, this meant Russia no longer sat at the table with other allies arrayed around it—that is "19 + 1" in NATO jargon—but rather sat as one of the club "at 20" tasked to make joint decisions and take joint action.

When asked at the press conference following the establishment of the NRC to explain what the difference meant in practice, then NATO secretary general Lord Robertson said it was in the "chemistry not the arithmetic." President Bush went even further in stating, "The NATO-Russia Council offers Russia a path toward forming an alliance with the Alliance." At the time President Vladimir Putin seemed completely relaxed about the prospect of other countries in the post-Soviet space eventually joining NATO. When asked at the post-summit press conference about Ukraine's seeking membership, he answered, "Ukraine is an independent sovereign state and will choose its own path to peace and security." Putin continued: "Such a conversation [between Ukraine and NATO] would be entirely appropriate and possible. I certainly don't see there being anything particularly tricky here, anything that need or that could cast a shadow over relations between Russia and Ukraine."[7]

In hindsight it was the lull before the storm. Over the next few years Putin would switch course in his domestic and foreign policies. Whereas he had come to power in 2000 first using the vocabulary of a reformer and talking about "Russia's Western vocation," the Russian leader was later to embrace an alternative autocratic ideology emphasizing "sovereign democracy." Yeltsin's anti-imperialist and pro-Western foreign policy line of the 1990s would also be cast aside and replaced by a new harder-edged nationalism. In a step-by-step fashion, Putin abandoned the policies of Western integration and the de facto alliance with the West promoted by Yeltsin and initially embraced by him after September 11, 2001. Whereas Yeltsin had spoken of the collapse of the USSR as the liberation of Russia from Communism, Putin famously remarked in the spring of 2005 that the Soviet Union's collapse "was the greatest geopolitical catastrophe" of the twentieth century.[8]

Russia's main goal was no longer to go West. Putin had instead opted for his own Eurasian path, which he would develop further as a concept in the years ahead. But now that Russia had decided it did not want to align itself with the West, it was even more determined that its neighbors not do so either. Thus, when the Rose and Orange Revolutions occurred in 2003 and 2004, respectively, they were greeted in the West as new democratic breakthroughs and a chance to extend the wave of democratization of the 1990s further eastward. In Moscow, however, they were seen as dangerous. The same Putin who two years earlier had suggested he was relaxed about the prospect of Ukraine joining NATO now reacted as if developments in Ukraine and Georgia were mortal threats to Russia. As Ivan Krastev has written, the Rose and Orange Revolutions were Moscow's equivalent of September 11, requiring a wake-up call to a new and underestimated threat. The prospect of liberal democracy and a pro-Western government taking root in the Southern Caucasus was seen as a challenge to Putin's new narrative of rebuilding the Russian state through "sovereign democracy" and to its power and influence in its former neighborhood. They could boomerang and echo in Russia itself, especially in the Northern Caucasus where separatism was already a major challenge.[9]

Moscow's reaction to the Rose and Orange Revolutions bordered at times on the hysterical and surreal. Russian spin doctors created a new wave of conspiracy theories directed against the West in general and the United States in particular to explain what was happening in Georgia and Ukraine. American NGOs were presumed to have almost magical powers in conjuring up revolutionary movements, and senior U.S. government officials were dubbed the "grey cardinals" alleged in the Russian press to be behind these color revolutions. Moscow quickly moved to develop a strategy to counter these developments and to roll back Western influence on its borders.

As the country most enthusiastically embracing Western-style reforms and the leading candidate for eventual NATO membership, Georgia rapidly became a special target and focus of this new Russian wrath. Moscow understood that if Georgia were to succeed in becoming the first viable democratic project in the Southern Caucasus and in joining NATO, such a development contained the potential to open up and transform the region. The great tragedy was that Moscow was unable to see that this kind of transformation could produce a new kind of stability that could also be in its own interest. Instead, Moscow viewed it in zero-sum terms, fearing that this trend would only produce the loss of influence and control. Moscow preferred to rely on old imperialist and colonialist habits of dominating the region through a divide-and-conquer strategy using local proxies. That is how Russia had managed the Southern Caucasus for centuries. Such habits did not die easily.

This tension was clear from the beginning of the Putin-Saakashvili relationship. In their first meeting, they are reported to have gotten along reasonably well. At that time, given how much Moscow despised Eduard Shevardnadze, Saakashvili may have seemed like the lesser of two evils. But the seeds of future problems were evident. Putin had asked Saakashvili to keep in his cabinet, in a key position of influence, a Georgian known to be corrupt and close to Russian intelligence—the then minister of state security Valery Khaburdzania. It was a sign that Moscow still expected to have a direct say and to interfere in the running of Georgia. It expected Saakashvili to play the same old colonial game of paying homage to its northern neighbor. But the Rose Revolution had been about breaking with that. Saakashvili refused and quickly reformed that ministry and "promoted" Khaburdzania to another senior but less sensitive post. Relations between the leaders soon deteriorated.

When President Bush or other Western leaders brought up Georgia with Putin, the Russian leader often went into an irrational rant. Kremlin aides admitted in private that they avoided raising issues or ideas associated with Georgia for fear of what the reaction at the top would be. Face-to-face meetings between Putin and Saakashvili became electric with anger and suspicion. Aides described their relationship as hatred mixed with a touch of admiration. Both were in a sense top-down revolutionary leaders trying to remake their societies. But they were going in completely different directions. Putin's project was about rebuilding a centralized and authoritarian Russian state and Moscow's sphere of influence beyond its borders. Saakashvili's was about remolding Georgia into a capitalist country and going West.

Witnesses say that Putin and Saakashvili spoke to each other with open and at times brutal candor. Putin was crystal clear that if Georgia expected Russian help in resolving issues like Abkhazia and South Ossetia, it needed to make a basic choice to accommodate Russia's interests. It needed to decide if—in the Russian leader's words—it was going to be a friend and an ally of Russia or not. Tbilisi it had to decide whether it was on the side of Moscow or the West—and Russian policy toward these conflicts would depend on that answer. If it opted to be a friend and an ally, it could expect Moscow's assistance in resolving these issues. If it chose another course, then it should not.

While Moscow officially recognized Georgia's territorial integrity, at times Putin would openly threaten to recognize the provinces and physically take them away from Tbilisi. Georgian officials recall one particularly candid, if not brutal, exchange on the issue between Putin and Saakashvili in St. Petersburg in the summer of 2006. Putin had made Saakashvili wait for three hours before receiving him to underscore who needed whom the most. The Russian leader made it quite clear that Georgia had a choice to make as to which side it was on. When Saakashvili or other senior Georgian officials asked what being a friend or ally meant in practical terms, the response was, "You know what you need to do." Georgia needed to abandon its pro-Western course and its NATO aspirations.

As a result of its choice, Georgia came under increasing political, psychological, and economic siege by Moscow to change course. Yet Tbilisi not only refused to buckle under but dared to fight back politically. Saakashvili refused to tone down his NATO aspirations or back off from his close ties with the United States. He refused to be intimidated by Putin and was reported to have referred to him as "Lilli-Putin." While he denied that accusation, it rang true to many who knew him. After having uncovered and quietly dealt with numerous Russian attempts to engage in dirty tricks and interfere in Georgian domestic politics, Saakashvili publicly outed four Russian intelligence officers and charged them with espionage in the fall of 2006.

Moscow responded by imposing a full economic embargo, banning trade as well as all transport and postal links. It is estimated to have poured millions of dollars into antigovernment activities and increased its covert activities as well. It launched pogrom-like harassment of ethnic Georgians living in Russia, closing down shops and deporting ordinary people.[10] Driving to South Ossetia in the spring of 2007, a European intelligence official recounted to me one Russian attempt after another to interfere in Georgian politics. When I asked how his capital responded to such reporting, he responded, "I don't dare report everything happening here. No one would want to hear it or believe me. It is the Wild West." At times it seemed like a John le Carré Cold War spy novel—only much more serious.

Perhaps the best weapon Moscow had at its disposal against Georgia was the frozen conflicts of Abkhazia and South Ossetia. They were in many ways the weak spot or chink in Tbilisi's armor. The simple fact that Tbilisi did not have control over 20 percent of its territory and Russia did—and that these regions were often centers of lawlessness, smuggling, and organized crime—did not make it easier to introduce market reform, a state of law, or greater democracy. Dealing with them diverted and absorbed political energy, capital, and resources. No one was more eager to resolve them than those Georgians responsible for the economy and for attracting foreign investment. The prospect of instability also scared off European allies who feared being pulled into a local ethnic war with Russia in the background.

It also cast a huge shadow over Georgia's NATO aspirations. How could these countries join NATO when its borders were not secure? What borders would allies be asked to defend in the future? To be sure, there could be workarounds for such issues. Germany joined the Alliance in the 1950s absent its eastern territories. The Alliance had survived with a frozen conflict called Cyprus in its midst for decades. The Baltic states had not all signed border treaties with Russia when they joined NATO. But no one had any illusions. Georgia's quest for NATO was harder. It was as if it were running a marathon with weights around its ankles. The conflicts slowed down Georgian reform, made the West more cautious to embrace Tbilisi, and gave Russia tremendous leverage for the simple reason that the key to their resolution lay largely in Moscow.

Putin had also moved to strengthen his and Moscow's control over the separatist leaderships in Abkhazia and South Ossetia. Georgia and South Ossetia had been working toward a possible peace deal and in 2000 they took a modest step forward by producing a working document called the Baden Plan. While it did not resolve all the issues, it pointed in a direction that could have potentially opened the way for a peaceful resolution of the conflict. However, Putin's rise to power soon led to Moscow's installing its own man in power in Tskhinvali—a former wrestling champion named Eduard Koikoty—with links to organized crime and an arrest warrant in his name. That change of power, in 2001, put an end to any debate in Tskhinvali over possibly suing for peace with Georgia—those willing to back reconciliation were then pushed out of the South Ossetian leadership. Shortly after becoming president, Koikoty is said to have held a closed meeting with a group of advisors where he reportedly dismissed the Baden Plan and instead unveiled a plan to gain independence for South Ossetia by launching a war against Georgia.

Many of the key ministries in Koikoty's government were subsequently taken over by former Russian intelligence officials with little or no link to Ossetia. Abkhazia managed to maintain a bit more of its autonomy but here, too, Moscow's grip tightened, as Abkhazia's defense ministers and chief of staff were Russians as well. Moscow also provided the lion's share of the budget for both the Abkhaz and South Ossetian separatist administrations. Starting in 2002, Putin initiated a dramatic expansion in the granting of Russian passports to the Abkhaz and South Ossetians. Russian passports were welcome as a way to travel, although in reality few residents ever left the country except to visit Russia. For Moscow it created a fake diaspora and another lever of control. Having handed out thousands of passports to individuals living on what it still recognized as Georgian territory, Moscow would subsequently claim the right to defend its newly minted "citizens."

Visiting Western officials were also exposed to Putin's wrath and his threats to use the frozen conflicts against Tbilisi. In late October 2006

Secretary of State Rice visited Moscow. In a private meeting with Putin after dinner in a hunting lodge outside of Moscow, the conversation turned to Georgia. Putin's tone immediately changed, and he went into a tirade against Saakashvili. He told Rice that if the Georgian leader ever moved against either Abkhazia or South Ossetia, Moscow would respond with military force and he would then officially recognize both Sukhumi and Tskhinvali. Rice responded that it was important that all sides, including Russia, practice restraint. She underlined to Putin that the United States firmly supported Georgia's territorial integrity and a peaceful resolution of the issues and would oppose the use of force by any side, including Russia. She warned Putin that military intervention by Moscow would have very real consequences for U.S.-Russian relations. The Russian president became furious, stood up, and walked out.[11]

Russian leverage over Georgia on the frozen conflicts derived from the importance Tbilisi attached to getting these lost territories back. Saakashvili had come to power promising not only democracy but reunification. Even though the responsibility for the loss of Abkhazia and South Ossetia lay with his predecessors, he made defending Georgia's territorial integrity the number one priority in his maiden speech as president. At times it appeared to Western diplomats that he mixed modern American-style politics and nineteenth-century Central European or Balkan nationalism. When Westerners suggested he forget about the conflicts, he not only pointed to past injustices, refugees, or the decrepit state of affairs in Abkhazia and South Ossetia; he believed that neither he nor his government could survive if he were seen as "losing" these territories.

This is where many outside critics believe that Saakashvili went wrong. They contend that he should have set aside the frozen conflicts as a problem he had inherited and blame them on his predecessors as opposed to making their resolution his priority. They claim that the Georgian public was far more interested in fixing unemployment than in regaining the lost territories. But such a judgment may to be too simple. While public support for Saakashvili's strategy of Western integration and NATO was high, hovering between 70 and 80 percent, support for regaining the lost territories was even higher. The Georgian public seemed to care far more than many Western observers wanted to believe. In any case, Saakashvili was not prepared to jettison his responsibility to try to regain the territories. It was the David the Builder side of him.

At the same time, Saakashvili actually marked a break with his predecessors' tradition of irresponsible and romantic Georgian nationalism in important ways. His concept of citizenship was not ethnic. He was a republican with a small *r*. He was willing to go further than any Georgian leader since independence in offering autonomy to South Ossetia and Abkhazia, but he was also fully committed to Georgia's territorial integrity. In his first months as president, Saakashvili faced a major political crisis in the southwestern Autonomous Republic of Adjara with its capital of Batumi. With a major port, it was a wealthy enclave run by an authoritarian narco-baron named Aslan Abashidze who had close ties to the mayor of Moscow, Yury Luzkhov.

Saakashvili managed to defuse the crisis peacefully and oust Abashidze by mobilizing society and using many of the same tactics of "people's power" that had been successful in the Rose Revolution. Abashidze was forced to quit in May 2004 and flew back to Moscow on a plane with the former Russian foreign minister and head of the Russian National Security Council Igor Ivanov, himself half-Georgian. Saakashvili proudly called it a "second bloodless revolution" and a new way of using democracy and civil society to wrest control from local separatist dictators. He promised to step up his efforts to regain Georgia's other two separatist provinces as well.

Moscow tolerated this move, perhaps because Abashidze was so unsavory that he could hardly be defended. But in Russian eyes it was hardly a recipe for how to do business. Moscow was top down whereas Saakashvili was bottom up. Putin subsequently warned Saakashvili not to expect any additional favors from him. As Saakashvili later recalled the conversation, Putin told him, "Now remember, we did not intervene in Adjara, but you won't have any gifts from using South Ossetia and Abkhazia." In the years that followed, Putin repeatedly referred to Adjara in talks with Western leaders as proof that Saakashvili could not be trusted to deal with the frozen conflicts. It was another example of a Russian modus operandi in which a small victory for the cause of law and order over a despicable narco-baron could be twisted and portrayed as evidence that the new Georgian president could not be trusted. After Adjara, Moscow moved to tighten its control over Abkhazia and South Ossetia.

Saakashvili's strategy had several components. Perhaps the most important one was to fix Georgia. No one wanted to live in a broken and failing state with rampant corruption and limited economic opportunity—least of all the alienated minorities in Abkhazia and South Ossetia. If Georgia harbored any hope of convincing these lost provinces to return, it would have to create a more democratic and prosperous society to attract them. It was a version of the magnet theory. Georgia's leaders understood in principle the direct link between their ability to reform Georgia and the frozen conflicts. The long-term hope was that the allure of a better life in Georgia would ultimately lead Abkhaz and Ossetians to conclude that opting to stay in a loose structure with Georgia was preferable to being independent or being annexed to Russia. Although this was not initially his main focus, developing that Western perspective for Georgia and offering the Abkhaz and South Ossetians a chance for a better life in a loose confederation with Tbilisi came to been seen as a key part of such a strategy.

A second priority for Saakashvili was to move beyond the disastrous legacy of his predecessor and make it clear that minorities had rights and a future in Georgia. While his opponents tried to paint him as a continuation of the crazy romantic nationalism of Gamsakhurdia, in reality he also tabled autonomy proposals that in principle went quite far. They involved offers of widespread autonomy that in substance came to independence through the decentralization of local decision making, free economic zones, disproportionate representation in federal structures, and constitutional guarantees of language and cultural rights within a loose federal structure. There were offers to allow ease and freedom of movement with North Ossetia through cross-border arrangements with Russia as well as a flexible approach to dual citizenship. Georgia's territorial integrity was sacrosanct, but everything else was negotiable.

Third, Tbilisi clearly saw the existing formats and peacekeeping mandates as one-sided and as part of the problem as opposed to part of the solution. This was the bone that perhaps stuck in the Georgian president's throat the most—and trying to change these mandates was one of his overriding objectives from the outset. Georgia had been forced to accept them at a time of extreme weakness to achieve a ceasefire. They also made it impossible for Georgia to solve these conflicts on its own. They needed to be changed if they were going to bring about an authentic peace process. Tbilisi wanted to see a step-by-step expansion of the international presence on the ground and a broader participation of the international community—starting with the United Nations and the OSCE and extending to the European Union. This plan was designed to dilute the de facto monopoly that Russia enjoyed. Changing the format was also important because the needs on the ground had changed. The original structures and rules were designed more for a truce and the separation of forces. What was needed now was something more geared toward confidence building and conflict resolution.

But Saakashvili did not just believe in carrots. He also wanted a stick. He wanted to pursue diplomacy but with the threat of force in his back pocket. One lesson he had drawn from the wars of the early 1990s was that Georgia needed a strong state and army that Russia would respect and would not be able to push around militarily. He did not believe that the kind of separatist leaders who ruled in Sukhumi and Tskhinvali would willingly abandon the status quo just like that. In his eyes they were way too comfortable and depended on the conflict in order to justify their rule. He wanted to convince them that the status quo was not tenable and would change—one way or the other.

He obviously preferred to do it peacefully and cooperatively. But he was also willing to keep the military option on the table—either to get their attention and strengthen his hand in negotiations or to use it if it ever came to a fight. Saakashvili wanted to mix it up and keep the separatists off guard. In conversations he was capable of switching with astonishing speed from talk of isolating and ratcheting up the pressure on the separatist leaderships to being conciliatory and tabling creative peace deals that went well beyond what anyone had previously contemplated or could have pulled off. It was also why some visitors came away unsure what his real bottom line was and whether he could be fully trusted.

So while launching his peace offensive and pursuing his own brand of secret diplomacy, Saakashvili also launched an effort to modernize and upgrade the Georgian police and armed forces. To some degree this was simply part of his broader strategy of building a strong state that could defend its citizens. He was also driven by his desire to qualify for NATO militarily. But he was also determined that Georgia would never again be easily defeated by a ragtag separatist militia, as it had been in the early 1990s. It was also a signal to a Russia that he felt would never take Georgia seriously unless it was strong and willing to defend itself. Building Georgian military strength was one way to reduce Russia's asymmetrical position and strengthen his. He wanted the Russians to know that if they provoked a fight with him, he was capable of fighting back. It was the Mannerheim in him.

How did the Abkhaz and South Ossetians—as well as Moscow—react to this strategy? The Abkhaz and South Ossetians stonewalled, further cut themselves off from Georgia, deepened their own cooperation, and appealed to Moscow to finally recognize their independence once and for all. When Tbilisi offered to secretly meet the Abkhaz or South Ossetians for quiet confidential peace talks outside the country, the latter usually demurred. The separatist leaders also understood full well that the source of their power was their alliance with Russia and anti-Georgian nationalism. Their identity was rooted in a sense of confrontation with Georgia. If these enclaves were truly opened up to the outside world, many of their leaders were unlikely to survive. They, too, needed a sense of siege and the image of a Georgian enemy at the gate to cement their rule. Every time Tbilisi made a new peace proposal, Saakashvili was attacked and further demonized.

Moscow enjoyed having it both ways. It continued to officially recognize Georgia's territorial integrity and thus portrayed itself as being constructive. In conversations with Western diplomats, Russian diplomats would point to the lobbying by the Abkhaz and South Ossetians for outright recognition as proof of the pressure Russia was under from the two separatist provinces and how difficult it was to ostensibly restrain them. At the same time, the unresolved status quo served Russian interests quite well. A resolution of the conflicts would, of course, have reduced its leverage over Georgia and would have given Tbilisi an open path to try to accelerate its integration in the West. That was the last thing Russia wanted. For a long time, the West assumed that Moscow was content to leave the pot boiling in these enclaves as a way of maximizing its influence and pursuing its goal.

The result was stalemate. Whereas Georgia wanted to start with various steps that would open up the conflict zones to the outside world and influence, the separatist leaders wanted to talk about status and recognition.

That was, of course, anathema for Georgia. Whereas the separatist leaders wanted to cement the status quo, Tbilisi wanted to overturn it. In spite of a plethora of peace proposals and plans over the years, the sides went around in circles, and none of these proposals ever got past first base. Moscow preferred it that way. Many in the West could live with it—and in a funny way the separatist leaderships had their own interest in the status quo, as unsatisfactory as it was. But it was a stalemate and a catch–22 situation that Saakashvili was constantly looking for a way out of.

Many of Georgia's partners, especially in Europe, were not sure about Saakashvili's policies either. They were scared by any talk of the use of force or hard power to regain the territories. But they were also nervous when Georgia rolled out its strategy to use soft power to solve the South Ossetian conflict, refusing to embrace such tactics in any meaningful way. They were not sure how serious Tbilisi really was about peace plans that never seemed to go anywhere or achieve anything. They were reluctant to support Georgia's desire to press Russia into changing the international peacekeeping formats and mandates—and often unwilling to commit police or any other forces to complement or replace them. Above all, they were nervous about Georgia's buildup of police and armed forces—especially the saber-rattling and loose talk of a possible land grab or military action.

To Georgian ears, the West was better at telling them what not to do than presenting a useful way forward. They heard the West's warning about the use of force, but when they asked how the West expected them to actually resolve these conflicts, the answer they received was not convincing. I was exposed to some of these dilemmas and the tension evoked while on a study tour to Georgia in the spring of 2006. We met with then defense minister Irakli Okruashvili. He was known for being the most vocal advocate of a possible military option to regain the lost territories. A native of Tskhinvali, he had boasted that he would resign as minister if Georgia failed to restore control over the breakaway province by January 1, 2007.

After he became defense minister, he and his staff studied past military campaigns in which states had used lightning strikes to achieve strategic surprise and major victories—for example, Israel in 1967, and Operation Storm in 1995, when Croatian, Bosnian, and Bosnian-Croat forces brushed by UN peacekeepers and crushed the Bosnian-Serb army in a matter of days, setting the stage for ending the fighting in Croatia and Bosnia. How much was serious and how much was bluff was never quite clear. Okruashvili also enjoyed offering to take visitors bear-hunting in the Kodori Gorge or other dangerous places close to enemy lines. Many people believed that his tough rhetoric and tactics had helped to precipitate heavy local fighting in South Ossetia during the summer of 2004.

Okruashvili was also emerging as a potential rival and challenger to Saakashvili. Allegedly the two men had initially agreed that the defense minister would play the role of the hawk in public whereas the president would be more restrained so as not to scare off Tbilisi's western allies. But Okruashvili's tough rhetoric struck a chord and his popularity started to grow. Following Zhavania's death earlier that spring, the posturing to become Saakashvili's heir apparent had intensified and soon there was talk about Okruashvili as a potential rival to the president. When we met with him in the Defense Ministry, his relations with Saakashvili were already strained.

Okruashvili asked our study group of diplomats, think-tankers, and journalists how committed the West was to helping Georgia regain its lost provinces. What strategy could we offer, he asked rhetorically, to help Georgia peacefully regain South Ossetia? There was an awkward silence. No one had an answer. "That's okay," the minister said. "I understand that for you this is not an urgent problem. You can live with the status quo. We can't." He went on to say that if the United States and Europe were not willing to assist Georgia, we should understand that Tbilisi might have to go its own way to resolve the conflict. The implications were clear. He was not ruling out the use of force. After the August war broke out, Okruashvili stated in an interview that Saakashvili and he had developed plans to take both Abkhazia and South Ossetia while he was still defense minister.[12]

What he did not say in that interview, however, was that it was also during that same period that the decision was made to abandon the military option for South Ossetia. Okruashvili resigned in mid-November 2006— less than two months before his self-proclaimed deadline for taking back South Ossetia. He and Saakashvili fell out over the frozen conflicts, charges of corruption, and his real or imagined efforts to position himself as a successor to the president. Okruashvili would end up a bitter foe, eventually seeking and receiving political asylum in France. But the debate he pushed while defense minister is nevertheless revealing as it underscored both Georgia's temptation to consider the military option and the constraints holding Tbilisi back. Even before he left office, the decision to abandon the military option for South Ossetia had been made.

The fighting in South Ossetia in 2004 had led to a debate within the Georgian leadership over the feasibility of the military option to regain Abkhazia and South Ossetia. In spite of Tbilisi's rhetoric, the reality was that Georgian military capabilities were actually quite limited. Georgia would never have enough troops to fight in both South Ossetia and Abkhazia and the country could ill afford a heavy and sustained defense buildup. Georgian leaders knew there was no support for such a move in the West and that even talking about that option was costing it support among the allies. Some in Tbilisi argued that if they could launch a quick strike and succeed within three days, the West might be prepared to accept such a fait accompli and recognize a new status quo. But they would have to fight and win on their own. If they lost, everyone understood that no one would come to Georgia's rescue.

It was also clear to everyone that Abkhazia was much more important than South Ossetia—politically, economically, and strategically. As a result, a decision was made to abandon planning for any military move in South Ossetia but to keep it open as an option for Abkhazia. Three arguments won the day in the Georgian cabinet against the use of force against South Ossetia. The first was the risk of provoking a war with Russia. The second was the realization that even if Georgia succeeded in South Ossetia, it would lose Abkhazia—and there was no comparison in the importance of the two in Georgian eyes. The third and final argument was that such a move would doom Georgia's chances for NATO. The person who took the final decision to abandon the military option against South Ossetia was Mikheil Saakashvili.

In 2005 the then Georgian prime minister Zurab Noghaideli put forward a new peace plan for South Ossetia. But the real shift in strategy came in late 2006 as Georgia opted to bank on the success of soft rather than hard power in South Ossetia. The idea was to take advantage of the porousness of the border and the intermingling of populations and to use soft power to appeal over the heads of the separatist leaders to the hearts and minds of the local population. The goal was to persuade them that a future with Georgia was not as bad as their own leaders suggested; that they would be better off in a loose confederation with a reforming Georgia that was starting to boom economically; and that Tbilisi had a fair offer for them that would respect their cultural autonomy. To back this up, Tbilisi set up an alternative Ossetian government in the town of Kurta north of Tskhinvali under Georgian protection. They started demonstration projects, ranging from free summer holidays to medical clinics to recreational facilities designed to lure and attract South Ossetians. It was called Project Sanakoyev.

One of the consequences of Moscow's increasingly tight grip over the Tskhinvali leadership and Koikoty's own tactics was that several Ossetian rebel leaders had broken ranks. They included a number of South Ossetian leaders who had been more open to trying to negotiate a peace deal with the Georgians but had since been expelled from the South Ossetian leadership. Some of those former South Ossetian rebel leaders had since gone to Russia, but others had headed to Tbilisi, where they were discovered by the Georgian government. One of those was Dmitry Sanakoyev. He had fought as a militia leader against the Georgians in the 1991–1992 war. He had subsequently been the de facto defense minister and later the prime minister of South Ossetia. As prime minister he had advocated burying the hatchet and starting a dialogue with the Georgian side the conflict—only to be pushed out and replaced by Koikoty, with Russian support.

With Georgian support, Sanakoyev now became the head of what was essentially a rival South Ossetian government based in the town of Kurta and supported by Tbilisi. The Georgians invested heavily in his administration, providing him with funds to build infrastructure projects and provide a better life for those living in the part of South Ossetia under Georgian control. Georgia also offered summer camps and other recreational opportunities for South Ossetian youth, including a "Disco for Peace" built at the end of a valley where Georgian and Ossetian youngsters could go dancing. Tskhinvali responded by declaring Sanakoyev a traitor and trying to prevent any of the citizens under its control from participating in such projects. The Disco for Peace stood empty—a symbol of the fear of the South Ossetian authorities to even let their youth go out for an evening of drinking and dancing with their Georgian counterparts.

Georgia had shifted strategy and embraced a new logic, one that was openly discussed with Washington: recover South Ossetia peacefully; bolster your credentials and case for NATO by focusing on gaining MAP (Membership Action Plan, a course of action leading to membership in NATO); and only from this position of greater confidence and strength contemplate in greater detail how to eventually recover Abkhazia. In the spring and summer of 2007 there was nevertheless a sense of possible movement on South Ossetia. Georgia had walked up to the line on the use of force then turned around and walked back and dropped that option. It had embraced a new strategy that it felt was gaining some traction on the ground. Russian diplomats were hinting at possible flexibility on South Ossetia and suggesting they might be ready to sack South Ossetian president Koikoty.

It was against this background that President Saakashvili decided to roll the diplomatic dice and make his most ambitious offer to resolve the South Ossetian conflict on terms amenable to Moscow. The idea emerged from a conversation between Saakashvili and Gela Bezhuashvili during the latter's stint as Georgian foreign minister. Bezhuashvili was one of the few key aides to Saakashvili who had worked hard to keep open lines of communication with key Russian officials. In June 2007 he proposed to Saakashvili that he call Putin and tell him that he had a very concrete plan to solve the South Ossetian conflict and that their foreign ministers should sit down to discuss it. Saakashvili made the call and Putin agreed. Bezhuashvili then called Russian foreign minister Sergei Lavrov to sketch out some of the key elements of his plan and agree on a time and place to meet.

The two foreign ministers met for a private dinner in Istanbul on June 24 at the Çirağan Palace Kempinski hotel, a former Ottoman imperial palace on the shores of the Bosporus. The Georgian proposal was far reaching. As opposed to pushing to delegitimize the Russian presence in South Ossetia, Tbilisi was now prepared to shift course and make Moscow the guarantor of peace there. Tbilisi was also willing to accept a special travel regime for South and North Ossetians. The package had a major economic component to develop energy and transport projects, including selling electricity to Turkey and Armenia. When Lavrov asked about NATO, Bezhuashvili responded that Georgia's NATO aspirations were best kept out of the package for the time being. But he also said that Georgia could be open minded.

At the moment, neither side trusted the other, but that could perhaps change over time if they managed to solve concrete problems together and build more trust.

The key question was, of course, who would run South Ossetia. The Georgians made it clear that they wanted to see Koikoty go but would not insist on his being replaced by Sanakoyev. Instead, they suggested internationally monitored elections be organized and that both sides allow the various South Ossetian leaders to compete for office. The Georgian side offered to turn this package into a treaty that would solve the border issues and drew a comparison to the 1921 Treaty of Kars, between Turkey and the Soviet Union. That treaty is one of the rare instances in international law where the local administrative structure of another country is secured by a treaty with another. Georgia was offering to give Russia a legal voice in its internal affairs in South Ossetia.

According to Bezhuashvili, it was an open and constructive conversation, with Lavrov listening and asking lots of questions. At the end of the dinner he agreed to report the offer back to Putin accurately but said he would not be making a recommendation one way or the other. This was something Putin, scheduled to arrive in Istanbul the next day, would want to decide himself. The next morning the details of the Georgian plan were leaked in the Russian press. When Bezhuashvili confronted Lavrov with the news story, the Russian foreign minister was equally surprised and furious. That leak effectively scuttled the plan as Koikoty immediately moved to shore up his position. Tbilisi speculated that the Russian Federal Security Service (FSB), which is responsible for maintaining the security of official phone calls, had monitored the conversation between the two foreign ministers and leaked the story in order to kill the plan.[13]

This failure notwithstanding, there was a widespread view in Tbilisi that Moscow would eventually cut its losses in South Ossetia and seek a deal. The conflict was simply too artificial and the province too small to be viable. Russia seemed to have much less of a strategic stake in it as well. Georgia had a policy in place to undercut support for the South Ossetian regime through soft power, which it thought was gaining traction. During my many visits to Tbilisi and in talks on the frozen conflicts, there was a clear difference in attitudes toward South Ossetia and Abkhazia. The Georgians were cautiously optimistic that they had a strategy that could work in South Ossetia and that time was on their side.

That was not the case in Abkhazia. It was both more important and a tougher nut to crack. That conflict had been bloodier and had left deeper scars. It was also more isolated, and Georgia had no access. The stakes were higher, as was the potential for escalation. Here Tbilisi did not yet have a political strategy. Nor did it believe time was on its side. The Georgians no longer had active military contingency plans for South Ossetia, but they had them for Abkhazia.

In spite of Washington's urgings that the Abkhaz issue be put on the back burner, Saakashvili had a hard time practicing patience. In the summer of 2007 he helped popularize a hit song about how Georgians longed to regain Abkhazia. Georgian Airways planes were named after Abkhaz cities. Saakashvili's own plane bore then name of Sukhumi. On the subject of Abkhazia, the military option was, in Georgian eyes, still very much on the table. And it was over Abkhazia that tension rose in the spring and summer of 2008, as the two sides almost came to war.

Other warning signs were also appearing on the horizon. In the fall of 2007, Bezhuashvili again met with Lavrov over a Scotch in New York on the margins of the annual UN General Assembly. The two men talked openly about the growing tension between Russia and Georgia, the risk that their countries might be headed toward war, and that they might end up personally fighting each other in the diplomatic trenches as their countries' respective foreign ministers. How could that trend be stopped? they asked each other. According to Bezhuashvili, Lavrov told him that Moscow would never let Georgia go West and join NATO. It simply feared that such a move would undercut its position in both the Southern and Northern Caucasus. Bezhuashvili pleaded that the opposite was true and that Georgia's democratic integration with the West would produce real stability in the region from which Moscow would benefit. But Lavrov was not buying it. The Georgian foreign minister headed home worried that his country was headed toward a clash.

CHAPTER 3

THE KOSOVO PRECEDENT

Diplomacy has its version of the Hippocratic oath—do no harm. Leaders and diplomats, like physicians, need to be aware of the consequences, intended or unintended, of their actions and of the potential collateral damage of their decisions. This means being aware of the impact that diplomacy in one area or region can have on another—and, if need be, refining or modifying such policy steps in ways that contain or limit those risks. The law of unintended consequences applies in international politics as well as in other areas of life.

In the spring of 2008, Western diplomacy in recognizing Kosovo did not heed that principle and inadvertently contributed to the summer's slide to war in Georgia. It supported Kosovo's independence without any coordinated effort to contain any spillover from that step into the frozen conflicts in Georgia. It also contributed to the war in the way it handled the issues involving Georgia and Ukraine and their desire for a Membership Action Plan (MAP) at the NATO Bucharest summit. In neither case did the United States or Europe intend to undercut Georgia. Their mistake was underestimating and being unprepared for how Moscow would use these crises as a pretext to move against Tbilisi.

In their handling of Kosovo, the United States and the European Union rarely connected the dots between what was happening in the Balkans and what might happen in the Southern Caucasus. We were too optimistic in our belief that we could compartmentalize the conflicts and handle each one separately and differently. The Balkans were obviously a priority for the West, which meant that the need to resolve Kosovo was the top concern driving Western policy. Georgia would have to live with the fallout of Western policy decisions there. Apart from simply reassuring Georgia that Kosovo would not set a precedent for frozen conflicts elsewhere, there was no attempt to handle these two sets of issues as an integrated whole. The West simply underestimated Moscow's deep-seated and long-standing anger on Kosovo and its willingness to retaliate against Western policy moves.

The West's decision to move ahead and recognize Kosovo while ignoring Russian objections may have been the right policy move for Kosovo and the region. The United States and leading European allies had their own arguably good reasons for supporting Kosovo's independence. It had been a decade since NATO's initial military intervention to halt Serbian ethnic cleansing, during which time Milošević was toppled and diplomatic efforts had failed to reach a consensual compromise on Kosovo's final status. I, too, was a supporter of Western recognition of Kosovo's independence. The desire to finally cut the Gordian knot on Kosovo and find a resolution after years of futile talks and deadlock was understandable. That was not necessarily the problem.

The problem was that the West did not develop any kind of Plan B for managing the consequences of that policy for Georgia—either on the ground or diplomatically with Moscow. This step increased instability and tension in Abkhazia and South Ossetia at a time when tensions were already high. Diplomatically the West's argument about the uniqueness of Kosovo was a double-edged sword that Moscow now used to pursue its own interests. Its message was clear: uniqueness in the Balkans will beget uniqueness elsewhere. If the West could act with impunity against Moscow's wishes in the Balkans, the Kremlin would show that it could act with impunity in the Southern Caucasus. All of this enhanced Georgia's vulnerability by handing Moscow a pretext to move against Tbilisi and helped trigger the Russian political and military escalation that culminated in war on August 7. After the West's recognition of provisional Kosovar independence, Russian leaders openly told their Georgian counterparts that they would now pay the price for Western policy on Kosovo—and they did.

As a result, there was no preventive strategy under consideration, let alone in place on the ground or in the diplomatic corridors of the West, to shield Tbilisi from or to mitigate such consequences—except for weak diplomatic talking points. That gamble backfired. Moscow meant what it said—and acted accordingly. There was no Western strategy to engage or protect Georgia from the collateral damage. And there was precious little that Georgia could do on its own to insulate itself from the fallout of Western policy decisions. There are steps the West could have and should have taken to prevent this from happening. It could have warned Moscow at the highest levels that retaliation against Georgia as a response to Kosovo's independence would be considered unacceptable and would have consequences for Russia's own relations with the United States, the European Union, and NATO.

The United States and the European Union could also have pushed for beefed-up and expanded UN and OSCE missions and international presence on the ground in the separatist provinces to help control dynamics there. An expanded international presence in the conflict zones would have provided greater transparency, mitigated the fallout of the Kosovo decision, and reduced the potential for Russian mischief. Or the United States and Europe could have been even bolder and pushed for full-scale internationalization of the management of these conflicts under the auspices of the UN—as it had done in Kosovo a decade earlier. The West neither took steps to deter Russia nor pushed for changes on the ground to protect Tbilisi and limit the fallout from Western policy decisions.

In Bucharest, NATO was looking for a compromise that bridged the internal divide in the Alliance on the future of enlargement in general and on the issue of whether to grant Georgia and Ukraine a MAP. The compromise that was eventually forged—not to grant a MAP but to make an unprecedented political pledge that these countries would eventually become Alliance members—satisfied the different political needs within the divided Alliance. It reconciled a deep divide on what to do about Georgia and Ukraine while preventing a diplomatic train wreck. The allies hoped it would reassure Kiev and Tbilisi by granting them an unprecedented long-term pledge for eventual membership without alienating the Russians and Putin, who had staked their reputation on preventing these countries from getting a MAP.

What looked good in theory and satisfied the divergent political needs of key NATO members elicited a very different reaction in Moscow. Putin's behavior at the summit itself and his subsequent comments to Western leaders, including President Bush, suggest that Moscow drew the very opposite conclusion from the one NATO had hoped for. Moscow may have concluded that the danger of Georgia's joining NATO was indeed real but, given the strong divisions in the Alliance, it was unlikely in the near term. It therefore decided it had to act soon to stop Georgia before the process gained momentum and became irreversible. In other words, instead of deterring the Russians, this compromise might have emboldened them. Like Kosovo, Bucharest helped trigger a series of Russian steps that led to war the following August.

By mid-2006 it had become clear that Moscow's policy on Kosovo was hardening and that the assumption that Russia would not stand in the way of a resolution of the Kosovo issue was crumbling. It was all part of the quasi-revolution taking place in Russian foreign policy and the hardening of Moscow's position on issues across wider Europe. However, the international community, and above all, the United States and the European Union, did not take seriously Moscow's threats that it would retaliate against Kosovo's independence by moving against Georgia. They concluded that Moscow was bluffing. The West was unwilling to run the risks of growing instability in Kosovo by, yet again, postponing a decision in favor of supervised independence. It therefore took a calculated policy gamble that Moscow's threats were not serious and that it could move forward on Kosovo without adversely affecting Georgia.

How the conflict in Kosovo on the one hand, and in Abkhazia and South Ossetia on the other, became linked is a saga involving international law, changing Western diplomatic priorities, and the dynamics of a resurgent Russia seeking to challenge the United States and Europe. It often had less to do with the facts on the ground than with the stakes of the changing dynamics of the West's relationship with Russia. A decade earlier the issue of

Kosovo had produced arguably the greatest crisis, as well as the greatest moment of collaboration, in Russian ties with the West since the end of the Cold War. The drama of the political and diplomatic effort to stop Serbian dictator Slobodan Milošević from pursuing the ethnic cleansing that culminated in NATO's military campaign is interwoven with the effort to build a new and more cooperative post–Cold War relationship with Russia.

NATO's decision to intervene in Kosovo to halt Milošević's brutal campaign had exacerbated Russia's worst fears about Western intentions and strategy. The problem from Russia's perspective was that the United States was once again acting as if it had the right to impose its will on the world—throwing its weight around in the UN Security Council, enlisting NATO, and pushing the OSCE to do its bidding. After Bosnia in 1995, an expanded NATO was now bombing Orthodox Serbs in a nation once closely allied to Russia and a cause célèbre among Russian pan-Slavic nationalists. To make matters worse, the Alliance did so without a full UN Security Council Resolution, thereby showing Moscow's UN veto right to be inconsequential. To Russians, it looked like American expansionism pure and simple under the guise of a new doctrine of humanitarian interventionism with NATO as the world's policeman.

The Kosovo conflict in the late 1990s also brought out the worst in Russian conspiracy theory. Few Russians could believe that the West was truly acting out of humanitarian concerns or that NATO would become involved in a place as strategically unimportant as Kosovo unless it was part of some larger master plan. Many Russians saw in Kosovo a sinister analogy to Chechnya. Like Chechnya, Kosovo was a Muslim-majority province on the border of a state with a Slavic majority. Like Chechnya, it was boiling with separatist passions. As absurd it sounds, as NATO moved closer and closer to military intervention in Kosovo in the spring of 1999, Russian politicians, military experts, and commentators speculated that this war was just a warm-up for a future war against Russia that would begin with the West's claims that it was defending human rights in Chechnya. Russian leaders bluntly warned that if Moscow accepted intervention in Kosovo, sooner or later the same model would be applied to Russia, and neither its seat on the UN Security Council nor its nascent ties to the Alliance would give Moscow a veto over U.S. actions.

Kosovo therefore became a remarkably sensitive issue for Moscow, touching on all of its reasons for fearing NATO and opposing its expansion. I was not part of the State Department team dealing directly with Kosovo at the time, but I had my own brief brush with Russian passion on the issue. When NATO started its bombing campaign in March 1999, Russia froze or broke off nearly all ties with the United States and the West, with a small handful of exceptions. One of them was a consultation I had scheduled in Moscow with Deputy Foreign Minister Yevgeny Gusarov on a new OSCE charter. As I arrived from the airport at the U.S. ambassador's residence, known as Spaso House, I found the entrance blocked by more than a dozen police cars and security personnel milling around. I made my way through the security corridor to find Ambassador Jim Collins studying an arrow imbedded in the outside wall of Spaso House. He explained that a man on horseback, dressed as Alexander Nevsky, had ridden by a few minutes earlier and attacked the residence with bow and arrow to protest NATO's intervention.

The Western view was, of course, different. NATO had taken the step of intervening and going to war only with great reluctance and as a last resort to prevent widespread ethnic cleansing and the slaughter of Kosovars by Milošević's brutal army. NATO would have acted with the blessing of the UN Security Council if the Russian Federation had not threatened a veto. What many in Moscow claimed was an awesome display of Western military might looked a bit different from the inside—a divided Alliance desperately trying to stay on course and manage its own division while fighting a war against a wily adversary with one hand tied behind its back. Rather than displaying Western strength, many thought NATO's campaign only revealed the Alliance's own timidity and indecisiveness.

A decade later it is easily forgotten how close NATO and Russia came to an actual military confrontation on the ground in Kosovo. The West and Moscow had not only wrestled over the diplomacy of how to end the war. One final sticking point was where and how Russian troops would be included in a NATO-led peacekeeping operation on the ground. Moscow finally agreed to the proposed Western solution, but hard-line elements within the Defense Ministry launched a last-minute attempt to surprise the West with a secret dash to grab the Slatina Airport, a key provincial airfield, which could have scuttled the peacekeeping force and sparked a NATO-Russian military clash. NATO in turn moved quickly to get to the airfield first and eventually defused the confrontation. But the danger of a military clash was real. It was arguably the closest NATO and Russia had come to fighting since the end of the Cold War.

But Moscow was often less focused on events on the ground than on the symbolism of the West's seemingly acting without Russia's consent on a key issue of European security. The domestic echo of NATO's bombing mobilized anti-Western forces in Russia and endangered the fragile government of Boris Yeltsin. Russia eventually came around and assisted the West in compelling Milošević to accept Western terms to stop the bombing—but not without dramatic diplomatic clashes, constitutional crises in Moscow, and mutinous and out-of-control Russian generals ignoring civilian orders. Although the war began over the furious objections of the Russian Federation, it ended in large measure because President Yeltsin and his special envoy, Viktor Chernomyrdin, eventually decided to ignore the military and nationalist calls for harsh action against the West and threw Russia's weight behind what were essentially American and NATO demands on Milošević to stop the bombing.[1] The Kosovo war of 1999 was both the most severe crisis of a nascent post–Cold War era as well as the most dramatic example of what U.S.-Russian collaboration could accomplish. But whereas the West moved on, scars remained on the Russian side, and Moscow's bitterness never completely dissipated. Yeltsin's national security advisor at the time was a rising former KGB officer by the name of Vladimir Putin who was directly involved in some aspects of the final diplomacy, including Russian attempts to occupy the Slatina airfield before NATO forces could arrive. By the end of 1999, Yeltsin had resigned and Putin had become president of Russia.

While Russia was subsequently fully included in the UN–mandated and led effort for the political reconstruction of Kosovo as well as the NATO-led peacekeeping force, Moscow neither forgave nor forgot. It saw NATO's intervention in Kosovo as creating a dangerous precedent of the Alliance's acting out of area without a full UN blessing, undercutting the strength of its veto. The idea of cooperation with Moscow in the Balkans becoming a model for the future ran out of steam and political will. Kosovo's legacy, like that of Bosnia before it, remained a very ambivalent one. In Russian eyes, Kosovo remained a cause célèbre for Russian nationalists—the penultimate symbol of Russia's impotence vis-à-vis the West under Yeltsin. It was an exercise in Russia's humiliation and exclusion that needed to be avenged and never repeated. Some scholars suggest that NATO's campaign in Kosovo did more than enlargement did to reshape Russian perceptions of the Alliance and that it was the beginning of the end of the post–Cold War strategic partnership between Russia and the West.[2]

Following Milošević's ouster in the summer of 1999, the West was not officially prepared to support Kosovo's independence. UN Resolution 1244 had acknowledged Serbian sovereignty while establishing a UN mission to prepare Kosovo for self-government, pending a political settlement on its future status.[3] NATO had gone to war to stop Serbian ethnic cleansing rather than to make Kosovo independent, although at that time many of us already wondered whether Serbs and Kosovars could ever again live together in the same state. There was a widespread view in Washington and Europe that Serbia's future was actually the key to regional stability. Without a successful and democratic Serbia, the Balkans would never be stable, and Europe would never really be whole, free, and at peace. The big prize in Western eyes, therefore, was a democratic, economically successful Serbia that would eventually become a member of the European Union and NATO. The issue was to reconcile that goal with the overwhelming desire of Kosovars for independence.

There appeared to be one way to square that circle. A Serbia that was free of Milošević, was truly democratic, and that confronted its nationalist demons could—so it was hoped—also embrace a different stance on Kosovo as well. The United States and Europe hoped that this new post-Milošević democratic Serbia would either reconcile with Kosovo in some new framework or recognize that this issue had become an albatross around its neck that it needed to shed in order to move forward. In short, the hope was that a new democratic Serbia would let Kosovo go and instead make a dash for the European Union and, ultimately, NATO.

For these initial years after the Kosovo war, the West concentrated on a policy of "standards before status" while hoping that democratic change in Serbia could help foster that kind of new attitude and policy. This meant improving governance in Kosovo, especially the protection of minority rights; giving Belgrade time for democratic transformation as well as for reconsideration of the plusses and minuses of a continued desire to dominate Kosovo; encouraging the European Union to offer Serbia the prospects of closer ties and eventual membership in return for progress made on war criminals and a sensible solution in Kosovo. In the meantime, the UN-led effort would focus on getting fledgling Kosovar institutions ready for the possibility that the Serbs could not be reconciled and that Kosovar independence might eventually have to come without Belgrade's acquiescence.

This policy suffered several setbacks in 2003 and 2004. The first came when Prime Minister Zoran Djindjić—the one Serbian leader who appeared committed to domestic transformation and who recognized the long-term advantages of accepting a highly autonomous or even independent Kosovo—was assassinated in March 2003. The second came in Kosovo itself when anti-Serbian riots broke out in March 2004. Those riots deeply shook Serbian faith in the Western commitment to protect the Serbian minority in Kosovo. In the meantime, the Balkans had been sinking as a policy priority as the terrorist attacks of September 11, 2001, followed by the Iraq war, diverted American attention away from Europe and an issue that was still seen by many as a Clinton Administration legacy. These factors all contributed to a loss of momentum and a stalemate on the ground as the Balkans were put on the back burner of Western political priorities.

But the years of failed attempts to reach a mutually satisfactory solution to Kosovo's future political status slowly but surely changed the center of gravity in Western thinking on the Kosovar issues to favor some kind of supervised independence. By the beginning of Bush's second term, the United States had decided that its initial policy approach on Kosovo had failed and that it was time to shift gears. Along with many Europeans, Washington concluded that the Serbs were unable to move beyond their own nationalism and would not be reconciled to the loss of Kosovo in the near future. Lagging reforms at home in Belgrade meant that the European Union could not move quickly or clearly enough on Serbian EU membership to offer a real carrot, and expecting the Kosovars to continue to wait for their independence was running the risk of provoking major instability on the ground.

This realization led to a series of diplomatic initiatives designed to engineer a soft landing for Kosovo. The hope was that the international community could manage a process leading to conditional supervised independence of Kosovo rather than making it come about through a unilateral declaration that could spark renewed conflict. In these efforts, the West was prepared to go the extra mile and work creatively to address Russian concerns and resolve the Kosovo issues within the UN framework. It was not prepared to run the risk of Kosovo exploding and new instability emerging. The West was bearing the lion's share of the responsibility and risk on the ground in Kosovo. It was above all the European Union that was offering to take over responsibility from the United Nations, play a leading role in resolving these issues, and eventually integrate these countries into European institutions. The United States and Europe were willing to work closely with Russia but expected that at the end of the day, Moscow would defer to them on the way forward.

But Belgrade and Moscow were moving in the other direction. The Serbian government interpreted this shift in Western policy as pro-Kosovo. In June 2006 it made a final attempt to approach Washington and European capitals with a proposed plan that would focus on local municipal authorities in Kosovo and then move forward in small steps. It was rejected by American and European officials as a delaying tactic. After that rejection, the Serbs effectively gave up on Western mediation and increasingly turned to Moscow for help and support for their position. In parallel and for other reasons, Russia under Putin was moving in a more autocratic and nationalist direction and was quite happy to embrace Belgrade. Flush with the wealth of petrodollars, the Russian leader had embarked on the project of rebuilding Russia's strength at home and influence abroad and reversing what many consider the humiliations of the 1990s. The Balkans were obviously not part of Russia's "near abroad," on which Putin was focused, but Moscow still felt that it had significant interests to defend there. It was determined to make clear to the West that nothing would again be decided in the Balkans without its approval and over its objections.

The similarities and differences between Serbia's conflict over Kosovo and Georgia's conflict over Abkhazia still ignite passionate debate. Both cases involved restive provinces governed by separatist ethnic leaderships that were seeking independence from central governments. It was the classic tension or clash between the principle of territorial integrity and self-determination—an issue that had bedeviled statesmen and lawyers for a long time. Under what circumstances does an ethnic group have the right to break away and become a separate state? The issue of whether and how state borders in Europe can be changed was at the heart of the Helsinki Final Act in 1975 and was put to the test with the breakup of both the former Soviet Union and Yugoslavia.

But when one moved beyond principles and into the real world, the differences between the conflicts in Kosovo and Abkhazia often seemed to be far greater than the similarities. One was the simple issue of demographics. In Kosovo, the ethnic majority of the population was some 90 percent Kosovar. In Abkhazia, the Abkhaz had been in the minority. The Georgian population had been almost three times the Abkhaz before the early 1990s, when it was ethnically cleansed with the help and involvement of Russia as an outside power. There was also a basic difference in the origins of these conflicts. Kosovar Albanians had been discriminated against long before the fall of Communism. In the former Yugoslavia they had been denied the kind of autonomy granted to other ethnic groups from the Slovenes to the Macedonians. The Abkhaz, on the other hand, had enjoyed a more privileged position. In many ways, they had been the privileged ethnic group in Sukhumi, enjoying disproportionate power and representation under Soviet rule. They revolted after Georgian independence in a fight to keep that position of power and privilege.[4]

Moreover, Kosovar and Abkhaz political leaders had dramatically different visions of self-rule. Kosovo's leaders were hardly model democrats, but over the years they had, with Western encouragement and pressure, put forward an extensive package of autonomy and minority rights for Serbian ethnic communities in Kosovo. In the case of Sukhumi, the Abkhaz leadership did no such thing, for it would have undercut their claim to power. Abkhaz leaders were very much aware that they had been in the minority before the war. They understood full well that any agreement allowing the return of significant numbers of Georgian refugees or granting those regions autonomy might turn into a slippery slope that would erode their power base and control. Instead, in this conflict it was Tbilisi that put forward plans for far-reaching autonomy, equal rights, and the resettlement of refugees.

There was also a basic difference in the moral justice of these conflicts. After a decade of gross human rights abuses, Serbian leaders launched in the late 1990s an ethnic cleaning campaign against Kosovo that over a number of years resulted in the deaths of 10,000 people and the displacement of 1 million more. Only after exhaustive diplomacy efforts did the international community and NATO go to war over Kosovo, and Serbian leaders were indicted on charges of war crimes for what they had done. To be sure, Tbilisi had pursued dangerous and foolish nationalistic policies toward both Abkhazia and South Ossetia in the early 1990s after Georgia had gained its independence. It certainly bore its share of responsibility for the bloodshed and atrocities that ensued and the wars it had lost. But it had not committed the same kinds of crimes that Milošević and the Serbs had. When it came to historical justice, it was the Georgians who had been expelled and ethnically cleansed by the Abkhaz with Russian support.

But perhaps the biggest differences between the two conflicts lay in how much the West cared about them and the legitimacy of the processes enacted to determine their outcomes. There was no comparison between the political priority given to the Balkans and that given to the Southern Caucasus. NATO had intervened twice in the Balkans in the 1990s to stop ethnic cleansing and war. The West had mobilized one of the world's biggest peacekeeping efforts ever, one that initially included the Russians. In some ways, modern UN-mandated and NATO-led European peacekeeping was born and developed in the Balkans. The UN mission in Kosovo had real authority and in many ways ran the province. The OSCE had significantly expanded its capabilities and role on the ground. The European Union had made economic reconstruction and the integration of the Balkans a top priority of its nascent common foreign and security policy. The Balkans were the showcase for the UN, OSCE, European Union, and NATO—and this was reflected in the quality of the diplomats and soldiers sent there as well as in the money that was showered on the region. Last and perhaps most important, these countries had a very clear prospect of becoming members of both the European Union and NATO.

In part because of how much the West cared, Kosovo had been the focal point of an intense diplomatic process to determine its future status. That process was sanctioned and led by the United Nations, and thus had full international legitimacy. That effort was not precipitate. On the contrary, it was deliberate and designed to build consensus and address the issues and concerns of key actors, including UN Security Council member Russia. Georgia and Abkhazia and South Ossetia, on the other hand, had none of that. They were not a top priority of either the UN, OSCE, NATO, or the European Union. Tbilisi suffered from that neglect and lack of interest. In contrast to its role in Kosovo, the UN mission in Abkhazia was small and had no real authority over or say in events on the ground; its mandate was largely limited to observing. The OSCE mission in South Ossetia was not much different. Attempts to beef up and expand either mission and to turn them into something more substantial were prevented most often by Russia or because people didn't even dare put them forward for discussion, as they assumed Moscow would block them.

A visit to Kosovo and then to Abkhazia or South Ossetia made the difference perfectly clear. The peacekeeping arrangements in the latter cases were flawed from the beginning, as they were dominated by Russia, which was itself a party to the conflict on the ground. The European Union and NATO devoted a fraction of the time and resources to the region. Moscow had no interest in and actively discouraged any expanded involvement by international organizations to promote any kind of reconciliation process on the ground. Had the international community been as centrally involved in managing the Abkhazia and South Ossetia conflicts as it was in the Balkans, the August war could have been prevented.

If the West was not paying enough attention to the possible consequences of its management of the Kosovo conflict for the Southern Caucasus, Tbilisi certainly was. It was well aware of the potential implications of the West's handling of Serbia's relationship with Kosovo for its own relations with Abkhazia. It saw a parallel between the dilemma it faced and the one confronting a post-Milošević democratic government in Belgrade. Both governments had come to power through color revolutions and civil mass movements. Both had inherited the albatross of these conflicts. Both were willing to acknowledge past misdeeds and offer far-reaching proposals for autonomy to resolve the issues. But both Belgrade and Tbilisi feared a humiliating result that a nationalist old guard could use to paint them as traitors and to undercut fledgling democratic transitions if they abandoned those conflicts.

Belgrade and Tbilisi had one more thing in common. Both were wrestling with the issue of a contested province whose future status lay largely in the hands of foreign powers. Tbilisi's desired solution for Abkhazia was extreme autonomy coupled with respect for overall Georgian sovereignty. Belgrade's preferred solution for Kosovo was much the same. Tbilisi also flirted in private with the idea of some kind of partition of Abkhazia that would allow Georgia a role in the part of the province that had been overwhelmingly populated by ethnic Georgians and to which refugees wanted to return. The idea of partitioning Kosovo and ceding the northern slice of the province to Serbia was also frequently floated as part of a possible final package to resolve that conflict as well. Last but not least, the two conflicts were playing themselves out on more or less the same political timeline.

As a result, Saakashvili desperately wanted to see Belgrade and the Kosovar capital, Priština, come to a voluntary accord because he hoped it would create a positive precedent he could then apply to a possible agreement between Tbilisi and Sukhumi. Alternatively, his second preference was for some kind of partition agreement between the Serbs and the Kosovars that could also create a precedent for a future peace plan between the Georgians and the Abkhaz—a version of which he would eventually table in June 2008. But the least desirable outcome in Georgia's view was one where Kosovo's independence came about without consensus and handed Moscow a pretext to act elsewhere. Saakashvili raised these concerns with both U.S. and European officials on several occasions. But he was repeatedly assured that Moscow was bluffing or simply positioning itself for maximum leverage and that there would be no consequences for Georgia from Western policy.

The West believed that Moscow's own concerns about Russia's territorial integrity would serve as a brake on its behavior. On more than one occasion, senior Russian leaders and diplomats had, while supporting Serbia in public, privately signaled that they would not try to stop what they referred to as "the inevitable"—that is, Kosovo's independence. But the West was misreading the changing political winds back in Moscow. Moscow had been brought back into the Balkan game by Belgrade, and the Kosovo issue had now become intertwined with Russian calculations on Georgia. In early 2006, Putin hinted at the change in policy when he announced that there was a need for "universal principles" to settle conflicts ranging from Kosovo to the frozen conflicts in Georgia.[5]

As Russian policy hardened in the course of the year, Western diplomats tried to assess what Moscow really wanted. Was it all about respect, or was Moscow really preparing to block independence? Russia's harder line also emboldened nationalist forces in Serbia. At the same time, Serbian leaders like Boris Tadić were leery of relying too much on Moscow's support. They understood that Russia's support was not driven by a love of Serbia but by broader geopolitical calculations—a fact that was communicated more than once by Belgrade to Tbilisi.

The result was the equivalent of a diplomatic wrestling match where the West mixed openness to working with Moscow with a warning that, if necessary, it was prepared to move forward on its own. The West hoped that this would cajole Russia into acquiescing to a compromise. The first step in that process was the plan for Kosovo's future presented in the spring of 2007 by the UN secretary general's special envoy for Kosovo, Martti Ahtisaari. He had concluded that the reintegration of Kosovo with Serbia was no longer viable, that the continued administration of Kosovo by the international community in its current form was not sustainable, and that, as a result, a supervised and conditional independence with the heavy involvement of the international community, particularly the European Union, was the only option.[6]

Russia refused to play along, however. In spite of private assurances given to Ahtisaari in late 2006 by Foreign Minister Lavrov that it would not try to stop the inevitability of Kosovar independence, Moscow now blocked the plan. Moscow officially complained that it had agreed to the principle of "standards before status" and then agreed to move to "standards and status simultaneously," but it now refused to endorse what it saw as "status before standards." After Putin again insisted on universal standards for settling the frozen conflicts in both the Balkans and the Southern Caucasus at the G–8 summit in Heligendamm in June 2007, the Western response was to launch another last-ditch effort to find a negotiated compromise via a United States-European Union-Russia troika, an initiative put forward by French President Nicolas Sarkozy. The effort was led by three seasoned diplomats, Wolfgang Ischinger for the European Union, Frank Wisner for the United States, and Alexander Botsan-Kharshenko for Russia. They had three months to find a last-minute solution. They came close when Ischinger—reaching into his country's own history of building practical cooperation between West and East Germany and avoiding tricky status issues—proposed a compromise that would allow both Serbia and Kosovo to maintain their different positions on status while allowing practical cooperation on the ground to move forward. Moscow initially appeared openminded about this compromise and Russian diplomats supported its exploration and development. In the end, Moscow torpedoed this proposal as well.[7]

The more the West seemed to push for a compromise granting Kosovo some form of independence, the more determined Russia appeared to be to take the issue hostage. This ran contrary to the West's desire to argue that Kosovo was a unique case that did not establish precedence in international law. This was the *sine qua non* for a common EU position on Kosovo from the outset because several member states had their own minority issues to worry about. If the United States, the European Union, and Russia could all agree that a compromise on Kosovo was unique, the thinking went that it would indeed be unique. But Russia refused to play along with this approach. Instead, it was trying to deter Western action on Kosovo by raising the specter that Western recognition there might force to it recognize the separatist provinces under its tutelage and control.

Moscow was playing hardball. But was it serious or was it bluffing? Was this a ploy to maximize Russian leverage and place pressure on the West to get a better deal on Kosovo? Or would a decision on Kosovo's independence indeed spark a spread of unilateral declarations of independence from the Balkans to the Caucasus? It was a dangerous game. Debate centered on the question of what did or did not constitute a precedent politically as well as under international law. Like beauty, it often seemed to lie in the eye of the beholder. In the final analysis, such details probably did not matter. Moscow's real motivation had little to do with the fine details of history, moral justice, or the principles of international law even though they were often cloaked in those terms.

Six months later Moscow would abandon those principles and do its own complete volte-face when it recognized Abkhazia and South Ossetia. Even before he began invoking the Kosovo precedent, Putin had on occasion threatened Saakashvili that he would use force to turn Abkhazia into another Northern Cyprus, recalling Turkey's 1974 invasion and subsequent occupation of the northern part of the island under the banner of defending a threatened minority. The vernacular would change but the threat to use force to create a fait accompli in Abkhazia, the issue he knew was Saakashvili's weak point, would continue to be part of his effort to bring Georgia to heel.

The debates over international law and the rights of Serbs were diplomatic shadow boxing for Moscow's desire to maximize its leverage and influence in what it considered its own backyard. It was also designed to send the message to the West that Russia was back and would be listened to. It was about Russian status and influence and the rules of the game, above all vis-à-vis the United States. Moscow had always viewed NATO's intervention in Kosovo as a demonstration of American power and its sphere of influence. Kosovo's declaration of independence over Russian opposition a decade later, once again under American leadership, was a further affront in Russian eyes. It confirmed their view that Washington saw the Balkans as a sphere of influence where it could do what it wanted.

Tbilisi was a perfect target for Russia's retaliation. Moscow wanted its response to be as painful to Washington as recognition of Kosovo was to Moscow. Georgia was the obvious choice because it was the place where Russia could underscore that it, too, had a sphere of influence in which it could make the West and, above all, the United States, pay a price. As Saakashvili was seen as a personal ally of Bush, he was the ideal target.

Tbilisi was well aware of the potential precedents and dangers involved in the Kosovo issue. Saakashvili followed the Kosovo debate in great detail and with keen interest. The parallels were all too obvious. If discussions went well and there was a deal negotiated between Belgrade and Priština, it set one precedent. If things went badly, it set another. Regardless of whether a solution involved partition, protracted autonomy, or independence, it would inevitably affect Georgia. Saakashvili could see the risks as well as the possible opportunities. Protracted autonomy involving the return of refugees plus international supervision was an idea some Westerners had floated as an option for Abkhazia. Another option suggested by the West was a negotiated partition, an idea that Saakashvili was toying with. This meant offering Moscow an interim solution along lines that divided Abkhazia into spheres with different levels of international, Georgian, and Russian presence.

The worst outcome on the Kosovo issue from Georgia's view was a forced unilateral declaration of independence. In that case Tbilisi feared it could end up completely exposed to Russia's wrath and retaliation. If Moscow recognized Abkhaz and South Ossetian independence, it would shatter the fiction that the international community fully supported Georgian territorial integrity. The problem was that there was very little Georgia could do about it. It had no influence over Western policy on the Balkans. While it thought a lot about these issues in private, it was cautious about even drawing attention to the issue in public lest it inadvertently strengthen linkages it did not want to exist.

On several occasions Saakashvili wrote Western leaders—including President Bush—urging them to keep Georgia and its vulnerabilities in mind as they worked for a solution on Kosovo. But he avoided the issue in public. He did not want to be an irritant or a problem to the countries that were his main supporters. Western officials involved with Kosovo, in turn, met with him and other Georgian officials to reassure them. But those meetings did little else than brief the Georgian side on Western thinking regarding Kosovo. Beyond verbal assurances, the West had no strategy or plan to shield Georgia. Tbilisi had to rely on Western assertions that Russia was bluffing.

While the United States and the European Union were at times divided on what to do about Kosovo, a critical mass of key countries eventually decided that they could no longer wait, Moscow's threats and warnings notwithstanding. They decided to call Moscow's bluff and move forward, creating a fait accompli on Kosovo, albeit in a careful manner, that left the door open for future rapprochement with Moscow. They did not believe that Moscow would move forward or allow separatist leaders in Abkhazia or South Ossetia to proclaim their independence. It calculated that it could recognize Kosovo and still preserve the status quo in these other conflicts. That calculation proved to be wrong, and there was neither a back-up plan nor arrangements to support Georgia or deal with the aftermath of that miscalculation.

Russia was not bluffing. On February 10, 2007, President Vladimir Putin spoke at the annual Munich security conference—perhaps the most prestigious transatlantic forum. It was the first time a Russian leader had been invited to speak there. I was among the crowd, anxious to hear what he had to say. Most of us expected that he would take advantage of this opportunity make a positive overture to the West. The Munich conference was perhaps the citadel of NATO conferences and the invitation to Putin had been seen as a gesture of friendship and partnership. However, it soon became clear that Putin had decided to deliver a stem-winder of an anti-Western speech that contained a laundry list of Russian complaints against the United States: unilateralism, unipolarism, NATO enlargement, missile defense and—of course—the possibility of Kosovo's independence.

The American delegation and much of the audience looked as if it were in shock. As Putin spoke, I texted Dick Holbrooke, who was also in the audience, asking him whether he thought Putin realized what he was doing and how insulting it was to the conference hosts. The Russian president's full-bore attack on the West and the United States in particular seemed completely out of place. Dick's response was, "This is intentional." After his speech, Putin left immediately, leaving behind a stunned audience to try to figure out if the speech was a game-changer and whether relations with Russia were at a turning point.[8]

On February 17, 2008, Kosovo declared its independence. Five days later, Putin and Saakashvili had a bilateral meeting on the margins of an informal Commonwealth of Independent States (CIS) summit in Moscow. Their discussion centered on Kosovo's recent declaration of independence and what it meant for Georgia. According to the Georgian record of the meeting, Putin said to Saakashvili,

There is an urgent need to react to what has happened in Europe on Kosovo. We are currently thinking how to deal with this problem. You shall remember that we are under huge pressure from the republics of the

Northern Caucasus, and we have to answer to their solidarity for Abkhazia and South Ossetia. We do not understand why the Americans have started their campaign of Islamicizing Europe. After the Albanians have swallowed Kosovo, they will try to expand further at the expense of Macedonia.

You know we have to answer the West on Kosovo. And we are very sorry but you are going to be part of that answer.

The Russian president went on to say that Moscow's response would not be a mirror image of what the West had done but that Georgia would be part of it. He added that it was not Georgia's fault. "Your geography," he said, "is what it is." He went on to elaborate about how Russia planned to lift the existing trade embargo the CIS had imposed on Abkhazia and South Ossetia in 1996 and how Russia would soon be expanding its political and legal contacts with these two provinces.

Saakashvili responded with alacrity, "With all due respect, what you are saying now does not make any sense to me. What does the situation in Georgia have to do with Kosovo? Nothing." He warned Putin that he should not have any illusions about the motives of the North Caucasian republics. They were supporting independence for Abkhazia and South Ossetia because they too desired to be independent—but from Russia. Putin responded by saying: "That is not a big problem for us. We will fix them"— and made a motion as if slitting their throats.

The Georgian president responded: "We are here to solve our conflicts, not to make them deeper and even more dangerous. You should aspire to play a more positive role when it comes to the problems of our region." He went on to plead for a different solution. "Georgia could be one of the best neighbors you have," he argued. "Let's sit down and talk about how to respect each other's sovereignty, territorial integrity, and how to take into account the vital strategic interest of both sides, including those questions you are worried about." It was an obvious hint that everything was on the table, including Tbilisi's NATO aspirations, if Moscow was willing to deal on the territories.

But Putin did not pick up on the implicit offer and instead swept aside the Saakashvili's remarks. He said his decision was final. "I am not here to talk about an exchange of territory for concessions. As for the disputed territories of Abkhazia and South Ossetia, in this regard we shall respond on Kosovo not to you but the West—America and NATO. You should not worry, it shouldn't bother you. What we will do will not be directed against you but will be our response to them." The conversation between the two leaders started to go around in circles and then downhill, but not before the Russian president delivered one more lecture on the perils of joining NATO:

> After NATO is expanded farther to the East, and Georgia is a member of the organization, you will have to follow the discipline of the bloc and will therefore be a threat to our nuclear and military capacity. Nobody will bother to ask your opinion [when it comes to decisions], the same way nobody will ever ask the Poles and Czechs their views [about proposed U.S. missile defense sites in Poland and the Czech Republic]. NATO's purpose is aimed against the sovereignty of Russia. . . .
>
> Condi [Rice] promised to send a paper confirming that Russian inspectors can be attending U.S. radars twenty-four hours a day. Where the hell is that paper? . . .
>
> After joining NATO your sovereignty will be limited, and Georgia, too, will be a threat to Russia.

Before the meeting ended, the Russian president delivered a parting message to the Georgian delegation: "You think you can trust the Americans, and they will rush to assist you? *Nobody* can be trusted! Except me. I'll provide what I promise," he said emphatically. "That is how it is." He went on to say that Medvedev would be taking over and handling these issues. At the press conference after the CIS summit, Putin publicly warned the West about the consequences of recognizing Kosovo's independence, saying that the decision would "come back to knock them on the head."[9]

The Georgian delegation left Moscow deeply worried. This was the first meeting with the Russian leader for David Bakradze, the new chairman of the Georgian Parliament. When Saakashvili asked him what his impression was, he responded, "I think it smells like war."

Russia's response to the Kosovo situation was not long in coming. On March 4 the South Ossetian Parliament called on Russia to recognize its independence. Three days later, Abkhazia followed suit. On March 6 Russia withdrew from its own unilateral sanction agreement against Abkhazia, which dated back to 1996, and henceforth considered itself free to establish contacts with the de facto authorities on the ground.

On March 13, the Russian Duma met in a closed session to discuss a report on Abkhaz and South Ossetian independence. On March 21, it adopted a special resolution endorsing their requests for independence. Konstantin Zatulin, deputy head of the Duma's committee on CIS affairs, warned that recognition should not be postponed too long as the window that had been opened by the West's recognition of Kosovo would not stay open forever. On April 14, an anonymous Russian diplomat was quoted in the Russian daily *Nezavisimaya Gazeta* as saying that Moscow should recognize the independence of Abkhazia and South Ossetia under two circumstances: if Georgia seriously undertook to join NATO and in the case of war.[10]

Shortly after the August war started, a senior Russian official sat down with a former American official from the Clinton Administration. He wanted to give Washington a heads-up about Moscow's goals for this war. The goals he laid out included:

- Establish full control over South Ossetia, eliminating pockets of Georgian control and building a security zone around them.
- Help the Abkhaz authorities bolster control over the largely Georgian-populated district of Gali in Abkhazia and drive Georgian forces from the Kodori Gorge.
- Establish a Russian security zone on the western side of the border between Georgia proper and Abkhazia around the city of Zugdidi.
- Force Georgia to sign a formal document renouncing use of force.
- Humiliate Saakashvili and keep him under increasing pressure at home in the hope that he will eventually be toppled, as Milošević was.
- Destroy Georgia's chances of ever joining NATO.

For anyone familiar with the Kosovo conflict, the parallels between the Balkans in 1999 and what unfolded in Georgia starting in August 2008 were obvious. It was almost as if the Russians had spent much of the subsequent decade carefully studying the West's political and military campaign in Kosovo and the Balkans and adapting it to their own ends. Moscow's terminology and rhetorical line of defense were almost a mirror image of the West's rationale on Kosovo a decade earlier. Russia justified its invasion of Georgia as a "peacekeeping" operation to end the Tbilisi government's "genocide" and "ethnic cleansing" of South Ossetia. Moscow suggested that Saakashvili was a modern-day Milošević and that, prior to their rescue by the Russian arm, the South Ossetians had been suffering under Tbilisi's thumb just as the Kosovar Albanians had suffered under Belgrade. This analogy turned reality, and history, upside down. It was all part of a strategy that had been in the works for some time. It was payback time for a grievance that Russia had borne against the West for nearly a decade.[11]

CHAPTER 4

DIPLOMATIC SHOOTOUT IN BUCHAREST

Recognizing Kosovo's independence was the first Western policy step that helped trigger a Russian backlash against Georgia and accelerated the path toward war. Six weeks later allies took a second step that also angered Moscow and provided an additional pretext for escalating pressure on its small southern neighbor. At the NATO summit in Bucharest, Romania, held April 2–4, 2008, allies engaged in a heated and at times dramatic debate over whether to grant Georgia and Ukraine access to NATO's Membership Action Plan (MAP), a program designed to help aspiring countries prepare better for eventual membership. The compromise eventually reached avoided granting MAP but instead made an unprecedented commitment to eventual membership for these two countries.

NATO's hope was that this compromise would not only bridge the gap among allies but provide Georgia the reassurance it sought. Alliance leaders also hoped that by sidestepping the MAP issue they could also avoid a clash with Moscow, which had warned NATO against taking such a step. But what made sense from an internal NATO perspective and, while not ideal, could be sold in Tbilisi and Kiev as a success and a step forward, was in some ways the worst of all worlds from Moscow's perspective. After all, the Kremlin's real goal was not just to prevent MAP but to stop any momentum to eventual membership. And Bucharest had done the opposite. Alliance leaders were now officially committed to something Moscow fundamentally opposed.

Had the Alliance stood fully committed and unified behind this goal, Moscow might indeed have backed down. Russia had opposed previous rounds of enlargement, too, but acquiesced in the face of a unified Alliance. But Georgia and Ukraine were a more neuralgic issue and the debate in Bucharest had openly shown how divided NATO still was about it. It was a commitment on paper and little more. The risk, in Moscow's eyes, was that the candidacies of Georgia and Ukraine would now start to gain momentum and become unstoppable. At the same time, division within NATO meant there was a window of opportunity in which these candidacies could still be undercut and stopped. But the time to act was soon. Thus, instead of taking the issue off the table, the NATO decision at Bucharest may have invited precisely the kind of Russian escalation vis-à-vis Georgia allies had hoped to avoid. Within two weeks of the conclusion of the Bucharest summit, Moscow launched a series of steps that seriously upped the pressure on Tbilisi.

How did the issue of an obscure NATO program called MAP come to play such a divisive role in Bucharest and a key role in sparking this conflict? Tbilisi had placed its hopes on NATO's helping it halt the downward spiral in its relations with Moscow. In Bucharest it had hoped for an endorsement from the Alliance of its pro-Western course. To Georgia, such backing was critical to maintaining momentum for reform at home and was seen as key to sending a message to Russia that Georgia was moving irrevocably West in spite of Moscow's efforts to stop it. And not least, Tbilisi saw NATO support as an important element of its long-term strategy to address the frozen conflicts. Closer ties with the West could help convince the populations in these provinces that life as an autonomous region of a Georgia heading West with a chance of joining the Euro-Atlantic community was better than being aligned to an autocratic Russia whose track record in the treatment of small minorities was hardly exemplary.

Based on the standards for new members developed by the Alliance in the mid-1990s, neither Georgia nor Ukraine was close to being ready for full NATO membership. They were looking for a kind of halfway house or shelter where they would be politically embraced, where their efforts and accomplishments would be recognized and reinforced, and where a signal would be sent to Moscow that these countries were becoming part of the Western orbit and that Moscow should keep its hands off. For these reasons, the issue of whether or not Tbilisi or Kiev would be granted MAP came to assume a political and psychological significance that far transcended the actual merits of this program. For a country besieged by Russia and under pressure at home to show that painful reforms were putting it on a Western path, MAP had become a kind of holy grail providing a political lifeline to the West.

The problem was twofold. The first issue was that MAP was never intended to answer that kind of political and strategic dilemma. I was part of the team in the U.S. government that developed the concept for the Washington NATO summit in 1999. MAP grew out of the experience with the first round of NATO enlargement to Poland, the Czech Republic, and Hungary and the realization that these countries were far less prepared than had been expected. Given the benign strategic environment and the belief that encouraging Central and Eastern European countries to consolidate pro-Western reforms was also a key factor in European stability, NATO had consciously raised the bar on what was required of new members in the 1990s. MAP was designed to jump-start and focus the preparations of future candidates by providing "advice, assistance, and practical support" to them at a much earlier stage.

The aim was clearly membership, hence the name Membership Action Plan. But it fell short of a pledge that they would get in. As we explained it at the time, NATO would grant MAP when the Alliance knew it wanted these countries to join but was not yet convinced they were ready. Joining NATO was like running a marathon. Countries had to run that race themselves and cross the finish line on their own. There were no guarantees. But MAP was like an intensive coaching effort that kicked in when they were getting ready to run that race. The burden of preparing was on them, but NATO members were determined to help them get across that finish line successfully. It was a kind of self-help program for these countries to not only get ready sooner and faster, but it also was carefully designed to stop short of a pledge that they would actually be admitted. It was focused on these countries' shortcomings and was not designed to deter aggressive action by anyone, certainly not Russia.

The standards in MAP that countries were asked to work toward were far more specific than anything NATO had previously demanded from aspiring countries. But they were still fairly general, and the assessment process was far from being immune to political influence. That, too, was deliberate. NATO wanted neither to create any sense of automaticity nor to tie its own hands. At the end of the day, whether or not a country joined NATO was a political and strategic decision, one informed, but not predetermined, by performance. NATO had raised the bar on performance in the 1990s in the face of a benign security environment—and it reserved the right to lower it again if strategic circumstances were to change. The penultimate criterion was whether Alliance members believed that the inclusion of a candidate served overall NATO interests.

To further muddy the waters, NATO had almost immediately violated its own, admittedly loosely written, rules by granting MAP to Albania during the height of the Kosovo crisis. Everyone knew that Albania was at best a decade way from eventual NATO membership. But NATO had to secure Albanian cooperation in the midst of the Kosovo war. If MAP was what it took under those circumstances, then that was what NATO was going to do. This move set a precedent that would play a role a decade later. If NATO members had bent the rules once before, would they do so a second time? It was a reminder that at the end of the day these were guidelines, and political leaders could override them if they felt the needs of a moment required it. It was a point the Georgians and Ukrainians would underscore when critics claimed they had not done enough to warrant MAP.

But that was precisely the rub—and the second problem. In reality, many NATO members were not at all convinced that enlargement should extend deeper into Eurasia or across the Black Sea or that bringing Georgia and Ukraine into NATO was in their or the Alliance's interests. As they were skeptical about the end goal, they were also hesitant to take even this modest step in starting down that path. Their opposition to MAP became the technical way in which they expressed these deeper political and strategic doubts. In the late 1990s, it had been relatively uncontroversial to extend

MAP to a set of countries. That was because there was a growing Alliance consensus that all of the countries from the Baltic to the Black Sea needed eventually to be anchored in the European Union and NATO—with the pace of that process determined by their individual performance. When it came to extending MAP to Albania, the decision was driven by NATO's war needs and by the fact that the Alliance had in principle crossed the Rubicon in believing the Balkan countries should sooner or later join NATO, too.

None of this was the case yet with Ukraine and Georgia. As an alliance, NATO did not yet have consensus on whether to expand deeper into Eurasia or into the Southern Caucasus. When NATO enlargement was first conceptualized and debated in the 1990s, apart from a few visionary individuals, no one had seriously thought about the process ever extending that far. When I was working on NATO enlargement in the State Department in the 1990s during the second Clinton Administration, the initial focus was on the countries composing the Visegrád Group (the Czech Republic, Hungary, Poland, and Slovakia) in the heart of Central and Eastern Europe. That was then broadened to include the wider swath of the region stretching from the Baltic to the Black Sea. When President Bush gave his landmark speech on NATO enlargement in Warsaw in June 2001, he officially embraced the goal of an enlarged Atlantic Alliance stretching in the East from the three Baltic states of Estonia, Latvia, and Lithuania in the north to Bulgaria and Romania on the western edge of the Black Sea in the south. That reflected the emerging consensus not only in the United States but in NATO at that time.[1]

For the first decade of the enlargement debate, therefore, the question of candidate countries in Eurasia or the Southern Caucasus was not really on NATO's radar screen in a meaningful way. Ukraine and Georgia had, of course, officially declared that they wanted to join NATO some day. The Alliance had also embraced what it called its "open door" strategy—leaving the door open to new democracies that qualified for membership and whose inclusion would serve the Alliance's own interests. It was a permissive approach in which NATO did not draw any lines or preclude any European democracy from membership. It was up to the individual countries to decide where they wanted to belong—a right enshrined in every OSCE document since the Charter of Paris—and for the Alliance to then conclude whether they met the standards for membership and whether their inclusion would advance NATO's own security.

While Georgia and Ukraine might have talked about joining NATO, such discussions were largely seen as pro forma. Their candidacies were not taken seriously in the West given the lack of democracy and reform at home. That calculus only started to really change with the democratic breakthroughs of the Rose and Orange Revolutions. Those breakthroughs brought to the fore a new set of leaders who seemed far more committed to building democracy at home and aligning their countries with the West. What had previously seemed a mirage was now starting to look like a real possibility—the prospect of democratic pro-Western governments in Tbilisi and Kiev who shared our values, wanted to be part of our Alliance, and now had a fighting chance to pursue the kinds of policies that would help them qualify.

For the United States and Europe, this raised the question of whether the initial vision of EU and NATO enlargement was too limited and whether the Alliance needed to think bigger—and embrace a new round of enlargement. It was a question the West was not eager to debate. Such a move was destined to be more controversial and consequential than the West's move into Central and Eastern Europe or even to the Baltic states. Proponents insisted that embracing these countries around the wider Black Sea was not only a moral imperative in the wake of their democratic revolutions, but that enlargement could strategically help lock in stability in Eurasia and around the Black Sea. The importance of a southern energy corridor bringing oil and gas from the Caspian Sea and Central Asia to the West was an additional rationale for this next round of outreach. Such a move, proponents argued, could shore up the southern flank of the Euro-Atlantic community against the wider Middle East to the south. While Moscow would not welcome this move, supporting democratic breakthroughs on Russia's borders would arguably eventually enhance Russia's own long-term prospects for more democracy.[2]

Opponents disagreed. They claimed that such a move was premature and risky. The questions started with the European credentials of these countries. Were they even part of Europe? Skeptics claimed that the democratic track record of these countries was unproven. In the case of Ukraine, people acknowledged the country's strategic importance, but also noted how divided the public was on the issue of NATO membership. In the case of Georgia, they pointed to the fact that in November 2007 Saakashvili had declared a state of emergency after opposition protests threatened to spin out of control. Critics also argued that a Western embrace might actually exacerbate the frozen conflicts or embolden Saakashvili to be more aggressive in handling them. Above all, they worried that such a move could catalyze a new and deeper confrontation with a Russia that was already turning against the West.

As a result, the debate over MAP in Bucharest was not just a debate about Georgia's and Ukraine's technical performance and whether they met the loose standards laid down in NATO doctrine. It was really a debate about the future of NATO enlargement and the Alliance more generally as well as about relations with Russia. MAP became the surrogate for the fight over the Alliance's strategic direction. Allies advocating MAP were not necessarily interested in the details of whether Georgia had or had not successfully completed all of its reforms. They believed it was necessary to embrace and reassure Georgia at this critical moment when so much seemed to hang in the balance, and to send a message to Moscow to back off and leave Tbilisi alone. If that meant being flexible on setting the bar for MAP, so be it. The Alliance had done that with Albania in 1999 and it could do it again.

Similarly, the countries opposing MAP were often using procedural or performance-based arguments to make larger political and strategic points. They not only had real doubts about the democratic reforms or preparedness of Georgia or Ukraine. Many of them simply thought enlargement had gone far enough in terms of straining NATO cohesion or irritating Russia. They had doubts as to whether NATO should take a first step in this strategic direction because they did not want to start a process they could not later stop. They were unsure if it served their national interest, feared it was a bridge too far for NATO, and above all worried about being pulled into a new conflict with Russia over Georgia. When they said that Ukraine or Georgia was not ready, they were also saying that they were not ready either, and that was what worried the Georgians and Ukrainians most of all.

Leading the arguments in favor of a further enlargement of NATO was the United States, where Georgia and Ukraine became a central part of President Bush's freedom agenda. Washington had support from the United

Kingdom, Canada, many new members from Central and Eastern Europe, and a few of the smaller West European members like Denmark. Skepticism was centered in Germany, France, Italy, Spain, and the Benelux countries. Nowhere was this split more apparent than between the United States and Germany. Here an important role reversal had taken place. In the 1990s, when it was a question of stabilizing those countries on its eastern borders, Germany had been the European country supplying the political muscle to get the enlargement process started. The idea of enlargement had first been voiced by German defense minister Volker Rühe. Chancellor Helmut Kohl was Washington's biggest ally on enlargement throughout the divisive debates over the first round of NATO enlargement—including in 1997 when Berlin deserted Paris to support the American position at the dramatic Madrid summit.

The United States and Germany had been the engines behind the first round of NATO enlargement. Kohl's friendship with and support of Bill Clinton were key to launching the first wave and in limiting the first round to three countries—Poland, the Czech Republic, and Hungary—while maximizing future chances for other candidates, above all the Baltic states. Washington and Berlin worked closely in developing the second part of NATO's dual-track strategy of reaching out to Russia and initiating a NATO-Russian partnership, as Clinton and Kohl were the two Western leaders in whom Yeltsin had the most confidence.

A decade later, however, Berlin's position was different. It had become one of the most skeptical allies about further enlargement. The reasons for and the consequences of that shift were critical for the NATO debate on Ukraine and Georgia. A lot had changed over the past decade as the traditionally close U.S.-German relationship had all but collapsed over the war in Iraq—reaching its lowest point since World War II. Chancellor Gerhard Schröder had made anti-war and anti-American sentiments a key part of his reelection campaign in 2002—and succeeded. Washington's frustration with Berlin was reflected in Secretary of State Rice's widely quoted remark to associates in the spring of 2003 that U.S. policy would "punish France, ignore Germany, and forgive Russia."

The enlargement issue was not a driving cause in the rift between Berlin and Washington but it affected it nevertheless. American and German views on enlargement were now a point of divergence as opposed to convergence. Following NATO's so-called Big Bang enlargement at the 2004 Prague summit, Germany's vision of an enlarged Europe based on an expanded European Union and NATO was essentially fulfilled. In reality, Berlin had initially been skeptical and privately opposed to Baltic membership in the European Union and NATO, but it had dropped those objections and subsequently supported their inclusion. Now that Germany was encircled by friendly allies, Berlin saw its national interest in the enlargement process as achieved. While it continued to support NATO's principle of an open-door policy rhetorically, it was a sated power. Its priority now was deepening cooperation with Moscow.

The latter had become increasingly fashionable and important after the Iraq war. The debate over the Iraq war had not only unleashed a new wave of anti-American sentiments, but also pushed Germany's geopolitical orientation eastward. When Chancellor Schröder broke with the Bush Administration to oppose the war, he embraced both France and Russia in order to find political cover and avoid isolation. What had initially seemed like a marriage of convenience now started to establish deeper roots as Berlin discovered new foreign policy options. One of the greatest ironies of the Iraq war is that it helped re-legitimate a pro-Russian lobby in German politics. Increasingly, it was now the relationship with Russia that captured the imagination of a growing part of the country's political class, not whether and how to extend the frontiers of democracy and freedom in places like Georgia and Ukraine. Whereas the United States and Germany had previously been the closest of collaborators on enlargement, a decade later they were leading opposing, feuding camps.

Washington had hoped for a shift in German strategic priorities when Angela Merkel succeeded Gerhard Schröder as chancellor in November 2005 and came to power determined to repair relations with the United States. She had grown up in Communist East Germany as the daughter of a Lutheran pastor. Growing up in the East had cured her of any illusions about Communism and Russia. Some observers would describe her as almost "Eastern European" in her outlook toward Moscow, and she was known for being among the clearest and toughest leaders in Europe when it came to dealing with the Russians. Merkel was one of the first European heads of state to extend a hand of support to President Bush during his second term in office when he sought to repair relations with the Continent. The two leaders would develop a relationship of close trust and personal friendship.

But the rift in American and German thinking on the future of enlargement was never fully bridged. While an Atlanticist, Merkel was not immune from the broader currents in German strategic thinking and society that had pushed Berlin farther away from Bush's Washington. She was in a coalition with the Social Democratic Party (SPD) and its foreign minister, Frank-Walter Steinmeier, who had distanced themselves from the United States under Bush and whose leaders at times spoke of the need to pursue a policy of "equidistance" between Washington and Moscow. The SPD now made the continuation of a "peace policy" that included friendly relations with Russia a core part of their foreign policy—which only reinforced its skepticism on further enlargement. The party also controlled the Foreign Office, which was now becoming the citadel of German advocacy for deeper cooperative ties with Moscow.

Tbilisi also damaged its own cause as it frequently lashed out against Germany, arguably the country that mattered most on the continent when it came to Eastern policy. Saakashvili's rants accusing Europe of appeasement were often directed at Berlin, which he saw as a kind of Trojan horse within the Alliance pursuing pro-Russian objectives and the major obstacle to achieving Georgia's Western aspirations. Tbilisi had no effective strategy to answer Germany's questions, overcome its doubts, or build public support in this major European country. For its part, Berlin thought Saakashvili was hyping the Russian threat to deflect attention from his own democratic shortcomings. They worried that he was a hothead who would pull Germany and other European countries into a conflict with Russia. In Berlin there was none of the enthusiasm about Georgian and Ukrainian membership in NATO that existed in Washington.

German skepticism about Georgia extended to Merkel as well. She had traveled to these countries prior to the breakup of the former Soviet Union, and she felt she knew how far they needed to go before they became part of the West. To make matters worse, her first meeting with Saakashvili had been a disaster. One could hardly imagine a greater contrast than that between the reserved chancellor from northern Germany and the overbearing, gregarious Saakashvili. When they met for the first time, on the margins of the annual Munich security conference, they talked past each other in a meeting both sides describe as bad. Merkel tried to underscore the importance of the rule of law and judicial reform, pointing to a German-funded program to train judges. Saakashvili, who believed the program was ineffective, dismissed the chancellor's concerns and tried to reassure her that Georgia was on the right track. She didn't believe him. He thought she had no feel for Georgia's local conditions or what he was trying to accomplish. Merkel's aides said it was among the worst meetings she had ever had.

Bush and Merkel disagreed on how best to handle Georgia's aspirations from the first time they discussed it at length, in Stralsund on the German Baltic coast in the spring of 2006. They would continue to discuss Georgia, and to disagree, over the next two and a half years, even as their friendship deepened. At times they would even joke about their different views. When Merkel visited Bush's ranch in Crawford in November 2007, shortly after Saakashvili had declared a state of emergency and cracked down on protestors in Tbilisi, the president joked with her to please not tell him "I told you so" about Saakashvili's democratic instincts, or rather the lack thereof. But Bush liked and admired Merkel. He felt that they had a common commitment to the advancement of freedom and democracy and that there was room for cooperation and compromise on the Georgia issue.

Bush understood that Merkel's problem with Georgia and Saakashvili was indeed about performance. He sensed that she was different from her Social Democratic vice chancellor and foreign minister, Frank-Walter Steinmeier, in whom he had less trust. The Bush Administration considered Steinmeier to be the heir of Gerhard Schröder and thought that he placed too much emphasis on not offending Russia and not enough on supporting freedom and democracy in wider Europe. However, Bush regarded Merkel as someone who would stand up to Moscow if she was convinced the cause was right. He felt that both he and Merkel saw the same weaknesses and shortcomings in Georgia. They did not disagree in their analysis of where Georgia was and what it needed to do.

They did disagree on what NATO policy should be. Bush believed that the best way for Georgia to overcome its flaws was for the West to embrace

Georgia even more closely and work with it, not keep it at arm's length and further its insecurities. The president was not naïve about Georgia or about Saakashvili's shortcomings. The question in his mind was how best to overcome them. The Central and Eastern European countries in NATO had not been perfect either, and many had had their own crises and near-death experiences on their path to membership. Bush felt that the best way to manage Saakashvili's unpredictability was to support Georgia, not discourage it. The country was taking extraordinary risks in trying to go West over Russian opposition, and Bush believed that a friend and ally had to stand by Tbilisi as a matter of principle.

Germany was not the only country skeptical about Ukraine and Georgia and reluctant to move forward on MAP. France was another skeptical player that mattered in NATO, but it was more of a wild card than many realized. President Jacques Chirac had initially been perhaps the biggest skeptic on NATO enlargement. Paris had historically leaned toward a smaller vision of Europe, was ambivalent about both America's influence and NATO's role, and had viewed its own close relationship with Moscow as a way of balancing the United States and Germany. NATO enlargement promised to dilute that vision and strengthen NATO and American influence. After resisting enlargement, France nevertheless reversed course, with Chirac championing a more extensive round of enlargement at the 1997 NATO summit in Madrid than Washington was comfortable with. That was an attempt by Paris to make the best out of a policy it had never really liked.

But by May 2007 Chirac was out and Nicolas Sarkozy was in. On this issue, as on many others, he was determined to set his own course. During his campaign for the French presidency, Sarkozy had presented himself as a foreign policy maverick, promising a break with the policies of his predecessor. Nowhere was this more evident than in regard to policies on the United States and Russia. He campaigned on improving ties with Washington and maximizing French and European influence by working with rather than opposing the United States. It was on the issue of Russia, however, that he drew the strongest contrast with Chirac. During the campaign he denounced Putin as a thug and a leader "with blood on his hands" and criticized Chirac for giving Putin the Légion d'honneur two weeks before Anna Politkovskaya's assassination. He pledged to put liberty and human rights at the center of French foreign policy and abandon Paris's cynical Realpolitik. The biggest difference between Chirac and him, he told visitors at that time, was that his predecessor was anti-Bush and he was anti-Putin.

Sarkozy, whose father was of Hungarian origin, also had a very different attitude toward Central and Eastern Europe. He criticized Chirac for ignoring these countries and telling their leaders to "shut up" in 2003 after they had supported the United States on the Iraq war. He was sympathetic to the Western aspirations of young democracies like Ukraine and Georgia during his campaign. As president, Sarkozy made a point of visiting capital cities in Central and Eastern Europe before traveling to Moscow. Whereas Chirac had refused to receive Saakashvili, the Georgian president was one of the first heads of state Sarkozy received in the Élysée Palace after his election. Unlike Merkel, Sarkozy liked Saakashvili. As someone accused of having autocratic tendencies himself, Sarkozy had a more relaxed view of Saakashvili's style and shortcomings. The two leaders were both big personalities and men of action, willing to take occasional shortcuts to get things done, leaving protocol and diplomatic niceties aside.

Many of Sarkozy's ideas on these issues were anathema to the French political and diplomatic class, which was steeped in Gaullism. The big question was whether Sarkozy's maverick approach and energy were sufficient to break from French diplomatic tradition or whether he would eventually be brought around to supporting more traditional French approaches. His appointment of Bernard Kouchner, a socialist humanitarian activist and founder of Médecins Sans Frontières, as foreign minister also seemed to signal a break with the past. Shortly after his election, Sarkozy joked to a group of friends that he was considering bombing the Quai d'Orsay, where the Ministry of Foreign Affairs is located. The only open question in his mind was whether he should let the diplomats escape first or not. A friend joked that if he let them escape, they might conspire to sabotage the changes he was planning to introduce in French foreign policy. It was Sarkozy the rebel.

Officially, France opposed MAP for Georgia and Ukraine and fully supported Berlin's position. But in meetings with visitors, including Americans, the French president strayed from the official script and from the idea that there was a common Franco-German position on this issue. He would tell visitors in private that he liked Saakashvili, sympathized with Georgia's aspirations, and wanted to help. The problem he had was not with Tbilisi's democratic shortcomings. Nor was he afraid to offend Russia. The problem he had was with Germany. He did not want to pick a fight with Berlin at a time when he and Merkel already had a testy relationship. The conclusion that Washington—and Tbilisi—drew from this, however, was clear. Sarkozy would be opportunistic. If Merkel could be moved, Sarkozy would not oppose a compromise. And if Germany and France came on board, the remaining opposition in the Alliance would crumble.

But counsel in Washington was also divided on the MAP issue. The opposition of a number of key European allies was obvious. Saakashvili's declaration of a state of emergency in late 2007 gave even his strongest supporters pause. The Bush Administration was entering its last year in office and was entering a lame duck period when its influence in Europe, while it had never been high, was waning even further. Leading officials at the highest levels in the administration had their doubts as well. Both Secretary of State Condoleezza Rice and Defense Secretary Robert Gates were initially prepared to compromise on MAP despite their own doubts about Georgia's preparedness and allied opposition. After the November 2007 crackdown, several senior American diplomats told their European counterparts in private that MAP was off the table. But they spoke too early—they had not checked first with President Bush. It was his view that mattered, and his support on MAP was still firm.

The differences within the top of the Bush Administration became clear to NATO secretary general Jaap de Hoop Scheffer in late February when he visited Washington. De Hoop Scheffer dined with Rice, Gates, and National Security Advisor Stephen Hadley on February 28, 2008, the evening before his meeting with the president. Over dinner Rice and Gates were in agreement with de Hoop Scheffer that MAP was a bridge too far. They thought it was better to pursue a compromise with the substance of the program but under a different label to ensure that this was not perceived as a Russian victory.

When de Hoop Scheffer went to meet the president the next morning, he was therefore stunned when Bush suddenly said that he had been thinking about the MAP issue the previous evening and was inclined to go for it at Bucharest. He was prepared, the president said, to put all of America's diplomatic clout in play in order to get it. The NATO Secretary General left the Oval Office wondering what had happened behind the scenes. In reality, Bush had always been forward leaning on MAP—much more so than his key lieutenants were. Rice and Gates realized they were not on the same page as the president. The National Security Council staff realized it needed an organized process to clarify U.S. policy and ensure everyone was on the same page. That led to a set of senior policy meetings and intelligence briefings—so called "deep dives"—with the president that would resolve those differences and formalize the president's instincts into an official U.S. government position.

What had motivated Bush to make that decision? In the president's mind, this issue was fundamentally a political one to be decided by leaders and not by diplomats. He, not his advisors, would decide U.S. policy on this issue. At these White House meetings, he challenged his aides as to why Washington should compromise. In his view, these countries were taking tremendous risks by trying to join NATO in the face of Russian opposition. The risks NATO was being asked to take were minimal in comparison. If Georgia and Ukraine were willing to stick their necks out, he argued, shouldn't the United States stand by them as matter of principle? The president was not frightened by the prospect of what would happen if the United States did not get its way. He wanted to fight for what he thought was right.

While NATO consisted of twenty-seven allies, Bush knew that the Alliance was divided right down the middle on the issue. He understood that MAP was controversial but he also had many leaders from NATO allies, largely but not only from Central and Eastern Europe, coming through the Oval Office that spring urging him to push for it. In Bush's mind, the final decision would boil down to a handful of countries and personalities who held the key votes—himself, Merkel, and Sarkozy—and who would be decisive in shifting the debate one way or the other. Bush also sensed a fault line in the German position. While Merkel and Steinmeier both opposed MAP, they did so for very different reasons. In Bush's mind, Merkel's thinking was not driven by concern over Russia, which meant she could still be persuaded to move. She, too, believed in the advancement of democracy and freedom and was willing to stand up to Moscow. He hoped he could personally appeal to those instincts over the heads of those in her government who focused, too much, in his mind, on Moscow. And if Merkel moved, Sarkozy would not prove an insurmountable obstacle. It was a Texas gamble but one the president was willing to make.

Thus, while the public debate on the pros and cons of granting MAP was waged in diplomatic corridors, in the halls of Congress, in the media, and in think tanks across the Atlantic, Bush remained quiet and his administration silent about its intentions in public—so quiet that many allies wondered what the hell the United States was doing. When asked what the U.S. position would be, American diplomats were instructed to say that the president had not yet made up his mind. Meanwhile, Bush ordered his National Security Council to open a private back-channel dialogue with Merkel and Sarkozy to explore a solution. The result is one of those diplomatic cases of what might have been. The draft language that was discussed in this back channel went far—and arguably might have been a much better compromise than the final results at Bucharest. If Merkel was negotiating on her own and not being held back by her foreign minister, Bush thought she might be more flexible and easier to persuade.

Saakashvili visited the White House in mid-March, some three weeks before the Bucharest summit. His visit overlapped with another exchange between Bush and Merkel on the MAP issue by videoconference. Before heading over to the White House, Saakashvili had received a phone call from the German chancellor. One week earlier she had publicly registered her opposition to MAPs for Georgia and Ukraine—initially at a meeting of senior military commanders but then in Moscow as well.[3] The White House was not happy. In calling Saakashvili, she wanted to underscore that she was not willing to support MAP for Georgia, and she urged him to consider a compromise on the issue in his upcoming discussions with the president. When Saakashvili met with Bush, he told him about his conversation with Merkel. Bush smiled and responded, "Leave Angela to me. You focus on Luxembourg."

Speaking to the press afterward, Bush noted Georgia's NATO aspirations and the fact that the Bucharest summit was coming up. "MAP," he underscored, "is not membership. It is a process that will enable NATO members to be comfortable with their country eventually joining. I believe NATO benefits with a Georgian membership. I believe Georgia benefits from being a part of NATO. And I told the president it's a message I'll be taking to Bucharest soon." A buoyant Saakashvili said, "I have to thank you, Mr. President, for your unwavering support for our freedom, for our democracy, for our territorial sovereignty, and for protecting Georgia's borders, and for Georgia's NATO aspiration."[4]

One of the key issues dividing the NATO allies was obviously Russia and the degree to which Moscow's opposition to MAP and any eventual Ukrainian or Georgian membership in NATO should be taken into account. Bush was not blind to Russian opposition. During his first meeting with the Russian president, in Slovenia in June 2001, he had famously said, "I looked the man in the eye. I found him to be very straightforward and trustworthy and we had a very good dialogue. I was able to get a sense of his soul."[5] The U.S.-Russian relationship had deteriorated since Bush's first term, but the two leaders had remained on cordial if not friendly terms. Bush had no illusions about Putin's growing authoritarianism or Russia's tougher foreign policy, which was fueled by petrodollars. But he too was committed to using his personal relationship with the Russian leader to avoid a fallback into a new cold war. Washington's motto was to cooperate with Russia where it could but to push back against Russian positions where it had to.

Already in the spring of 2007 Putin had told Secretary of State Rice and Secretary of Defense Gates that bringing Georgia into NATO was a "red line." Moscow had of course used similar language in the 1990s about Poland and other Central and Eastern European countries, and the warning did not set off major alarm bells. It was nevertheless another sign that Russian policy was hardening toward the West and toward Moscow's neighbors. Bush nevertheless refused to back down in his support for Georgia. He believed that publicly supporting Saakashvili had an important deterrent element in relation to Moscow and that embracing Tbilisi would help keep it on course and prevent it from doing anything desperate. His strategy was to lean forward and cooperate with Russia on one track but push forward on NATO enlargement on a second, parallel track. That strategy had worked in the 1990s. But this was a different Russia. Moscow's strategy was also to work together with Washington where it could on issues of common interest. It, too, now had a second track where it was determined to stop further enlargement.

Putin and Bush had asked their respective national security teams to try to put together a new strategic framework agreement as the Bush presidency wound down. The two leaders wanted a document that captured and codified the work accomplished together and to lock in an agenda that would continue once they both left the scene. Somewhat to the White House's surprise, Putin invited Bush to visit the Black Sea resort town of Sochi immediately following Bucharest for a bilateral summit to finalize the agreement. It was supposed to be a chance for the Russian president to say farewell to the outgoing American leader. Before agreeing, President Bush had to weigh the options and determine how the outcome of Bucharest might affect a Sochi event.

Success and failure each carried their own risks. If Bush succeeded in getting MAP at Bucharest, there was a danger that Putin would scuttle the summit in protest or would turn Sochi into an ugly confrontation that would make his Munich speech look tame. Bush was ready to accept the invitation only if he was confident this would not happen. On the other hand, if Bush failed to get MAP or if the United States backed off its position, a Sochi visit to sign a new deal with Moscow could look as if he had sacrificed the interests of Ukraine and Georgia in order to enhance U.S.-Russian relations. As the president weighed these risks, he concluded it would be best to take the bull by the horns and talk to Putin directly. Some ten days before Bucharest, Bush phoned Putin.

The U.S. president told Putin he was ready to come to Sochi but only if he could be confident that Putin would not pull another Munich stunt at the NATO summit. He wanted Putin to know that he intended to fight for MAP at Bucharest and, in turn, he wanted to ask Putin what his intentions were. Putin responded to the president's question by joking that it sounded as if the American president were afraid of what he might do. Bush replied that he was worried because he knew that Putin had strong feelings on the MAP issue as well and could overturn the table at the summit. If that was likely to happen, the two leaders would have a "dustup" and Bush would then be unable to come to Sochi. Bush told Putin that he would push for MAP in Bucharest, and Putin responded that, although the two leaders had their disagreements, he pledged there would not be a confrontation in Bucharest. Based in part on that assurance, Bush decided to accept Putin's invitation to Sochi—and to fight for MAP in Bucharest.

In the final weeks before the summit, Bush continued to insist that the United States work privately and not put public pressure on Germany or others to support MAP. When NATO foreign ministers met in early March, allies expected the United States to finally put its cards on the table and come out in support of MAP. But instead Rice was instructed to ask a series of philosophical questions challenging the opponents of MAP. From those questions, one could discern where U.S. sympathies lay. But this was not the kind of hard-charging campaign allies had expected. Instead, Bush preferred to use the back channel in a final search for a MAP compromise with Merkel. Washington and Berlin were actually not far apart in their analysis of Georgian strengths and weaknesses. The two key points on which they did disagree were the wisdom of embracing Tbilisi closely and the signal that such an embrace would send to the Russians. Washington proposed language that would assure the Germans that MAP was not a guarantee of membership and that it would not push for membership for several years to come.

In return, Berlin proposed language that would have given Georgia essentially all of the substance of MAP without the actual label. But Bush would not go for it. He had made up his mind to fight for MAP. At the end of the day, he was comfortable with the idea that the Alliance would have an open argument and would vote him down—even though that had never happened openly at a NATO summit for as long as anyone could remember. He preferred to fight for the principle, to rely on his powers of persuasion, and to bank on the traditional clout of the United States in NATO to still get his way.

The final decision to go public with the U.S. position was made on Air Force One prior to a stop in Kiev en route to Bucharest. From Air Force One, his aides called sympathetic allies to let them know that Washington had decided to fight and to ask for their support in what was to become the diplomatic equivalent of the showdown at the O.K. Corral. Speaking in Kiev, Bush stated that the United States strongly supported Ukraine's request for MAP, adding, "We are proud to stand with you in Bucharest and beyond."[6] Arriving in Bucharest, the president was asked by the press for his assessment of Georgian and Ukrainian chances of getting a MAP. He responded,

[MAP for] Ukraine and Georgia is a very difficult issue for some nations here. It's not for me. I think these nations are qualified nations to apply for Membership Application. And I said so on Ukrainian soil. I said so in the Oval Office with the President of Georgia. And I haven't changed my mind because it's—one of the great things about NATO is that it encourages the kind of habits that are necessary for peace to exist.

On Russia's possible reaction, Bush went on to say, "I have always told Vladimir Putin, my friend, that it's in his interest that there be democracies on her border and that he doesn't need to fear NATO; he ought to welcome NATO because NATO is a group of nations dedicated to peace."[7]

This set the stage for a NATO summit that was far more dramatic than had been expected. Only a few months earlier, some diplomats had been worried that the summit might be a bit sleepy. It was Bush's final NATO summit, European allies wanted to bid him adieu graciously, and no one felt the need to launch major initiatives. In reality, they were already looking ahead to his successor—calculating that it was better to save whatever new ideas or concessions they might have for the Oval Office's next occupant. Afghanistan was, as always, a major issue. NATO was expected to extend invitations to three new Balkan members, the so-called Adriatic Three—Albania, Croatia, and Macedonia. While many still had doubts about their readiness and there was still a dispute over Macedonia's official name, there was also a clear sense that it was time to wrap up business in the Balkans and move on to the bigger challenges facing the Alliance.

Instead, Bucharest became the most dramatic NATO summit since the Madrid meeting in 1997, when the Alliance had debated enlargement's first round.[8] Once again, the key issue dividing the Alliance was the future scope of enlargement. The headlines on the eve of Bucharest were also dominated by a second dispute over the official name of NATO candidate Macedonia, officially known as the Federal Yugoslav Republic of Macedonia (or FYROM). The dispute had been going on for years as Greece opposed the use of the name Macedonia as potentially irredentist; Athens now dug in its heels to successfully block an invitation to Macedonia over this issue. As important as that issue was locally in Greek and Macedonian domestic politics—governments in both countries were at risk of falling over the issue—

this was a dispute about history, identity, and domestic politics. It was not about NATO strategy; everyone, including the Greeks, agreed that Macedonia should receive an invitation—and the eventual compromise specified that an invitation would be issued as soon as the matter of the name was settled. The dispute nevertheless absorbed much of the conversation at the opening heads of state dinner and gave the saying "it's all in a name" a whole new meaning in NATO circles.

The real rift was over Georgia and Ukraine. At stake here was not semantics but strategy. Separate dinners were held by heads of state and foreign and defense ministers in an attempt to hash out a compromise, but without success. The United States had the support of Canada, the United Kingdom, and most of the Central and Eastern European countries, but it had arguably waited too long and had never conducted an all-out campaign to turn skeptics into supporters. Germany, too, had lined up its supporters opposing MAP—they were the same nine or ten countries that had been skeptical all along and included Belgium, the Netherlands, Greece, Luxembourg, Italy, Spain, and Turkey. Some countries were sitting on the fence, waiting to see which way the debate would go.

The reality was that NATO was divided right down the middle—and, given the Alliance's consensus rules, that gave the group opposed to granting MAP the advantage. So long as Berlin held the line, there would be no MAP. The real question was what kind of compromise, if any, would emerge. Dinner broke up with little progress having been made. NATO leaders asked Secretary General de Hoop Scheffer to come up with a compromise proposal that would be reviewed early the next morning and discussed when the North Atlantic Council (NAC) met at 0900. In a rare late-night meeting, President Bush huddled with his key staff to review the bidding. He was still determined to keep fighting and not settle for the lowest common denominator. Hadley and Rice were sent to negotiate for the United States at the early-morning session, but Bush insisted that any small group discussion also include both the Poles and the Romanians.

Shortly after 0630, a small group of advisors representing key NATO member states gathered to hammer out a compromise. They included the United States, Germany, France, the United Kingdom—and the Poles and the Romanians. The language of de Hoop Scheffer's first compromise was immediately vetoed by Berlin as being too close to the American position. A second compromise was in turn vetoed by Washington. The negotiation quickly became focused on the United States and Germany, with Polish foreign minister Radosław Sikorski providing input. Finally, there was a new compromise proposed. Its essence was a generic commitment of allies toward Ukrainian and Georgian aspirations; the start of a period of "intensive engagement" by NATO with these countries regarding the MAP applications as a step toward eventually joining the program; and a first assessment of their progress at the next ministerial meeting, which was scheduled for the end of the year. The text was circulated to NATO delegations before the NAC officially reconvened at 0900. Washington's advice to the pro-Georgian caucus was: take it because we won't get anything better.

But the advocates of granting Georgia and Ukraine MAP were not mollified so easily. Reading the proposed draft de Hoop Scheffer had circulated, Lithuanian president Valdas Adamkus was quite disappointed. In his view, it was not enough. He got out of his chair and walked around the table to where Bush and the U.S. delegation were sitting to see what the U.S. president thought. Bush told Adamkus, "It was the best we could do." Clearly Bush was not going to push for anything more. Adamkus returned to his chair, angry. The United States might have been prepared to abandon the fight but he was not. He had decided to try to fight for better language. Polish president Lech Kaczyński also looked at the proposed compromise and immediately rejected it. The allies' commitment to eventual membership was too weak, and the period of "intensive engagement" was seen as creating yet another step on the ladder toward eventual membership. Rather than moving Ukraine and Georgia closer to membership, another hurdle had been added. Romanian president Traian Băsescu sat in his chair reading the draft language. He was not only a strong advocate of MAP and the official host of the summit, but he felt a special bond with his neighbors around the Black Sea. In his eyes, the compromise was not only a rejection of MAP at the summit he was hosting; it did not even offer a clear perspective on the issue. He turned to his delegation and said, "I don't like this. It is not even close to what we expected." He asked his country's NATO ambassador, Sorin Ducaru, "Can't we try to get something better?"

Băsescu then stood up and walked over to Kaczyński, who, flanked by the head of his chancellery, Anna Fotyga, and Foreign Minister Sikorski, was also studying the draft text. Băsescu suggested that they not accept the language and push to see if there was not still a chance of getting something better. Kaczyński agreed, saying, "I am with you." In the meantime, Lithuanian president Valdas Adamkus had come over to join them and voice his skepticism as well. All three leaders agreed to push for better language and asked their key advisors to come up with a fix. By this time the leaders of several additional Central and Eastern European allies had gathered and voiced their support, too.

When de Hoop Scheffer convened the council, it quickly became clear that the compromise wouldn't fly. The secretary general then asked the delegations to leave the room so that the discussion could be continued in a smaller format—heads of state plus one advisor each. As people were leaving the room, the three Central and Eastern European leaders again huddled to discuss what to do. Seeing this, Chancellor Merkel walked over to them and asked how they could resolve the issue and arrive at a compromise. The first proposal of the three presidents was to modify the text to make it clear that Georgia and Ukraine would receive MAPs the following December at the scheduled NATO foreign ministers meeting; they suggested language along these lines. Merkel rejected this out of hand.

Kaczyński said, "We cannot let Russia have a veto. This is not fair to Georgia and Ukraine. This is not how NATO works." Merkel responded, "This is not about Russia and whether it has a veto. This is about whether these countries are ready and if we think this is the right time to take this step." Băsescu then stepped in and, looking at Merkel, asked, "Do we agree that these countries deserve to become NATO members and that no one has a veto?" Merkel reiterated that this was not the point and that everyone agreed on that. Adamkus stepped in to echo Băsescu's point: "Do we agree that these countries should become NATO members?" Merkel replied, "We agree on that. Where we don't agree is on timing." The response of the three presidents was immediate and spontaneous: "Then let's write that down!"

In the meantime, some chairs had been brought, and the four leaders were now seated in a semi-circle. A small crowd gathered around them, peering over their shoulders, to see what was happening. Listening to Merkel, the Central and Eastern European leaders sensed an opening. NATO had never before stated explicitly that a country would become a member. None of them had ever had such a pledge. Most of their Western

European counterparts, in all likelihood, would never have suggested this approach. They doubted if Merkel's foreign minister would have either, but he was not in the room. If Merkel agreed, it could be a major step forward.

Merkel then took out her pen and wrote on a sheet of paper: "We agree today that Georgia and Ukraine shall one day become members of NATO." After studying the wording, Băsescu said: "Madame Chancellor, in our part of the world saying 'one day' means nothing and does not commit you to anything—it means never." Kaczyński chimed in: "Absolutely." Merkel agreed to delete "one day" but instead insisted on the addition of a phrase at the end of the sentence: "if they so desire." Kaczyński, Adamkus, Băsescu, and the other Central and Eastern European leaders then pushed again for language that would say that the first review would be the last. Merkel refused.

While the language was being typed up, the full delegations returned to the room, and de Hoop Scheffer reconvened the meeting. In the meantime, the Polish delegation had had second thoughts. Someone had realized that the phrase "if they so desire" might be used against Ukraine, where public support for NATO was weak. Kaczyński took the floor to state that Poland would not agree to the phrase and that the Alliance should encourage, not discourage, Kiev. The phrase was subsequently dropped with the clear understanding that it was simply self-evident that a country could not become a NATO member against its own will. But the Central European NATO members had, working with Merkel, succeeded in getting a better deal than the United States had. British prime minister Gordon Brown leaned over to President Bush at the Council table and half-jokingly said, "I am not sure what we did here. I know we did not extend MAP. But I'm not sure we didn't just make them members of NATO."

The question now was how Russia would react—and whether Putin would keep his promise to Bush not to create a problem at the summit. As he rushed out of the room with the final compromise text, NATO assistant secretary general Martin Erdman ran into Russian deputy foreign minister Alexander Grushko, who was nervously hovering by the door. Grushko asked, "MAP? What about MAP?" Erdman told him there was no MAP but warned that there was a sentence that might be even worse from the Russian perspective. He quickly read him the sentence but then hurried off with the only copy of the compromise text in his hand. Exactly what the Russian diplomat had heard or understood was not clear.

A first glimpse at the official Russian reaction came that evening when Putin arrived in Bucharest for dinner. It was the first time a Russian leader had ever attended a NATO summit. Yeltsin had refused to attend the Madrid summit in 1997, when the first round of enlargement was launched, and Putin had avoided the Prague summit in 2002, when the Big Bang round of enlargement was concluded. Moscow's very public goal had of course been to ensure that Georgia and Ukraine did not get MAP. Technically, of course, NATO had not given it to them. But these countries had received something that was arguably better and stronger—an explicit political promise from NATO heads of state that they would one day became members. That had never happened before. When Putin arrived in Bucharest later that evening for dinner, he seemed to be in a good mood and to enjoy himself through dinner. Many diplomats breathed a sigh of relief, thinking they had dodged a bullet.

The next morning Putin was tougher. He showed up late for his first meeting with Secretary General de Hoop Scheffer to sign a transit agreement allowing NATO supplies for Afghanistan to pass through Russian territory. Putin started out by congratulating de Hoop Scheffer for having stood up to the Americans and denying MAP to Georgia and Ukraine. This was a big step, he quipped, for it showed that NATO was truly a democratic organization where the United States did not always get its way. De Hoop Scheffer tried to explain why that assessment was wrong and how NATO really worked. He also made it clear that NATO had made a commitment in principle to bring Ukraine and Georgia into the Alliance and that the question was no longer whether but when they would join. Putin continued his rant and, while signing the transit agreement, continued to lecture the secretary general on how the United States and its NATO allies had it all wrong in Afghanistan.

In his opening remarks to the NATO-Russia Council, de Hoop Scheffer repeated that the Alliance had made a commitment the previous day that Ukraine and Georgia would one day become members of NATO and that the question was no longer whether but when these countries would join. When Putin made his speech, Bush was watching closely to see if their gentlemen's agreement would hold. Putin was clear but measured. A mid-ranking Russian diplomat had given NATO interpreters an advance copy of Putin's speech. He chose to pass over the toughest remarks. On NATO enlargement, Putin said that on the whole Moscow was satisfied that the Alliance had handled the issue the previous day by not granting MAP. He said that if the issue had been handled differently, he probably would not have signed the agreement on transit routes.[9] On Kosovo, he repeated Moscow's opposition to independence but claimed Russia was acting responsibly and was still willing to work with the West. "You put us into a very complicated situation but we are trying to wriggle and behave carefully, without destroying the situation and without provoking military conflicts," the Russian leader claimed.

He still had tough words for Georgia and Ukraine. He criticized Tbilisi for thinking that joining the Alliance would help resolve the conflicts in Abkhazia and South Ossetia. "To solve these problems," he continued, "they do not need to enter NATO." Instead, what was needed was patience and dialogue on the ground. Although by this time Putin was already expanding ties with the two separatist regions that directly undercut Georgian sovereignty, he suggested that "we have been trying to help them, to help Georgia restore territorial integrity." He also insisted that Moscow had no intention of recognizing Abkhazia and South Ossetia. "We have been very responsible, very balanced, and we call on you to be careful as well."

The Russian president was even tougher on Kiev—describing Ukraine as an artificial creation and a state whose final formation was not complete. He noted that large parts of Ukraine were dominated by ethnic Russians and had been given to Ukraine by Moscow in an arbitrary fashion under Stalin, and asked, "Who can say that we do not have interests there?" The issue of NATO membership, he claimed, could threaten the very existence of Ukraine. "We should act very, very carefully. We do not have a right to veto [such a decision] and we probably don't even want one, but I want all of us to realize, when deciding such issues, that we have our interests there as well." At the press conference afterwards, Putin was also polite, but he was clear in reaffirming his opposition to NATO enlargement. Russia viewed "the appearance of a powerful military bloc" on its borders "as a direct threat" to its security, he said. "The claim that this process is not directed against Russia will not suffice," he continued. "National security is not based on promises."[10]

Did NATO leaders reach a historic compromise at Bucharest on the future enlargement of NATO? Or did they blunder in making a decision that would help catalyze the Russo-Georgian war four months later? Did the

Bucharest decision, along with Kosovo's declaration of independence, provide the trigger for a set of Russian actions and Georgian reactions that culminated in war on August 7? There is a clear trajectory in the escalation of Russian rhetoric and concrete pressure on Georgia that commenced in the spring of 2008, continued through the summer, and culminated in early August. Such timing hardly seems a coincidence. And when we take a close look at the content of the NATO decision in Bucharest, we can see how NATO's Bucharest compromise could have contributed to such a decision in Moscow.

The Bucharest compromise was a decision in principle to enlarge NATO to include Ukraine and Georgia. In some ways, it was similar to the compromise NATO had reached in January 1994, when it had stated that enlargement was not a question of whether but when. Many NATO leaders left Bucharest thinking they had managed to bridge the divide in the Alliance between those wanting to give a concrete perspective to Georgia and Ukraine and those firmly opposed to granting MAP. The Alliance had skirted that political minefield. Achieving that compromise was their definition of success. Designed as a technical program to accelerate practical cooperation with candidate members, MAP had become hostage to Alliance politics and a kind of fetish its original authors had never anticipated. While some NATO ambassadors were horrified that their heads of state had given an unprecedented commitment to these countries, many thought it a small price to pay for peace in the Alliance.

It was only later, after the dust had settled, that serious doubts about the Bucharest compromise started to set in and grow. The real measure for the success or failure of any NATO strategic decision is not only whether it meets the political needs of its members but what its impact is in the real world. It is precisely on that point that the Bucharest compromise is open to question. The Alliance was also trying to square the circle of reassuring Georgia and Ukraine without alienating Russia. It was part of NATO's overall dual-track strategy from the mid-1990s in which enlargement was accompanied by a parallel effort of outreach to Moscow. It was something NATO had pulled off successfully with Yeltsin during the first round of enlargement in 1997 and with Putin during a second round in 2002. Essentially, NATO was taking steps to bring new members closer to and eventually integrate them into the Alliance while simultaneously deepening its ties with Moscow to show that its intent was not hostile and that it wanted to include Moscow as part of the broader Western community.

But it did not work a third time, in Bucharest in 2008. The compromise NATO came up with did not reassure the Georgians nor did it avoid provoking the Russians. We will turn to Tbilisi's reaction in the next chapter. But the conclusion Moscow drew may have been a very different one than NATO had hoped for. To Moscow the Bucharest compromise suggested that the danger of Georgia and Ukraine eventually joining the Alliance had just become very real. Alliance heads of state had never before made such a political commitment to candidate members. At the same time, Bucharest had also shown how divided the Alliance was and how U.S. influence was on the wane. It was the first time in memory that a U.S. president had been rebuffed in such an open manner on a key issue at a NATO summit. Whether and when NATO would overcome these differences was unclear.

The Bucharest outcome might have not only failed to deter Moscow; it might have emboldened it. Instead of taking the issue off the table with Russia, it might have provoked precisely the kind of steps Moscow would take in the following months that eventually produced war in August. After all, from a Russian perspective there was now a real possibility that the candidacies of these countries would start to gain momentum if they were not stopped. And Moscow may have drawn the conclusion that the Alliance was now more committed than before to actually bringing in Georgia and Ukraine but was unable to do so in the short term unless and until its own deep internal differences were overcome. To Russia, that meant there was a window of opportunity to exploit NATO's disunity and to thwart Georgia's path to membership. How long that window would remain open was unclear. If Moscow was determined to stop Georgian membership, it had to act quickly. And what better way than to continue to escalate pressure on Tbilisi until it cracked?

After the August war, a debate emerged over whether Russia might have been prevented from attacking had the Alliance actually granted MAP in Bucharest. Would MAP have deterred Moscow? One can only speculate. In the eyes of this author, it is doubtful. The Alliance's problem was its lack of cohesion and unity. The differences on Georgia and Ukraine were out there in public for everyone, including Russia, to see. The Alliance underestimated

Russia's determination to prevent Georgia from ever joining NATO. A more strongly worded communiqué by a still-divided Alliance would not in all likelihood have deterred Moscow. The only deterrent to Russia would have been a unified and powerful signal of NATO commitment that enlargement was indeed inevitable and that trying to stop it would have real consequences. I doubt that granting MAP in Bucharest by itself would not have sent that signal. The real problem was the deep divide in the Alliance that made it painfully obvious that NATO was not ready for such a commitment.

At the end of the day, there is no escaping the fact that the problem in Bucharest was NATO's lack of unity and its failure to reach a commitment to help Georgia on the ground in meaningful ways, which could have deterred Russia's later actions. Given this lack of consensus, an important question is whether less would actually have been more. What was it that Tbilisi needed most—strong political statements of support, or real engagement on the ground and substantive cooperation? Would Georgia have been better off with a compromise focused on building practical engagement and putting a NATO presence on the ground? Such a compromise had been floated several times in the run-up to Bucharest. It was referred to as "MAP without MAP"—a package that would have granted Georgia and Ukraine the practical benefits of the MAP program but with a different label—either National Action Plan (NAP) or even Georgian Action Plan (GAP). Sometimes, in strategy as in life, less can be more.

There is an important codicil to the Bucharest summit, albeit one that's still somewhat opaque and shrouded in controversy. It came out of the meeting that took place in Sochi, where Bush and Putin journeyed for their own bilateral summit and to sign a new strategic framework agreement. The meeting was supposed to be a personal way for Putin to say goodbye to Bush and to sign an agreement that both captured what they had accomplished and left a framework for the successors to both presidents. It was largely a celebratory event—the two presidents and their delegations dined on pickled wild mushrooms, blini and caviar, and koulebyaka with salmon and crab, while the State Academic Ensemble of Folkdance of Adygheya and the Kuban Cossack Chorus provided musical entertainment. In the eyes of the American delegation, this was not a summit designed to do heavy diplomatic lifting. It was not a time to pick fights or score points. Contentious issues like Georgia had been dealt with at Bucharest. It was about Putin wanting to have a last dinner and a pleasant evening with his friend George Bush before the two of them left office.

Several weeks after Bucharest and Sochi had passed, the so-called memorandum of conversation, or memcon, from Bush's meeting with Putin in Sochi was finally typed up and circulated among senior officials. In the White House, a senior staff member from the vice president's office who had not been at Sochi read it closely, first with surprise and then with concern. In his view, that record showed that Putin had used stark and threatening language about Georgia that could be read as the Russian president testing Bush's resolve. The president had said nothing in response. In diplomatic practice, especially in sensitive conversations at the most senior levels, silence can be considered a signal that a suggested action, even if unwelcome, would draw no meaningful response. Indeed, the silence allows both sides to interpret the conversation as they wish. Given the risk that the Russians might interpret Bush's non-response as an implicit "green light" to act against Georgia, that staffer raised the issue to a more senior level.

Bush's aides who had attended the Sochi meeting with the president and who took the notes had not detected anything new or different in Putin's anti-Georgian remarks. After all, it was hardly a secret that the Russian president hated Saakashvili and was just looking for an excuse to slap down Georgia. The U.S. side had become accustomed to his tirades, and the United States was already on the record as supporting Georgia. Was this just more of the same, or something more ominous? Had the president, while enjoying the fete that Putin had prepared to bid him farewell, inadvertently signaled that the United States would not strongly oppose a Russian move against Georgia? Although this was a president who had coined the slogan "no more Yaltas," some who saw the memcon worried that the president had been vague in sending the message to Putin to leave Georgia alone.

CHAPTER 5

DIPLOMACY FAILS

The evening after the NATO Bucharest summit ended, Swedish foreign minister Carl Bildt had dinner with Saakashvili in Tbilisi. Bildt was eager to hear how the Georgian president assessed the NATO summit results. Saakashvili had been lobbied hard by President Bush to put a positive spin on the Bucharest outcome in public and had done so. Nevertheless, he was dismayed at the lack of European support for Georgia and at what was being widely reported as an American "defeat" in Bucharest. The key question, he and Bildt agreed, was how to overcome European, specifically German, skepticism and opposition to Georgia's Western aspirations. The Georgian leader recalled that he had sat next to Sarkozy at lunch in Bucharest and that the French president had told him that Georgia's rejection was not his fault and had blamed it on Merkel. It may have been disingenuous but it simply fueled the Georgian president's anger at Berlin.

Bildt argued that the best way to convince skeptical allies like Germany to be more forthcoming was to improve Georgia's democratic performance—starting with well-conducted parliamentary elections scheduled to take place in May. After all, Merkel's primary objection on MAP had been not the relationship with Russia but the state of Georgian democracy, although the same could not be said of the views of Foreign Minister Steinmeier. Saakashvili brushed off these concerns as a pretense. He didn't believe Berlin would support him even if Georgia were a model democracy. He was confident that his party would do well in the elections and complained that the opposition in Georgia was hopeless to work with. The only people who would not vote for him, he suggested, were those who still longed for the old Soviet days and their privileges—in essence, voters not to be bothered with.

It soon became clear, however, that the immediate issue on Saakashvili's mind was not NATO but the potential loss of Abkhazia—and that the Bucharest outcome had done little to lift his sense of siege or to assuage his concern that Russia's stance might amount to something ominous. He saw no political opening in Abkhazia and was convinced that Moscow was slowly but surely trying to turn the situation against him. "It would be one thing," he said, "if there was a status quo situation, but the problem is that we are losing the status quo." Putin had twice threatened him personally and told him that he would make Abkhazia a second Northern Cyprus if Georgia continued to pursue its goal of going West. Moscow was now using the Kosovar declaration of independence to move against him. The Abkhaz leadership was not interested in a political dialogue with Tbilisi and, he continued, they were just a bunch of criminals anyway. Negotiating with them was hopeless.

The key lay in Moscow, Saakashvili said. But the problem was that Russia was not interested in dealing either. It had lifted the economic embargo on the conflict zones and was now talking about making major investments there to prepare for the 2014 Sochi Olympics, which would be tantamount to economic colonization. Russia had also started, he claimed, a new military buildup in the region. Georgian intelligence had detected military personnel from several Russian units being quietly brought into Abkhazia to familiarize themselves with the terrain. What made him even less hopeful, Saakashvili continued, was the European Union's reluctance to speak out about any of this. He could not understand why it was so hard to acknowledge what was happening on the ground. Instead, many Europeans were starting to tell him that Georgia should just accept the loss of Abkhazia.

Georgia, Saakashvili stated with great emotion, would never, ever accept that. He went on to talk about how Georgia was upgrading its defenses with the help of Israel and Ukraine. What should I do, he asked rhetorically, when the Abkhaz refuse to talk with us, Russia illegally builds up its own military position, and plans to flood these conflict zones with investments and workers—thereby for all practical purposes taking over the place—and the Europeans say we should just accept Abkhazia as lost? Saakashvili went on to say that he had discussed the situation with both Bush and Rice when he was in Washington and had noted a certain degree of understanding of the fact that Georgia, too, had its red lines that could not be crossed.

Bildt wondered whether Saakashvili was thinking out loud about a possible Georgian military operation against Abkhazia—and he was worried that the Georgian president seemed to be interpreting his talks with Bush as some kind of flashing yellow light for military action if things continued on their present course. Saakashvili even recalled how in Bucharest a triumphant Croatian president Stjepan Mesić had told him—half-jokingly, half-seriously—that Georgia might look at the Croatian example of Operation Storm. During the war in Bosnia in the mid 1990s, Zagreb had successfully made its own land grab that created new military facts on the ground and had helped set up the negotiations that eventually led to Dayton. NATO had protested at the time but quickly moved on as it realized that Croatia's gains had actually made the resolution of the conflict more rather than less likely. A decade later, criticism of that move had been forgotten and Croatia had just been invited to join NATO.

Bildt spent the next hour trying to convince Saakashvili that such thinking was folly, that a military solution was a chimera, that fighting Serbs was completely different from fighting Russians, and that Georgia still had years of time. The only way forward, he emphasized, was a comprehensive diplomatic process that would bring a political solution. Bosnia and the Balkans were not the same. The key thing in a war was not to win the first battle, which Georgia might do successfully, but the final one. That was something Georgia could never do, given Russia's overwhelming military superiority. Bildt nevertheless left the dinner worried. He immediately let his American colleagues know about the conversation, including his concern that Saakashvili was misreading the signals coming from the Bush Administration.

Washington was stunned by Bildt's report. Senior officials went back and reviewed the records of the Oval Office meeting between Bush and Saakashvili. The president had been clear that he would support Georgia, including at Bucharest, but he had underscored that there were to be no surprises and no use of force. Washington nonetheless moved to reinforce the message and leave no doubt. On April 17, U.S. ambassador John Tefft delivered a strong message from the president to Saakashvili that the United States opposed any military actions and that Tbilisi, if it acted, would stand alone. The Georgian president responded that Bildt had misunderstood their conversation, that he never thought Bush had given him any kind of flashing yellow light, and that Georgia would not use force unless it were provoked or attacked.

Bildt's conversation was one of several alarm bells that went off in the spring of 2008 as Georgia and Russia seemed to be headed toward a possible war over Abkhazia. The reality was that Saakashvili had come away from his last meeting with Putin in late February, after the recognition of Kosovo, convinced that Putin was preparing for war. That is how he had interpreted the Russian president's final remarks to him in Moscow. Throughout the spring an anguished debate took place within the Georgian leadership over how Tbilisi should respond. Saakashvili's inner circle was divided, with one group advocating a preemptive Georgian military move to try to seize parts of Abkhazia. The hope was that Georgian forces could bypass and avoid fighting what was then a relatively small contingent of Russian peacekeepers, seize the largely empty stretch of land short of Sukhumi, and then hunker down and negotiate a diplomatic solution with the assistance of the international community. Others thought such a move would be a disaster. Saakashvili was somewhere in between these two views; he was skeptical about the military option but wondered what the alternative was.

The danger of a Russo-Georgian war, in turn, sparked a set of last-minute diplomatic moves to try to head off such a confrontation. A time-honored rule among diplomats faced with a tough problem or a looming crisis for which there is no apparent answer is to start a diplomatic process. Launching such a dialogue between the parties can help stem the momentum of a crisis or prevent a slide toward war. People are less likely to start shooting at each other if they are talking to each other. And while such a dialogue may not always look promising, sometimes new opportunities emerge that can be built on. A time-honored tactic of military strategists, however, is to use diplomatic talks and negotiations as a cover to create the impression of negotiating while actually using the time to make final preparations for a military assault. Talking and preparing for battle are not mutually exclusive. History is full of examples.

As tensions escalated in the spring of 2008, Washington and Berlin—as well as Tbilisi itself—launched diplomatic initiatives in the hope of stopping the downward spiral in Georgian-Russian relations. These initiatives ultimately turned out to be too little too late. Did they fail because the West was asleep at the wheel and was not reading the strategic signals coming from Russia and was therefore not forceful enough in pushing back on Moscow and Tbilisi, or was this a classic example of Moscow practicing the art of strategic deception while completing its own preparations for war? Throughout this period, Russian officials used both front and back diplomatic channels to tell their Western counterparts that their military steps were simply a deterrent to prevent the Georgians from acting rashly and attacking Abkhazia. They claimed to have intelligence that Saakashvili was planning such an attack and explicitly warned both Washington and European allies that Tbilisi was allegedly using them in a classic example of the tail wagging the dog.

During this same period, Georgia was trying to use all of the means at its disposal to attract the attention of the outside world and to invoke all the clauses and mechanisms that had been set up to prevent such escalations. The OSCE Istanbul Charter of 1999 had posited that security in Europe was based on two pillars—security between and also within states. It was an attempt to draw the lessons from the Balkan wars of the 1990s. What Georgia was facing was arguably exactly the kind of crisis the authors of that document had tried to anticipate and prepare for. But when Georgia tried to invoke the crisis mechanisms of the OSCE for assistance, there was little response. Similarly, when NATO set up the Partnership for Peace in 1994, the founding document contained provisions allowing partners to seek consultations with NATO in a crisis. When Georgian officials informally inquired at NATO about holding formal North Atlantic Council (NAC) consultations about the deteriorating situation, they were told they would be better off not doing so as the Alliance did not want to get involved. When the war broke out in early August, the North Atlantic Council managed to hold one meeting and issue a statement. Secretary General Jaap de Hoop Scheffer interrupted his summer holidays for a single day. The Supreme Allied Commander Europe (SACEUR) didn't even bother to break his vacation. And the NATO Military Committee only managed to meet when the fighting had all but stopped. For an Alliance that has claimed for itself the role of crisis manager across Europe as a whole, it was not an impressive performance.

It was just one more example of how a European security system that had been set up to provide transparency and early warning, to prevent strategic miscalculation, and to prevent crisis and war would fail in the spring and summer months of 2008.

The ink on Kosovo's declaration of independence was barely dry when Moscow took the first steps in what would become a sustained and significant escalation of political and military pressure on Georgia that culminated in the outbreak of war on August 7. On March 6, Moscow rescinded a 1996 Commonwealth of Independent States (CIS) decision on sanctions banning the delivery of weapons and military aid to the separatist regions and started openly arming the separatists.[1] Two weeks later, on March 21, the Russian Duma adopted a resolution urging the government to recognize Abkhazia and South Ossetia and to protect its "citizens" in these regions.[2] On April 3, President Putin sent a letter to the separatist leaders in which he pledged his support for Abkhazia and South Ossetia via means that are "not declarative but practical."[3] It was Moscow's response to Kosovo, just as Putin had threatened Saakashvili a few weeks earlier.

Alarm bells immediately went off in Tbilisi. These Russian actions threatened to cross what Georgia considered its own red lines—lines that, if crossed, could compel them to respond, perhaps even militarily. The first red line for Tbilisi was Russian recognition of the conflict zones. The second was large-scale ethnic cleansing of Georgian citizens living in the conflict zones. Although there were more ethnic Georgians living in South Ossetia, it was in Abkhazia that the Georgian government felt most vulnerable, because there was very little it could do if Sukhumi took steps against Georgians in border areas like Gali, which were beyond its reach. The third red line for the Georgians was a systematic Russian military buildup that essentially amounted to annexation and rendered a negotiated and peaceful resolution to the conflicts impossible.

The last scenario, however, looked as if it were now starting to become reality. It is precisely what Georgia believed Moscow was proceeding to implement in the spring and summer of 2008. Throughout the spring of 2008, Georgian officials told their allies that they would not survive as a government if they did nothing and simply acquiesced in losing Abkhazia and South Ossetia. The United States and European allies repeated their refrain that no matter what Moscow did, Tbilisi should not get into a fight with Russia that it could only lose. The two sides were talking past each other. All eyes were on Abkhazia. It was widely considered the more important of the two separatist provinces and the one where the potential for a conflict was greatest. It was also on Abkhazia that the Georgian Ministry of Defense's contingency planning was focused in the spring of 2008 as Tbilisi agonized over what to do.

After the NATO Bucharest summit, Moscow's campaign against Georgia intensified further. Putin had kept his promise to Bush not to create a scene at Bucharest, but this did not mean that Russian opposition was softening, nor did it prevent other senior Russian officials from speaking out. Soon after the Bucharest communiqué had been issued, Dmitry Medvedev, who had become president of Russia in May, issued a statement saying, "We will provide effective assistance to South Ossetia and Abkhazia in return for NATO's decision."[4] The head of the Russian General Staff echoed that sentiment when he said, "We will do everything [necessary] to prevent Georgia from joining NATO."[5] On April 16, Putin had signed a decree establishing direct legal and diplomatic ties with Abkhazia and South Ossetia.[6] In spite of all of the problems between Moscow and Tbilisi, Moscow had always paid lip service to Georgia's territorial integrity—as Putin had pledged to his NATO counterparts some two weeks earlier. This decree was a direct blow against that core principle and marked a significant hardening of Russian policy. The European Union, NATO, OSCE, and the leading Western powers all condemned the Russian move and urged Moscow to rescind the step, but to no avail.

On April 20, a Russian MIG–29 fighter aircraft shot down an Israeli-built Georgian unmanned aerial vehicle (UAV) that was conducting surveillance over the conflict zone. UAVs were not covered under the initial ceasefire in the early 1990s, but the UN had subsequently deemed such flights to be a violation of the existing agreement. This Russian action nevertheless clearly constituted an act of military aggression. Moscow did not want prying Georgian eyes watching whatever military preparations were taking place in Abkhazia. The drone captured and transmitted video footage of the attack. Russia initially denied responsibility, but a subsequent investigation by the UN's monitoring mission based in Abkhazia concluded that the fighter aircraft was Russian, that it had been directed by radar located at the Sukhumi airport, and that it had fired the heat-seeking missile that de-stroyed the drone.[7]

The ante was being upped. On April 18, the separatist government in Sukhumi claimed that Georgia was reinforcing its troops along the Kodori Gorge. The United Nations Observer Mission in Georgia (UNOMIG) in-vestigated the claim, but could not find any evidence that Georgian troop in-creases had taken place. Valery Kenyakin, the Russian special envoy for CIS countries, declared that Moscow was prepared to "act through military means" if Tbilisi made a military move in Abkhazia. Three days later, Moscow again claimed that Georgia was reinforcing its presence in the Kodori Gorge in preparation for an invasion and announced that it was de-ploying 400 additional paratroopers from the Novorossiysk Airborne Divi-sion to reinforce its peacekeeping contingent in Abkhazia and to establish several new checkpoints along the Enguri River. This move was made with-out the required prenotification of the Georgian side and was thus in viola-tion of the CIS agreement on peacekeeping operations. In early May Moscow reported that its troop presence in Abkhazia had been increased to over 2,500 soldiers. Georgian intelligence estimated the number was closer to 4,000. Around the same time, the Russian air force issued a nationwide call-up for military helicopter pilots with experience flying in mountainous areas.[8] One of the Russian pilots the Georgians captured during the August war was a reservist who had been called up several months earlier and knew the terrain from of the country having served there during Soviet times.

In mid-May the Russian media started broadcasting stories that a war in Abkhazia was imminent and that the Georgians were planning to attack Abkhazia from both the Kodori Gorge and the Gali region. In reality, it was almost impossible for Georgia to invade from the Kodori Gorge. That gorge was separated from both the Georgian and Abkhaz sides by 4,000-meter mountain ranges and was therefore largely inaccessible. The Georgians had armed police units there that were the equivalent of light infantry and were capable of putting up a significant fight in mountainous terrain if attacked, but they had little offensive capability. There was only one road leading down the gorge into Abkhazia that could easily be blocked by Abkhaz or the Russian forces deployed there. Trying to move in from Senaki would have entailed a more conventional assault and would have been more plausible—

and was one of the scenarios Tbilisi had planned for. But in the summer of 2008 the Georgians, with one brigade in Iraq and another in pre-deployment training, lacked the forces to carry out anything more than a very limited operation from Senaki.

Tbilisi was increasingly jumpy. Parliamentary elections were scheduled for May 21, and it was not clear how such security issues might impact the result. Saakashvili's ruling party ran a campaign focusing on jobs and pensions and downplaying security issues, but the danger of war lurked in the background. The deployment of Russian paratroopers had initially led Saakashvili to conclude, for example, that the feared Russian offensive might be in the works. The day the deployment was announced he had phoned National Security Council secretary Alexander Lomaia to say, "It has started"—only to call back shortly thereafter to admit it was a false alarm. But it was a sign of how tense the situation was. When the result of the Georgian elections came in on May 21, Saakashvili's party won a clear victory, with 59 percent of the vote—a victory even greater than the president had achieved in January. Discontent in the country was growing, but the opposition was unable to capitalize on it and put together a clear alternative. Russia's saber-rattling had had little effect.[9]

Moscow would step up its campaign on other fronts as well. In early May NATO and the Russian Chiefs of Defense met in Brussels as part of ongoing NATO-Russian consultations. The Russian defense chief, Army General Yury Baluyevskiy, stunned his NATO colleagues when he warned them that there could be a war in Georgia during the summer unless steps were taken to avoid such a conflict—and he urged NATO nations to cancel a scheduled exercise involving NATO and U.S. troops lest they end up getting caught in a conflict there and being killed. Baluyevskiy again suggested that Moscow had intelligence that Saakashvili was planning an unspecified action to regain Abkhazia by force to divert attention from his domestic troubles. At the time, NATO thought it was just standard Russian bluster and political posturing against Tbilisi. In retrospect, it might have been a warning that went unnoticed.[10] After the meeting, NATO and Russia activated a back channel that had been set up between the Supreme Allied Commander Europe (SACEUR) and the Russian General Staff in the 1990s. But even that did not translate into proactive steps to stabilize the situation on the ground. The Alliance was preoccupied with Afghanistan and had lost much of its Cold War ability to interpret and respond to this kind of strategic signaling.

On May 30, Georgia took a step to de-escalate the situation when Ambassador Irakli Alasania announced to the UN Security Council that Tbilisi would no longer conduct UAV flights over Abkhazia. Hopes that Russia would reciprocate were dashed the next day as Moscow again stepped up the pressure by announcing that it was deploying another 400 railroad troops to Abkhazia to "rehabilitate the region's railway and road infrastructure" between Sukhumi and Ochamchira.[11] It was another illegal and ominous move. Georgian deputy foreign minister Grigol Vashadze responded at the time, "No one needs to bring railway forces to the territory of another country unless a military intervention is being prepared."[12] His words were accurate. Those Russian engineering troops completed their renovation in early August, just in time for Moscow's invasion. The refurbished railways and roads would help move Russian forces and supplies when Russia invaded from Abkhazia in August.

By now alarm bells had started to ring throughout the West as well. The Bush Administration had a problem. Georgia's attempts to go West were widely considered—rightly or wrongly—an American project with which President Bush was directly and personally associated. Washington had been a driving force behind both Kosovo's independence and the MAP campaign for Georgia in Bucharest. Russian warnings that U.S. support could have consequences for conflicts like Abkhazia and South Ossetia had been ignored. But what if Moscow was serious? Some American officials did worry that the MAP issue had been left hanging at Bucharest and that this uncertainty might tempt Moscow to go after Georgia. There was little doubt in Washington's eyes that the Russians were meddling, seeking to provoke Saakashvili, and were just waiting for the Georgians to make a mistake they could exploit. Washington knew that Saakashvili was worried that he was losing part of his country and that, in desperation, he was flirting with the idea of a land grab in Abkhazia.

Matt Bryza was the senior working-level American official in the State Department responsible for Georgia and the person who bore the brunt of Georgian frustration—but he was also the person with whom they shared their most sensitive fears and thoughts. Georgians, from the president down, had talked to Bryza—but also to his EU counterpart, Peter Semneby—on occasion in years past about the possibility of a Georgian military move in Abkhazia. Such conversations were never official and tended to take place in moments of real or imagined desperation. Sometimes they involved Georgia's responding to events on the ground to protect citizens in trouble. But at times they also entailed the option of Georgia's taking and seeking to hold a piece of Abkhazia—usually the areas that had been predominantly populated by Georgians before the war. Many of us referred to it as the "land grab" scenario. Such conversations usually took place in private settings—at Saakashvili's home, in his chancellery late at night, or during one of Georgia's favorite pastimes—drinking. Maps were brought out or drawn on napkins as Georgian officials thought out loud about what-they-would-do-if scenarios.

Moscow's escalation in the spring of 2008 created precisely such a moment. American officials knew about Bildt's conversation with Saakashvili. They were hearing the same things through their own channels as Tbilisi agonized over how to respond to the growing fear that Abkhazia was being lost. The repeated American response to Georgian talk about possible military action was: Don't do it. If you get into a fight with Russia, you will be destroyed. The Georgian retort came in several parts. They first insisted that they might do better militarily than the Americans thought. This was often coupled with a plea to provide Tbilisi with Stinger missiles to help stop a potential Russian airborne assault. Such requests were considered but eventually denied by Washington. The Georgians also said they had a window where such a move was still feasible, but it was closing as Moscow launched its own military buildup. If they were to move, they had to do so before it was too late.

Tbilisi was becoming desperate. It saw itself losing Abkhazia—once and for all—as Moscow moved bit by bit to consolidate its hold over the province. If they did not act soon, Georgians argued, they would never have a chance to regain their territory. Moreover, they worried that the ongoing uncertainty and tension—a kind of "phony war" or undeclared conflict— was frightening off Western investors. Again there were voices in Saakashvili's inner circle arguing that it would be better to consider a limited military option now that would at least preemptively draw a clear line in Abkhazia and end the uncertainty. The issue came up during the visit of a Georgian delegation to the State Department in April to see Assistant Secretary of State Dan Fried. As he recalled in a subsequent interview:

> That was the first time that I used language that if the Georgians went in, they might win the first battle and perhaps the second. But that would be the last battle they would win because the Russians would subsequently come in hard and destroy them. They would do so with glee. Do not give them that opportunity, I told them.[13]

Also in April, National Security Advisor Stephen Hadley was sufficiently worried that things in Abkhazia were starting to spin out of control that he convened a series of meetings in his office in the White House. He wanted to kick-start a diplomatic effort to prevent this sixteen-year-old low-grade conflict, over two small mountainous regions in the Caucasus, from erupting into war. The answer Washington came up with was to attempt to reframe the problem from one where Georgia saw itself in a lose-lose situation—either acquiesce to losing Abkhazia, or launch a military move—to one where Tbilisi could see light at the end of the tunnel and a peaceful resolution of the crisis. To do that, Washington needed to change the narrative and terms of reference for the conflicts and for Georgia more generally. It knew many key allies distrusted Saakashvili and were reluctant to embrace him. They thought he was part of the problem and feared that a closer Western embrace would only embolden him.

Washington's view was the opposite—namely that the best way to get Tbilisi to abandon any military option was to embrace it, demonstrate Western support, and show Georgia that there was indeed light at the end of the tunnel. The U.S. goal was to help Saakashvili avoid the trap Washington thought Moscow was laying, in which the leader had to choose between losing these territories and going to war. That trap had to be diplomatically preempted and a new perspective for an eventual resolution of the conflicts created. Washington also wanted to be sure that if Russia made any additional moves toward recognizing Abkhazia and South Ossetia, it would be Moscow and not Tbilisi that would end up isolated as the odd man out.

There were three elements to the U.S. plan. The first was to show critics and nervous allies that Georgia was serious about peace by further elab-
orating on its own peace plan, which Saakashvili had announced that spring.
That included Tbilisi reaching out directly to talk with Sukhumi and talking to the Abkhaz. Saakashvili had turned skeptical about the utility of dealing directly with the Abkhaz, but Washington had received signals that the
Abkhaz, while having no desire to return to Georgia, were also keen to be
more independent from Russia and open to the West. No one knew for sure
how serious that desire was or, given Russian influence, how far the Abkhaz
would go. But Washington wanted to test those signs by starting a process
of low-level practical cooperation that would initially create people-to-
people contacts and start to open up the region to the outside world.

The second part of the strategy was to provide Tbilisi with greater reassurance against Russian moves. The key here was to begin to address
Georgia's long-standing demand that Moscow's monopoly of the peacekeeping presence on the ground finally be broken and a step-by-step process
launched to internationalize that presence. Washington was urging the European Union to start to bring in European police trainers or monitors to
augment the Russian peacekeeping presence in Abkhazia, including the
Upper Kodori valley, which was considered the most dangerous flashpoint.
In return for movement toward a greater international presence on the
ground and the opening up of the region to the return of refugees, the Georgians would have to issue a non-use-of-force pledge.

The third part of the strategy was to move beyond the current formats
for negotiating Abkhazia's future status. Washington agreed with Georgia
that these formats had long outlived their utility, were one-sided, and needed
to be transformed. Since the early 1990s, the Friends of the Secretary General—a group of countries, consisting of the United States, Germany, France,
the United Kingdom, and Russia—had been the main vehicle for dealing
with Abkhaz issues, but Washington was prepared to move beyond this format. It wanted to take a first step in that direction through a series of ad hoc
meetings aimed at implementing the fleshed-out Georgian peace plan, which
would evolve over time into a new forum based on direct contact between
Georgian and Abkhaz representatives without Moscow's supervision. The
plan also envisaged the eventual creation of a new council that would bring

the European Union into the picture as an actor. In mid-May Bryza flew to the region to lay out this strategy to the Georgians and the Abkhaz. He found interest in both Tbilisi and Sukhumi in spite of their many differences. That effort was reinforced by a visit by Georgian UN ambassador Alasania to Abkhazia as well. But the initiative stalled when first Saakashvili and then the Abkhaz got cold feet.

What was unfortunately missing from the plan was a clear and un-equivocal message to Moscow that any moves against Georgia would have real consequences in Russia's relations with the United States and the West more generally. But Washington, and even more so, Europe, had by this time defaulted to the comfort zone of blaming both sides and calling for both to show restraint. They could not agree on which side was more to blame for the deterioration in relations and whether the Russian provocations were real or manufactured by overzealous and jumpy Georgians. It was, of course, much easier to be diplomatically tough with the Georgians than with the Russians. Nevertheless, there is little evidence that either the United States or Europe weighed in clearly and consistently at the highest levels in Moscow to warn against the consequences of Russian aggression. While everyone knew that Moscow and the West were at loggerheads over the issue, there was a tendency to simply agree to disagree with Moscow on the issue. Agreeing to disagree with the Russians on Georgia was not the same as deterring Moscow from acting.

The United States was not the only country that got active diplomati-cally in an effort to head off the danger of war. The European Union was also increasingly concerned about the danger of a war breaking out over Abkhazia as well. When the European Council met in May, the growing sense of danger and urgency finally motivated the European Union to over-come its twin fear of ending up in a face-to-face confrontation with Russia or being pushed around by an unpredictable Saakashvili, and to become en-gaged in parallel diplomacy with Washington. The European Union's foreign policy czar, Javier Solana, traveled to the region in early June to offer a greater EU role, which was welcomed by all sides. In the following weeks, the European Union developed a set of small but nonetheless real confi-dence-building measures ranging from holding conferences in Sukhumi and Brussels to sending a border support team and offering to host additional meetings in Brussels to bring the conflicting parties together. Internal divisions prevented the European Union from taking bolder steps, but it was a start. Although they initially agreed to such steps, the Abkhaz and South Ossetians ended up backing out at the last minute.

Germany also stepped forward to play a key role. Berlin was the leading power in Europe articulating and shaping policy to the east. It had close ties with and a major investment in a partnership with Moscow, but it also had historic ties to Georgia. It was also the chairman of the Friends of the Secretary General. It saw itself as having a special responsibility for the Abkhaz conflict and was reluctant to cede that role to the European Union. It, too, saw the deteriorating situation on the ground in Georgia. Berlin knew and feared that a conflict between Georgia and Russia could jeopardize Europe's, and above all, its own, relationship with Moscow. Germany's calculations were driven not only by the need to assist Georgia but also the desire to avoid a confrontation with Russia that would damage everyone's relations with the West.

Berlin stepped forward with its own plan—quickly dubbed the Steinmeier Plan—that also envisioned a three-phase approach but with different emphases than the American one. Its first phase put the onus on the Georgians by asking them to make a non-use-of-force pledge up front—the key Russian demand—in return for a general agreement on the principle of refugee return and a mutual withdrawal from the Kodori Gorge. The second phase focused on confidence-building measures between the Abkhaz and the Georgians, especially in the economic realm. This was to be backed up by an international donors' conference to finance specific practical projects. The third phase was a settlement of Abkhazia's political status with the help of international mediation. When the Germans presented the plan to allies in late June, Washington went along with it in spite of some misgivings. Washington nevertheless wanted Berlin to assume responsibility for bringing the Russians on board and believed the German plan could be shaped to accord with the fundamentals of the U.S. plan. The most important thing was to get the process going and to get people to start talking before it was too late and they started shooting.

Tbilisi welcomed Berlin's engagement but was still wary. Germany was a heavy hitter in the region, and Berlin's special relationship with Moscow could in principle help Tbilisi. The problem was that the Georgians did not trust the Germans—and vice versa. They thought Berlin was naïve about Russian intentions and was too willing to accept Moscow's claim to a special sphere of influence in the Caucasus. They blamed Berlin for torpedoing their chances for MAP at Bucharest and especially distrusted Foreign Minister Steinmeier, who they saw as the main cheerleader for close German-Russian ties. Germany was Saakashvili's favorite punching bag and the country he would lash out against most often in his tirades about European appeasement.

Tbilisi also thought Berlin's plan was front loaded, with the Georgian side being asked to make the major concessions before getting enough in return. By negotiating the plan with the Russians in the Friends group before sharing it with Tbilisi, Berlin was almost guaranteeing that Georgia would reject it. This was the inherent problem in the Friends process as well as more generally. Russia was de facto a party to the conflict but was being treated as a co-mediator with the other major allies. At the same time, Tbilisi did not want to say no to the Steinmeier Plan or be blamed for its failure. They were happy that the Germans were finally showing signs of interest in Georgia and were willing to come to the region. They hoped that when Steinmeier saw the reality on the ground, German thinking and policy might evolve.

These initiatives never got off the ground for several reasons. One was a lack of Western unity. None of the parties on either side of the Atlantic could ever quite speak with a single credible voice—neither to Georgia or to Russia. Both saw the same deteriorating situation, but they disagreed on how to proceed. Whereas Washington believed that the best way to influence Tbilisi was to embrace it, European allies were less trusting and worried that such support might encourage Saakashvili to be even more assertive. They were concerned about being drawn by what they saw as a reckless and impatient Georgia into a conflict with Russia that was not in their interests. They were shocked when they heard Georgian officials speculate about a military move. Germany had had to wait patiently for nearly half a century before an opportunity emerged for its "frozen conflict" with East Germany to be resolved—and on peaceful terms. Many Europeans felt Georgia should be able to show strategic patience as well and had little sympathy for Saakashvili's hurry.

Europe's reticence was, from the U.S. perspective, the wrong approach. The further European allies distanced themselves from Tbilisi in the face of what the Georgians saw as aggressive Russian moves, the more Georgian disappointment and distrust of Europe deepened, and the more European influence waned. Restraining the Georgians required Europe to lean forward and not backward in the saddle. The Europeans were also reluctant to push Moscow too hard, especially on changing the existing diplomatic formats. They preferred to work with Moscow and within the existing framework in spite of its flaws. They saw their task as finding common ground and searching for solutions with, rather than against, Russia. Some of the Europeans thought privately that Abkhazia was lost anyway and were reluctant to invest large amounts of political capital in trying to either push Russia on this issue or to help Georgia recover it.

In short, the Europeans wanted Washington to deliver the "tough love" and rein in the Georgians. But they were reluctant to take steps to satisfy the key Georgian demands that would have helped the United States do so. Washington basically agreed with those Georgian demands but either wanted or needed the Europeans to take steps to carry them out. The core of the American plan was after all a greater presence and role for the European Union in Abkhazia—on the assumption that an American presence was too provocative. The allies were reluctant to take that responsibility and were not always pleased by Washington's desire to draw them further into assuming such responsibility. By mid-June, it was clear that the strategy was not coming together. What was on offer to Georgia was too little to reassure Tbilisi and was not changing the dynamics on the ground. In Washington, Fried went to Secretary of State Rice to urge her to become personally involved in trying to halt the downward spiral.

The second reason the strategy did not work was because of Russia. It was a key member of the so-called Friends group on Abkhazia and nominally the country responsible for pushing forward the peace process on the ground, but it did nothing of the sort. Indeed, it repeatedly tried to undercut or sabotage any moves it could not control or did not like. American negotiators were constantly frustrated by trying to work with their Russian colleagues to develop some initiatives only to find Moscow pulling the rug out at the last minute over some procedural or other issue. Every time it came to taking a next step that might de-escalate the situation or lead to direct Abkhaz-Georgian talks or confidence-building measures, it seemed that Moscow would find some way to undermine the initiative or reverse Abkhaz interest. It felt like a diplomatic slow roll. This all strengthened the sense in some quarters that Russia's half-hearted diplomatic efforts were simply part of a strategy of deception and a cover while Moscow completed its military preparations to attack.

June was a dramatic month in the internal Georgian decision-making process as well. The Georgian government was looking for a way to push back against Russian moves. It was also trying to mobilize Western attention while avoiding steps that would give Moscow a pretext for further action. One option under debate was to simply cancel the mandates of the Russian peacekeeping forces. What was perhaps most galling to the Georgians was Moscow's exploiting its internationally sanctioned position as an ostensible "peacekeeper" to pursue its neo-imperialist goals. Technically, Georgia had to agree to the renewal of this mandate to allow Russian forces to remain on Georgian territory. Yet the original agreements had granted both sides an opt-out clause. A number of Saakashvili's advisors were urging him to pull the plug. Such a move would put Moscow on the spot—Russia would then officially become an "occupying force." Opting out would set a clock ticking that would officially give Russia ninety days to withdraw its forces.

Tbilisi was under no illusion that Moscow would simply pack up and leave. But the hope was that such a move would dramatize Georgia's plight and underscore its legal and moral protests over what was happening. In Georgian eyes, this would simply drop the farce that Moscow was a neutral peacekeeper. The Georgians were not expecting miracles. They were looking for a legal and nonmilitary way to halt Moscow's escalation and force a shift to some kind of new security mechanism on the ground. Tbilisi did not take this step in mid-June after repeated American and European interventions and assurances. They feared that when the dust settled after such a move, Georgia could be even worse off. While the formats were flawed, they believed they were better than none at all. They also worried that such a move would start the countdown to confrontation with Russia. As part of the effort to forestall this Georgian move, both Rice and Steinmeier agreed to visit Tbilisi in July. The West's message was: Give us a chance to try to restart the diplomatic process.

In June, Georgian and Abkhaz leaders also quietly met under NGO auspices in Sweden to discuss the latest version of the peace plan that had been developed in the spring by Bryza and Alasania and that had seemed to spark some interest in Sukhumi. It was a chance for the Abkhaz and the Georgians to talk without having Russia in the room. That plan included a free economic zone allowing Abkhazia to establish external economic ties, a pullback of security forces from the demarcation line, an international civilian police presence in several ethnic Georgian districts in Abkhazia along the border to deal with local organized crime, and, finally, a non-use-of-force pledge by Tbilisi. But whereas in May the Abkhaz had shown interest in such ideas, they now took a tougher line with the Georgians. At the same time, they made it clear to EU diplomats that they welcomed greater European engagement on the ground.

In parallel, however, Tbilisi decided to roll its own diplomatic dice one more time. It placed its hope in Dmitry Medvedev and in the chance that the new Russian president did not harbor the same hatred of Georgia that Putin had and might be more open to a new dialogue or peace initiative. Saakashvili spoke to Medvedev on the phone on June 2 and then met him on June 6 in St. Petersburg on the margins of a CIS summit. The Georgian side was desperate for any sign of progress. Putin had always rejected the Georgian offer for a bilateral presidential summit meeting, but Tbilisi was hoping Medvedev might be more open to the idea. Saakashvili was accompanied by Deputy Foreign Minister Grigol Vashadze and National Security Council Secretary Alexander Lomaia. Vashadze had recommended that Saakashvili first try to find some common ground with the Russian president rather than starting with the conflicts. Both leaders were lawyers by training, and Vashadze urged Saakashvili to start talking about their common efforts to reform their countries to set a positive tone.

Saakashvili followed the script, avoiding even mentioning the conflicts and instead talking about legal and economic reform issues, how much the two sides potentially had in common, and the need to improve bilateral ties. Eventually Medvedev started to get restless and raised the issue of the conflicts himself. Saakashvili then pulled out maps he had brought along and placed them on the table, using them to outline the destabilizing effect of recent Russian moves such as the modernization of the railroad, as well as specific steps that could be taken to de-escalate the situation. The two leaders went back and forth. After forty-five minutes, a Russian aide signaled that it was time for the meeting to end.

As the meeting ended, Medvedev noted that the two leaders needed more time to discuss such complicated issues and suggested they meet again somewhere in the south of Russia. Saakashvili proposed a bilateral summit before the end of the summer and Medvedev agreed in principle. Saakashvili assumed this meant they would meet in Sochi. He concluded that that could be the perfect place and opportunity to try to cut the Gordian knot on Abkhazia and elaborate on the issue of how Georgia and Russia could work together in Abkhazia to make the Sochi Olympics a success. He saw the Olympic Games an opportunity to create a new positive dynamic for regional cooperation as opposed to even more confrontation.

Saakashvili had been thinking about what Georgian and Russian bottom-line interests were in Abkhazia and whether there was a way to square the circle between them. For him, the most important thing was to get Georgian and international access to those parts of Abkhazia that had been largely inhabited by Georgians before the war and allow the return of refugees. He did not have to get Georgian control over all of Abkhazia. He decided to put down on paper, in a letter to Medvedev, a package deal he had been toying with in his mind for some time. Working with Vashadze and a small team, the Georgian president put together his boldest proposal yet regarding Abkhazia.

In a letter dated June 21, Saakashvili proposed an interim solution on Abkhazia that, while it carefully avoided the word "partition," amounted to a split of the province into two areas—one opened to Georgian influence and the other firmly in Russian hands. The former would encompass the Gali and Ochamchira districts, which were among those districts that had been predominantly populated by ethnic Georgians before the war and where the remaining Georgians were concentrated. It was to become a free economic zone jointly administered by either a mixed Georgian-Abkhaz or international administration that would allow the Abkhaz to trade with the outside world. Tbilisi was also proposing mixed law enforcement agencies, supplemented with international involvement and supervision, to deal with the organized crime problem in the border areas.

In return, Tbilisi was willing to unilaterally commit to signing a non-use-of-force pledge, to abandon efforts to overturn the CIS peacekeeping mandate, and to accept the presence of a redeployed and reconfigured Russian peacekeeping presence. It was also willing to work with Moscow to make the Sochi Olympics—a huge prestige project for the Kremlin—a success. Most important, Georgia was willing to live with and sanction a de facto Russian presence in the rest of Abkhazia for the foreseeable future. This was not "land for peace" nor a formal partition. It was something in between, cast in terms of an interim solution. But it was a deal that allowed both sides to address their core needs and save face. Georgia would get access and a say—with international oversight—in local governance in those parts of Abkhazia that mattered most to Tbilisi and where a majority of the population was Georgian. While Tbilisi dreaded the word "soft partition" and on paper would remain committed to the principle of territorial integrity, that is what was on the table.

The letter was hand delivered in Moscow on June 23. Given its sensitivity, no one wanted to send it through normal diplomatic channels. The Russian Foreign Ministry's initial response was polite. But it did not take long for Tbilisi to realize that its hopes were, yet again, misplaced. On July 3, Russian deputy foreign minister Grigory Karasin hand delivered Moscow's official response to Deputy Foreign Minister Vashadze in Tbilisi. When Vashadze opened the letter and read the contents, he knew the initiative was dead. Russia had refused to pick up on the key openings in Georgia's package even though many of these initiatives contained ideas Moscow itself had been pushing earlier. Instead, it was raising the bar for any dialogue by adding new preconditions. Following the meeting, Vashadze headed over to the president's chancellery. He stuck his head into the office of National Security Council Secretary Alexander Lomaia. "Is there anything in the letter?" Lomaia asked. Vashadze replied, "No, the letter is empty. We are going to have a hot summer." The next morning South Ossetian forces tried to assassinate Georgian ally Dmitry Sanakoyev with an improvised explosive device (IED) while he was driving in a convoy near Tskhinvali and launched attacks against a Georgian school bus and police car. That, too, was a signal. The time to talk had passed. The situation was escalating.

On July 6 Saakashvili traveled to Kazakhstan for the tenth anniversary of the capital of Astana as well as a birthday party for the Kazakh leader, Nursultan Nazarbayev. There he hoped to talk again with Medvedev, who was attending too. But Medvedev had little desire to see him. The Russian president displayed none of the openness Saakashvili had sensed a month earlier, and he refused an official meeting with Saakashvili despite persistent Georgian efforts to arrange one. As the leaders were sitting down for dinner, Saakashvili tried to pull Medvedev aside and urged him to move forward with the summit idea the two leaders had tentatively agreed to in June. Medvedev equivocated, saying that Georgia was a problem he had inherited, not created—implying that he wanted little if anything to do with it. It was also premature, he added, to have a summit before they had some concrete results to show lest people be disappointed. When Saakashvili said the situation could hardly get worse, Medvedev responded, "It can get much worse," and walked away.

Several days later, on July 9, Secretary of State Rice arrived in Tbilisi. As her plane landed, four Russian fighter aircraft violated Georgian airspace yet again. It was an unusual way for Moscow to welcome America's top diplomat to the region. On the plane, Rice had huddled with Fried to go over what they were trying to accomplish. Rice understood that Saakashvili felt he was in a bind, that the Russians had him spooked, and that he believed he was in danger of losing Abkhazia. The Georgian leader had lost confidence in the West and no longer believed Washington or its allies had any red lines they were ready to defend against Russian encroachment. Nor did the Georgians particularly like the Steinmeier Plan or trust the Germans. The question was whether Rice could reassure Tbilisi and convince Saakashvili that there was still a peaceful way to resolve the Abkhazia question without a war.

Saakashvili and Rice met in the president's chancellery and continued their talks at the rooftop restaurant Kopola, which had a fabulous view over Tbilisi. Rice told the president he had to agree to a non-use-of-force pledge. "Your refusal to do so," she said, "is not getting you anything because you have no option to use force, and you, I, and the Russians all know it. So refusing to give a non-use-of-force pledge is gaining you noth-ing." Saakashvili responded that he was willing to do it, but that it should be part of a broader package. Rice suggested that Fried and his counter-parts sketch out such a package right then and there. The American and Georgian delegations went down to the end of the table to work on a draft. Negotiations continued after dinner at the Tbilisi Marriott. After several hours, they had agreed on a modified version of the German plan includ-ing a non-use-of-force pledge. On the plane the next day Rice immediately called Berlin to make sure they could live with the changes that had been made to the German plan.

Prior to departure, Rice and Saakashvili held a press conference, during which Rice underscored U.S. support for Georgia's territorial integrity and a peaceful solution to the conflicts. While criticizing recent Russian moves, she made it clear that the United States was still committed to working within the Friends of the Secretary General process and pushed Georgia to engage with both Russia and Abkhazia. In turn, Saakashvili pronounced himself willing to engage in such a dialogue but went on to accuse Russia of no longer acknowledging Georgia's jurisdiction over an essential part of its territory and of mounting an "unprecedented" challenge to European post–Cold War order. "This is their reaction to NATO expansion plans," he said. "This is their reaction to the independence of Kosovo. This is their re-action to the increasing U.S. presence in the region. Looks like some people have not noticed the Cold War is over."[14]

After Rice left, a frustrated Saakashvili prepared his own fallback plan. He instructed his National Security Council to again draw up plans for Georgia to withdraw from the existing peacekeeping agreements with Rus-sia on Abkhazia. He coupled it with a unilateral non-use-of-force pledge to address Western concerns and Russian complaints and to underscore that such a step was not a prelude to military action. He was going to issue the non-use-of-force pledge but on his own terms. The paperwork and diplo-matic instructions were drawn up and ready to go. The date set was July 16.

The plan was put on hold pending the visit of German foreign minister Steinmeier to the region. Berlin was not happy that Washington had revised the plan that had previously been agreed upon. Whereas Washington thought it was saving the plan by ensuring Georgian buy-in, Berlin feared it was undermining it. At the same time, it could hardly complain that Rice had worked to bring the Georgians on board. Steinmeier now journeyed to the region to meet Saakashvili and the Abkhaz separatist leader Sergei Bagapsh and went on to Moscow for meetings with the Russian leaders. At each stop, he managed to squeeze out an unenthusiastic agreement from the different parties to the plan to meet yet again, in Berlin, at the end of the month. It was a small but important step forward and gave diplomats some hope that the worst had been averted as they prepared for summer holidays. But it was like herding cats. German diplomats were still trying to work out the details for the next meeting when war broke out.

The Rice and Steinmeier visits led the Georgians to conclude that they had bought time and that the immediate danger of war was over. But it was only the lull before the storm. The Georgians started to relax, and many of the key lieutenants in Saakashvili's circle asked permission to go on vacation for a much-needed break. Saakashvili himself headed to Italy with his family. I caught up with him over lunch in the Ukrainian resort city of Yalta in late July at a conference organized by the foundation of the Ukrainian oligarch Viktor Pinchuk. I had just published an op-ed in the *Washington Post* warning that war might still be coming. Saakashvili and I discussed whether the window of vulnerability was closed or not. Joining us at lunch was Elmar Brok, a prominent German member of the European Parliament. He said that he had recently met Vladimir Chizhov, the Russian ambassador to the European Union, in Brussels. He had told Chizhov that he was planning to visit Georgia in September. As Brok recalled the story over lunch, he told us the ambassador had smiled and said, "You might want to go earlier. September may be too late." It was.

CHAPTER 6

THE BATTLE

On July 29, 2008, South Ossetian separatist forces started shelling Georgian peacekeepers and Georgian ethnic villages. A week later Russia and Georgia were on the verge of war. In Washington on the morning of August 7 Assistant Secretary of State Dan Fried read an e-mail from the U.S. ambassador to Georgia, John Tefft, and had his "oh sh—" moment, realizing that something was going badly wrong. At Secretary Rice's morning senior staff meeting, he warned that events in Georgia were in danger of spinning out of control, that this crisis seemed different from previous ones, and that the senior echelon of the U.S. government had to pay attention. By that time, however, Georgian forces were already deploying to the edge of the conflict zone and Temuri Yakobashvili, Saakashvili's special envoy, was in Tskhinvali for his last-minute and ultimately unsuccessful mission to defuse the conflict. By late afternoon Washington time, war would already be underway.

Moscow would deploy some 40,000 forces to Georgia between August 7 and 12. Nearly 20,000 Russian forces were deployed in South Ossetia through the Roki Tunnel and another 20,000 were in Abkhazia. The total of the Russian forces was more than three times the size of the Georgian army. It was a force whose size and capability far exceeded anything needed to come to the support of endangered Russian peacekeepers or to pacify a small separatist province the size of Rhode Island. It was a force that had been assembled over a long period of time for a different purpose. It was not only the scope and size of that deployment that points to many months of preparation. Everything, from the modernization of military bases and railroad infrastructure, to the increased deliveries of advanced weapons systems and matériel to both Russian and separatist forces in the months prior to the invasion, as well as the prepositioning of key elements of the Black Sea fleet, suggests a major undertaking planned well in advance.

Starting in late spring, the Georgians claim to have observed at least twenty-six large containers of Russian military equipment being brought into Abkhazia. Those illegal shipments included a large number of BMP/BTR armored vehicles, D–30 type howitzers, SA–11 BUK antiaircraft systems, BM–21 GRAD rocket systems, and ZSU–23–4 Shilka antiaircraft systems. Smaller quantities of the same weapons systems were imported into South Ossetia and pre-positioned in the Java district. By late 2007 new special Russian mountain brigades had been formed in the North Caucasus—the Thirty-third Brigade in Botlikh, Dagestan, which was subsequently deployed in South Ossetia, and the Thirty-fourth Brigade in Zelenchuk, Karachay-Cherkessya, used in Abkhazia. Senior Russian officials such as Nikolai Makarov, the chief of the General Staff, spoke openly after the war about how the Ministry of Defense had to handpick senior commanding officers from units across the country to lead Russian forces in battle in Georgia.[1] Such a process took time and planning.

The land, air, and sea assaults of the Russian armed forces were augmented by attacks in cyberspace. It was the first time in history that an invasion on the ground, in the air, and at sea was coordinated with an orchestrated online cyber offensive, leading some analysts to term it the "fourth front" of Moscow's invasion. While Western governments were careful about publicly linking the Russian government to those attacks, in private they are much more open about what role Moscow played. Georgia had experienced initial, sporadic cyber attacks in late July, including an attack on the presidential Web site on July 19 that lasted less than twenty-four hours. The real wave of attacks commenced the afternoon of August 8, when the Russians began to block, re-route, and seize control of Georgian cyberspace in earnest. Georgia's presidential Web site was taken under external control and started showing a slide show of pictures of Adolf Hitler interspersed with photos of Saakashvili.

Different groups of cyber warriors executed different kinds of attacks on Georgian infrastructure. For example, the attacks on the president's Web site were led by a different group than the attacks executed against the banking sector. In addition to the presidential Web site, some thirty-eight important Georgian Web sites were attacked—including those for the Foreign Ministry, National Bank, Parliament, the Supreme Court, the Central Election Commission, and the U.S. and UK embassies, as well as the local offices of several international organizations and news agencies.

The purpose of these attacks appears to have been multiple. The defacement of the president's Web site was designed to embarrass and humiliate the Georgian government and demonstrate the insecurity of its cyber infrastructure. The attacks against the political and informational Web sites were intended to reduce the capability of the government to get its message out and to communicate to the outside world. The banking sector appears to have been targeted with the goal of economic disruption. Some of Tbilisi's allies, such as Poland and Estonia, stepped in and allowed the Georgian government to use their Web sites as an alternative platform to communicate with the outside world and the public.

This cyber offensive was massive, coordinated, and sophisticated. Yet it was the attacks on the banking and financial sector that were in some ways the most interesting and revealing. They involved hundreds of systems routed through many countries, including Turkey and the United States, in an attempt to cover their origins. They were executed with a different set of actors using a different set of computers than, for example, those attacks executed against the president's Web site. They all began and ended within thirty minutes of one another—commencing at 1715 on August 8 and halting at 1245 on August 12. The latter was approximately the time when Moscow announced its initial ceasefire—demonstrating a degree of discipline, coordination, command, and control.

That is not the only example of Russian fingerprints. Cyber war experts inside and outside Western governments who have studied the attacks note that the Russian military has placed a growing priority on cyber attacks in its doctrine and strategy. One of the key forums used in the attacks—Stop Georgia.ru—appears to have been part of a bulletproof network that relied on shell companies to mask the involvement of Russian intelligence. Analyses conducted based on data provided by security companies and other sources suggest that the attacks were coordinated by individuals deeply involved in and coordinated with the political and military assault on Georgia. If one aligns the timing and scope of the cyber attacks with the unfolding campaign Russia was conducting on the ground, in the air, and by sea, it becomes clear that these cyber attacks were part of a larger campaign's political and military objectives. Attacks on this scale and level of sophistication require the professional planning and resources that only a state sponsor could provide.[2]

Evidence that Russia's attack on Georgia was—to use the words of Secretary of State Rice—"premeditated" is wide and varied. It starts with the detailed military planning and preparations as well as the cyber attacks described above. It includes the fact that Moscow started putting pressure on Israel to curtail the growing involvement of retired Israeli military and security experts in support of Tbilisi's defense modernization and to stop Georgia's procurement of Israeli technology and hardware[3] in the spring of 2008. It extends to the placement, discussed earlier, of nearly fifty Russian journalists in Tskhinvali several days before the attack started. In late July, Georgian counterintelligence received reports that Russian doctors and medics were being recruited to be sent to Tskhinvali and to arrive at the local hospital in early August. None of these pieces of information is definitive. Each of them is like an individual stone in a mosaic. In isolation and by themselves they are curious. But when put together they form a bigger picture and tell a larger story.

The picture that emerges is of a methodically prepared long-term buildup for a confrontation with Georgia. The precise details of Moscow's political and military campaign goals presumably lie buried somewhere in the Kremlin's archives. Clearly, Moscow was not fully ready for war and Saakashvili's move late on August 7 does appear to have been a tactical surprise as both President Medvedev and Prime Minister Putin were initially caught off guard by the outbreak of hostilities. Putin was, of course, in Beijing, and Medvedev managed to convene the Russian National Security Council only at midday on August 8. Russia's massive preparation notwithstanding, Saakashvili's move had created an element of tactical surprise, thus leading to speculation that Moscow's real move may have been planned for several days later. But that tactical surprise must be seen against a broader backdrop of a strategic campaign that had been in the works for many months.

What were Russia's military objectives? At a minimum, the Russian objective was probably to consolidate Abkhaz and South Ossetian independence—most likely as a prelude for their eventual annexation to Russia. After all, Putin and other Russian leaders had told Georgian leaders on more than one occasion and with varying degrees of candor that the price of their trying to go West against Russia's wishes could be the loss of these territories. The bigger question was whether this was the end in itself or a prelude to a more ambitious strategy of regime change. It seems unlikely that Moscow would have engaged in such an extensive military buildup and preparations solely for two separatist provinces that it already more or less controlled. At the same time, Moscow might have hoped that by seizing the territories and putting Tbilisi under pressure, it might precipitate a dynamic that would discredit the government and lead to its fall—regime change through indirect means.

Was it a trap? Moscow was undoubtedly aware of the agonizing discussions in Tbilisi over how to respond to what the Georgian government saw as a policy of creeping annexation. It, too, must have known that Saakashvili did not think he could survive politically if he lost South Ossetia or Abkhazia. Georgian communications were often insecure, and understanding the thinking of Saakashvili's inner circle was a top priority for Russian intelligence. Perhaps Moscow was presenting the Georgian president with an unspoken choice: either you acquiesce to the creeping annexation and run the risk of being toppled domestically—or you choose to fight and be crushed militarily. That was the corner—or trap—into which Moscow had maneuvered Tbilisi. It was the price Moscow wanted to extract from Georgia to punish it for its desire to be an independent country and to pursue the right to choose its own alliances as reflected in the principles of the OSCE Charters of Paris and Istanbul.

Pavel Felgenhauer, the well-connected defense correspondent for the Russian independent newspaper *Novaya Gazeta*, would subsequently write in the Russian press that "it is perfectly obvious that the Russian intervention in Georgia was planned in advance" and suggested that the Kremlin had decided "already in April" to begin the war in August. That plan, he argued, was for "the Ossetians to intentionally provoke the Georgians" and then "any response, harsh or soft [by Tbilisi] would be used as an occasion for the attack."[4] As he put it subsequently, "The war would have happened regardless of what the Georgians did. Whether they responded to the provocations or not, there would have been an invasion of Georgia. The goal was to destroy Georgia's central government, defeat the Georgian army and prevent Georgia from joining NATO."[5]

What was surprising was that the war happened in South Ossetia. The evidence and the buildup over the spring and summer suggested that the confrontation was going to take place in Abkhazia. Abkhazia was far more important strategically. It was Georgia's number one preoccupation, and Tbilisi was struggling to find an effective strategy. It was where Georgian defense planning had focused, where the Georgians had built up their own military capabilities, and where Saakashvili had contemplated a military move. The Russians had focused their own military buildup there since the spring in an attempt to deny the Georgians any military option and to create their own. In June, Georgian intelligence had issued an estimate on a possible military confrontation with Russia in Abkhazia—but predicted it would happen in the fall.[6]

It didn't happen in Abkhazia. One can speculate on the reasons. Perhaps it was the fact that there was a significant buffer zone in Abkhazia. Or there might be truth to the unconfirmed reports that the Abkhaz leadership had some element of autonomy and was reluctant to play the role of provocateur assigned to it. Abkhaz and Georgian forces were not intermingled as were the forces in South Ossetia but were separated by a river and limited in numbers and equipment. It was harder to start a war in Abkhazia resulting from an escalation of local tensions. Somebody had to make the first move. The Georgian temptation to use force had actually dwindled in the spring of 2008 because Moscow's significant reinforcements meant that Tbilisi's window of opportunity to act militarily was closing.

In any case, Abkhazia went quiet in July after several months of being on the brink of a conflict. Two weeks later, things suddenly started percolating in South Ossetia. There the regime of Eduard Koikoty was more malleable. It was also more vulnerable and worried that it might be bargained away one day in some peace deal between Moscow and Tbilisi. It may have seen a military conflict as a cynical way to paradoxically ensure its own survival. In South Ossetia, the intermingling of populations and forces within shooting distance of each other made it easier to stage provocations and spark a crisis that would ultimately produce the war. All South Ossetia had to do was start shooting and killing Georgian civilians and peacekeepers— then see how Tbilisi responded.

A vignette of Russian thinking and war planning is provided by an August 15 dinner in Gori attended by Russian general Vyacheslav Borisov, deputy overall commander of Russian airborne forces and commander of the Pskov Seventy-sixth Airborne Division; his deputy, General Alexandr Kolpachenkov; and senior Georgian officials. After the successful conclusion of the war, Borisov became the commander of Russian military forces during the occupation of Gori and, in the absence of a civilian government, the Russian generals were the de facto governors in the region. Borisov was an old-style hard-drinking Russian general notorious for his coarse language and anti-Western outbursts. The Georgians were keen to maintain good relations with him and his staff as the occupying force. They were heavily dependent on the Russian military's leniency and cooperation in delivering food to the occupied villages, as well as in evacuating wounded servicemen and the elderly.

That evening local Gori officials invited Borisov and Kolpachenkov to dinner. In addition to the two Russian generals, Alexander Lomaia, the Georgian secretary of the National Security Council, was at the table, along with a few other Georgians. The food on the table was simple—a loaf of bread and some cheese, a can of fish with tomatoes, boiled sausages, a couple of bottles of lemonade, and—of course—a bottle of vodka. During dinner Lomaia asked the two Russian generals why they were in Georgia and what their orders had been. Kolpachenkov did not seem surprised by the question. It was almost as if he had been waiting for it to be asked.

He raised his right palm and pointed his left index finger. Look, he said, this is Georgia, a country stretched from west to east. This country, he continued, is "easily accessible." What you do, he said, is you cut the country into pieces by invading through Abkhazia in the west and through South Ossetia in the east, then you bomb the major air- and seaports to cut the army off from any supplies, and then you sit back and watch and wait until the suffering population brings the government down. Lomaia responded that the general was being remarkably candid. Kolpachenkov replied—with a slight smile—that he was just a simple soldier.[7]

Saakashvili's order was issued at 2335 on August 7. The Georgian armed forces were being asked to fight a battle for which they were neither prepared nor trained to fight. Contingency planning in the Ministry of Defense had been largely focused on Abkhazia, where Tbilisi had thought the likelihood of a conflict higher, so there had been no active contingency planning for South Ossetia since Okruashvili resigned in 2006. The Defense Ministry had assumed that the main front would be Abkhazia. They had assumed that the South Ossetians and the Russians might try to open a second front in South Ossetia. But the Georgian goal in such a scenario was simply to try to limit any spillover from South Ossetia and focus on Abkhazia. When Georgian defense planners received the order that afternoon of August 7 to prepare for possible action in South Ossetia, they looked at the skeleton plans they had on the shelf and discarded them. They were out of date and useless. They drafted a new plan from scratch on the spot.[8]

Another very real constraint was that the Georgian armed forces had only enough men to fight effectively on a single front. Tbilisi had five brigades. The elite First Infantry Brigade had been deployed to Iraq, making Georgia one of the largest non-American contributors there, in an attempt to gain favor in Washington and strengthen the Georgian case for NATO. Georgia's Second Infantry Brigade had served in Iraq and had returned to its base in Senaki, in western Georgia, close to the border with Abkhazia. The Third and Fourth Brigades were in Kutaisi undergoing pre-deployment training for Iraq. A fifth brigade was essentially a training brigade. Georgia could deploy two brigades to fight in South Ossetia and pull a third brigade over from Senaki—but only at the price of leaving the Abkhaz front uncovered. Making matters worse, a few weeks prior to the outbreak of war, the Georgian army had—after months of being on high alert—issued orders lowering their readiness to the lowest possible levels, eventually releasing up to 50 percent of their soldiers. A significant portion of Georgia's small tank force had also been sent back to Tbilisi for refurbishment and upgrading and was unavailable when the battle broke out.

But the biggest constraint was that the Georgian army was simply not trained or equipped to fight an adversary like the Russian army. Perhaps the greatest irony was that Georgia's own NATO aspirations may have also indirectly contributed to that lack of preparedness. While Georgians clearly saw Russia as their main threat, they also wanted to join NATO. To qualify for the Alliance, however, they had to conform to Alliance doctrine and standards, which de-emphasized territorial defense and instead asked candidate countries to focus their preparations on peacekeeping and other so-called new missions. Tbilisi decided to write its threat assessment to conform to NATO standards and to de-emphasize the chance of a conflict with Russia. Training and procurement were focused on the same goals.

Nowhere was this more true than when it came to the United States, which, given its strong political support for Georgia, was extra careful about its defense training programs. In order to avoid provoking Moscow, American training was specifically tailored not to focus on territorial defense.[9] Washington's Georgia Train and Equip Program (GTEP) was initially a response to Moscow's demands for Georgia to allow Russian troops into the Pankisi Gorge in 1999 to pursue Chechen terrorists. Subsequent training focused on specific counter-terror capabilities and helping Georgian forces prepare to deploy to Iraq. The United States and other NATO allies also refused to sell Georgia modern weapons systems that Moscow might have found provocative. For example, Tbilisi wanted to acquire shoulder-held Stinger missiles, which are in many ways an ideal defensive weapon and would have been important weapons in any effort to resist a Russian helicopter and airborne assault. After Georgia requested Stingers in the fall of 2007, the United States sent out a Defense Department team to determine whether Tbilisi was capable of safeguarding such weapons and preventing them from being stolen or falling into the hands of terrorists. That team reported back that Georgia was fully capable of doing so. But the sale of such a system, which arguably could have elevated Georgia's defense capability, was eventually blocked. The United States and Russia had an agreement to limit the sales of such systems, and Washington would not make an exception.

When Georgian forces moved out very early on August 8 after an artillery barrage, they did so undermanned, with a plan that had been drawn up hastily in the previous twenty-four hours and had never been exercised.

Their forces had not yet been trained to operate together in combined arms operations at the brigade level, and they faced an adversary—the Russian army—that they were neither equipped nor trained to fight against. The Russian army was the adversary they had always feared the most but, in an effort to maximize their chances for getting closer to and eventually into NATO, it was also the adversary on which they had consciously chosen not to focus their defense preparations. It was not a good way to start a war.

The South Ossetian city of Tskhinvali is like a bowl, surrounded by heights to the west and east. The Georgian plan envisioned a three-pronged advance, through the center of the city and around the heights on both sides. The main Georgian effort in the center focused on passing in and eventually through Tskhinvali to the north of the city, where many of the most vulnerable ethnic Georgian villages were located. The command of that task force was given at the last minute to General Mamuka Kurashvili, who had just left his position as the commander of Georgia's peacekeeping forces in the Joint Peacekeeping Command and was familiar with the city and its surroundings. His task force consisted of a hodgepodge of different units that had been hastily assembled and had never worked together before. They had a large contingent of police special forces because the Georgians envisioned selective targets and pinpoint operations.

Kurashvili had almost no staff and no command post, and his radios were not interoperable with those of the two infantry brigades deploying on the left and right flanks and in the surrounding heights. The western zone was assigned to the Fourth Brigade, which was given the mission of securing the ethnically Georgian village of Avnevi and the high ground west of Tskhinvali near the village of Khetagurovo, from which South Ossetian artillery had been firing at Georgian peacekeepers and villages. The Third Brigade was given the same responsibility of protecting Georgian-controlled villages in the eastern zone, securing the high ground, and suppressing artillery fire against the Georgian villages and peacekeepers there.

In their attempt to secure Tskhinvali and move through the city to the Georgian villages to the north, the Georgian task force became bogged down in initial fights with local South Ossetian, Russian, and North Caucasian units, who were either embedded or had already arrived in the city. While Tskhinvali was largely evacuated of civilians, there were more South Ossetian and Russian forces in the city than the Georgians had expected. These Russian forces in all likelihood included some of the units whose movements out of Java the previous day had been spotted by Georgian reconnaissance and had precipitated Saakashvili's decision to fight. The large number of enemy forces meant that the Georgians had to pull additional units into the city from their other two brigades, including those tasked to block the main and bypass roads into the city against Russian incursions from the north.

The Fourth Brigade deployed to the northwest of the city would end up doing the lion's share of the initial fighting against Russian forces in Tskhinvali that first day and suffered the most serious losses. One of its battalions was ordered to hold the critical Dzara bypass road leading out of Tskhinvali to the north to prevent Russian forces from entering the city. When the main task force under Kurashvili ran into trouble in Tskhinvali, several units of the Fourth Brigade were pulled off for reinforcement. One of those units was the Forty-first Battalion. As it moved back into Tskhinvali from the north, it encountered a group of armored infantry carriers of the Russian peacekeeping forces, conspicuous by the large blue circle painted on its side with the yellow Cyrillic letters *MC*. Georgian forces had orders not to fire upon Russian peacekeepers unless they were fired on first. The Georgian battalion commander of the Forty-first Battalion, Major Shalva Dolidze, gave the order not to fire and to let the Russian peacekeeping forces pass. It was the last order he gave. The Russians approached the Georgian forces and suddenly opened fire, killing Dolidze and a number of his staff officers.

The Georgian forces suffered from many problems. One of the most serious was that they lost effective command and control early in the fight. Assessments conducted after the battle concluded that both communications and intelligence were ineffective. Radios did not function properly, and commanders often had to stay in touch by mobile phone or even in person. They also suffered from constant political interference in the military chain of command. The Georgian forces found it was also a mistake not to have taken the time to clear individual buildings in Tskhinvali as Georgian forces had moved through the city to take up positions farther north. Enemy forces were hidden and embedded there and attacked Georgian reinforcements moving through the city from behind. Several times, Georgian units fought their way through to the northern edge of the city only to find themselves unable to communicate with their command post or to receive reinforcements and were forced to fight their way back south.

Georgian forces had initially enjoyed modest success. Tbilisi had moved some of its artillery units forward to the Georgian enclave of Tamarasheni, north of Tskhinvali, to bring them within range of the Roki Tunnel. Czech-made Dana self-propelled artillery and Israeli-built GRADLAR artillery using cluster munitions wreaked havoc on a Russian column heading south from the Roki Tunnel, and Georgian artillery inflicted damage on Russian forces moving from Java to Tskhinvali. The Russians were also slowed by the breakdown of their own equipment on the single road coming down from the north. By the morning of August 8, Georgian forces controlled large parts of Tskhinvali as well as the surrounding heights.

However, heavy fighting in the course of the day forced the Georgians to pull back into the city the forces that had been supposed to defend the northern approaches. Russian artillery and air attacks started to take their toll as Russian and South Ossetian forces counterattacked. They reached the outskirts of the city, where they were stopped again by Georgian artillery. The battle seesawed back and forth and as dusk approached, fighting ceased and both sides regrouped. The biggest problem was the sheer numbers of Russian forces coming down from the north; the incessant air attacks by Russian aircraft and helicopters also took their toll.

Meanwhile, Washington was scrambling to find out exactly what was happening. The United States had pulled most of its intelligence assets monitoring the Caucasus out of the theater to focus on the fighting in Iraq and Afghanistan. As a result, the eyes and ears of the American intelligence community were initially unable to provide a comprehensive picture or confirm specific details on exactly what was happening on the ground. In the absence of clear information, competing narratives or explanations circulated among key policymakers over what and who was to blame and just how far the Russians might go. Washington also had some one hundred military advisors on the ground when the war broke out, largely preparing Georgian troops for their mission in Iraq, whose safety needed to be taken care of. Washington was furious that the Georgians had moved in spite of dozens of warnings over many months not to do so. Other officials wondered whether they had underestimated the Russian threat and whether the Georgian warnings throughout the previous months might have been accurate after all.

Many senior American officials hoped at this point that the conflict could still be limited to a Russian move to push the Georgians out of South Ossetia. That would soon change. President Bush was in Beijing at the opening of the Olympic Games. (We will turn to his initial encounters with Vladimir Putin shortly.) But one thing was clear. The Bush Administration had made the building of a Europe that was whole and free from the Baltic to the Black Sea a central part of its legacy. Regardless of what mistakes Tbilisi had made, Moscow had violated that basic concept and broken some of the cardinal principles upon which European security was supposed to be based. Nevertheless, Washington feared that Moscow was now going to take full advantage of Saakashvili's mistake and hit him hard. As one senior U.S. official put it, "We knew Russia had been salivating for this moment. Our policy had to be to break it, to stop it and to contain it."

Absent a strong American role and response, Georgia could be crushed within a matter of days. Washington quickly settled on a handful of central goals. The first one was to simply stop the fighting as soon as possible and limit Moscow's tactical military gains on the ground. The second was to prevent regime change through force of Russian arms and the toppling of the democratically elected Georgian government of Mikheil Saakashvili. The third was to make it clear to Moscow that it would pay a price for its action and hopefully compel it to conclude that this attack had not been worth it. Washington wanted to deter Moscow from any temptation to embark on similar adventures in the future—be they elsewhere in the Southern Caucasus, against Ukraine, or even against NATO members, such as the Baltic states. Whatever gains Moscow might make on the ground militarily, Washington wanted to impose a strategic diplomatic and economic price that would prevent Russia from considering moves in the future against any of its other neighbors.

At the same time, Washington did not want to act unilaterally or allow this confrontation to become a U.S.-Russian fight that could spark a new cold war or even escalate into a military confrontation. In the eyes of President Bush, this was not a U.S.-Russian conflict, and it would be a mistake to let it become one. The administration saw the risk that an American lead could quickly turn this into a U.S.-Russian confrontation—and encourage some European allies to run rapidly for the exits. The Bush Administration knew it was still unpopular in Europe and understood that its ability to unify the allies was limited. It was yet another example of how U.S. policy was constrained by a deterioration in U.S.-European relations and in the American public image after the Iraq war.

Bush also feared that the media would make the danger of a U.S.-Russian confrontation, and not Russian behavior toward Georgia, the story. This would not only distract from the real issues but run the risk of becoming a self-fulfilling prophecy. Bush worried that Putin would exploit a strong American response to further beat the drums of anti-Americanism on the continent as well as strike all the anti-American chords in Russian society. In short, the administration wanted a tough response but it wanted Europe to take the lead. It wanted to be involved but behind the scenes to limit the danger of the situation becoming a U.S.-Russian clash.

The American decision to step back and not try to lead was a big decision that had consequences for Georgia and for how the war would be stopped. Washington understood that this meant it would have less influence, but it was prepared to run that risk. It was not the stereotypical response critics might have expected. Whether it was the right decision is a question historians will debate. As former national security advisor Steve Hadley put it, "The message we wanted to send to the Russians was: This is not the U.S. acting with its friends to penalize you. This is the response of the international system of the twenty-first century saying to you that the rules of the nineteenth century no longer apply." Washington wanted Moscow to conclude that the world was rallying against Moscow and the actions of the Russian army, thus underscoring how out of step Russia was with twenty-first-century Europe.[10]

During the initial forty-eight hours Washington hoped that the Russo-Georgian war could be limited and contained. While Russian president Medvedev was brutal in his depictions of Saakashvili in his phone conversations with President Bush, official Russian demands were still limited, and Washington initially thought they could be met in an interim ceasefire. Senior Russian officials assured Washington at this point that Moscow was not seeking regime change but a restoration of the status quo. The administration wanted to believe that assurance, but it was clear that Russia was amass-

ing an armada of military force far in excess of what was needed for South
Ossetia. Washington was looking for a way to nip the conflict in the bud, to
de-escalate the conflict before it broadened or before Russian military success
whetted Moscow's appetite and tempted it to escalate and topple Saakashvili.

Rice and her European counterparts spent much of August 8 and 9 talking to both the Georgian and Russian sides, seeking to broker a stop to the
fighting and defuse the crisis. Washington proposed a plan based on an immediate ceasefire, the withdrawal of Russia and Georgian forces to the August 6 status quo, and a new international peacekeeping force to be deployed
in South Ossetia along with new elections there. Saakashvili agreed in principle. Rice was on the phone with Russian foreign minister Lavrov working
through the idea. Lavrov initially seemed open to the plan, telling Rice that
if the Georgians stopped fighting, Moscow would find a way to respond.
But he would not commit. And the military reality on the ground was
quickly turning against the Georgians and to Moscow's advantage.

Prime Minister Putin had arrived in the North Caucasus town of
Vladikavkaz and taken personal command of the operation. He is reported
to have been appalled by the initial inability of Russian forces to take
Tskhinvali, the breakdown of Russian tanks and other equipment on their
way through the Roki Tunnel, as well as the ambush and wounding on
the morning of August 9 of the commander of the Fifty-eighth Army, General Anatoly Khrulyev. Georgian forces ambushed Khrulyev's column,
complete with journalists, as it approached Tskhinvali, seriously wounding the commander, destroying a number of vehicles in the column, and
killing a number of officers and soldiers around him. The image of the
Russian Fifty-eighth Army commander surrounded by casualties, pounding the soil with his fists, and yelling that his entire battalion had been destroyed was captured by at least one Russian journalist traveling with the
column. It was hardly the image the Kremlin wanted.

Georgian officials insist that Putin's arrival led to an escalation of the
Russian military campaign, including significant reinforcements to bolster
the Russian effort. They claim the Russian prime minister gave the lead in
the operation to the Pskov Seventy-sixth Airborne Division as opposed to
the Fifty-eighth Army, ordered the pullout of paramilitary forces that did
an excellent job of terrorizing local civilians but were not delivering the

military victory he wanted, and ordered the mobilization of some of the Russian army's remaining top units. He also ordered an escalation of Moscow's air campaign against Georgia. Moscow flew over 400 bombing sorties against 36 targets across the entire country during the five-day war and is reported to have flown 120 sorties on August 9 alone. Some of the targets were more than 300 kilometers away from Tskhinvali, underscoring the breadth of Moscow's campaign plan.

Some Russian analysts have disagreed and instead suggest that all that was happening was that the full force of Moscow's invasion plan was becoming visible through the fog of war. Tbilisi was feeling the full weight of the mass of the invasion force that was finally making its way through the Roki Tunnel and into South Ossetia.[11] In any case, the flow of Russian reinforcements through the Roki Tunnel was now giving Moscow vast numerical superiority and was being felt on the battlefield. With its Second, Third, and Fourth Brigades already committed, the Georgians had effectively run out of forces to commit to the battle. Georgia's First Brigade was trying to return from Iraq to defend their country. The final brigade in the Georgian army—the Fifth—was a training brigade and was not ready for combat action.

Making matters worse, on August 10 Tbilisi was also receiving intelligence that Moscow was about to open a second front in Abkhazia, where no fighting had yet taken place but where an equally large invasion force was being assembled. The Georgians had been receiving regular updates on the activities of the Black Sea fleet task force, which, along with the Fifty-eighth Army, had taken part in the Kavkaz 2008 exercises that so closely resembled training for the invasion. Russian marines were soon landing at the Abkhaz port of Ochamchira. Troops from the Volgograd Twentieth Motorized Rifle Division were arriving via the newly modernized railroad, and troops from the Seventh Airborne Division were landing in Sukhumi. Russia would eventually amass some 20,000 troops in Abkhazia. On August 10 a Russian armored column crossed the Inguri River and entered western Georgia from Abkhazia. The Georgians withdrew ahead of them and offered no resistance. The Russians occupied Zugdidi, the port of Poti, and the key Georgian military base at Senaki.

The Georgian army was simply too small to fight a two-front war. The military imbalance between the two sides was growing by the hour as Russian reinforcements poured in through the Roki Tunnel and arrived by air, land, and sea in Abkhazia. Georgia's small army was being ground down. Moscow's escalation of the air war was overwhelming Georgia's limited air defenses, which, bolstered by the recent purchases of the Israeli-made Rafael Spyder and Ukrainian SA–11 air defense systems, had initially performed well. Tbilisi claims to have downed seventeen Russian aircraft—fourteen planes, one Blackjack Tupolev 22M3 strategic bomber, and two helicopters—during the course of the war. But the air defenses, too, were now being overwhelmed. Georgian Defense Ministry officials recall how at one point on the morning of August 9 they faced some twenty-eight Russian aircraft attacking Georgian targets. Moscow was now also attacking with SS–21 Tochka and SS–26 Iskander missiles. On the evening of August 9, the Georgian Defense Ministry received a phone call from the Pentagon warning them that six Russian strategic bombers had taken off from Moscow and were headed in their direction. The Pentagon provided coordinates; the estimated time of arrival was in twenty-two minutes. When the Georgians checked the coordinates, they realized the bombers were targeting Tbilisi.

Over the weekend Fried also received an on-the-ground assessment from Ambassador Tefft in Tbilisi. Tefft had concluded early Saturday that the Russian goal was not to retake South Ossetia or to avenge the loss of Russian peacekeepers. When Moscow started bombing Georgian ports and other targets across the country, Tefft knew it was about destroying the regime of Mikheil Saakashvili. Reports of large numbers of Russian reinforcements continuing to pour in through the Roki Tunnel, as well as major Russian reinforcements arriving in Abkhazia, only strengthened that view. When he sat down with his staff on Saturday morning to sift through the information the embassy was receiving, it was clear that this was all-out war. Moscow wanted to annihilate Georgia. Tefft cabled back to Washington that everything the United States had at stake in Georgia could go up in flames if the West did not act—and fast.

At dawn on August 10, Georgian armed forces received orders to fall back and establish positions south of Tskhinvali. There they continued to be subjected to relentless attacks by Russian helicopters and aircraft—as well as SS–21 Tochka and SS–26 Iskander ballistic missiles. It was also early on August 10 that Washington concluded that Russian goals were not limited to taking back South Ossetia. It was a posture to destroy Georgia—which is exactly what it was starting to do by taking down infrastructure across the entire country. Early that morning, Deputy Assistant Secretary of State Bryza told Secretary Rice that the Russian military offensive threatened to overwhelm the Georgians. Washington needed to do something to stop the fighting before it was too late, the secretary responded. She decided to place a call to Russian foreign minister Lavrov. That conversation was a turning point in Washington's assessment.

In that call, the Russian foreign minister not only demanded that Georgian forces return to their barracks and that Tbilisi issue a non-use-of-force pledge. He now insisted—for the first time—that there was an additional Russian condition for ending the war, namely that Mikheil Saakashvili had to go. Moscow's goal of regime was change was now out in the open. According to former secretary Rice, she immediately told Lavrov that such a demand was completely unacceptable, as President Saakashvili was a democratically elected leader. Lavrov protested that this was a confidential conversation, but Rice retorted, "The Secretary of State of the United States and the Foreign Minister of Russia do not have a confidential conversation about the overthrow of a democratically elected government. I am about to get on the phone and tell everyone I can possibly find that Russia's war aim is the overthrow of the Georgian government."[12] Lavrov was furious. Rice proceeded to call her key European counterparts to brief them on the Lavrov conversation. Later that same day, the United States convened the UN Security Council, where Ambassador Zalmay Khalilzad publicly announced—over the protest of the Russian ambassador—that the Russian side was now calling for regime change.[13]

Had the United States misread or been taken in by Moscow's initial assurances that its aims were limited—or had Moscow's own war aims shifted? The EU's Special Representative Peter Semneby, on the ground in Tbilisi, e-mailed back to Brussels reporting that Georgian forces would probably not be able to hold out for more than another twenty-four hours—and that Russia might be able to take Tbilisi within another twenty-four hours if it so chose. It was now clear to everyone that Russia's aim went well beyond restoring the status quo in South Ossetia. Russian forces had breached the borders of the conflict zones and were threatening Georgia proper. They were bombing targets hundreds of kilometers away from the original fighting. This was about regime change. Back in Brussels both NATO and the European Union were scrambling to issue statements to stop the fighting as Western capitals realized they had underestimated the seriousness of the situation.

The next morning—August 11—Georgian forces were ordered to withdraw, initially to Gori but then eventually to Tbilisi to defend the capital if need be. Saakashvili now faced the second big decision of the war, after his initial decision to fight the Russians late on August 7. Tbilisi had unilaterally announced its ceasefire and had withdrawn its forces from South Ossetia. But Russian armor and ground forces were still on the move in South Ossetia and Abkhazia with massive reinforcements being pulled in from across the Northern Caucasus and other parts of Russia. The Russian air force continued to bomb across the country. Moscow had by now also occupied western Georgia and was poised to enter the main Georgian city of Zugdidi—invading Georgia proper. They had essentially cut the country in half and were poised to go farther. The Georgian defense line was broken. The army was withdrawing to Tbilisi and preparing to make a last-ditch stand in case the Russians stormed the capital city.

The question now was what Tbilisi would do next. With Russian tanks less than two hours away from the capital, the Georgian leadership had to decide whether to fight to the end and try to defend Tbilisi as the final symbol of Georgian statehood, to prepare for a partisan war à la Chechnya or Afghanistan, or to sue for peace, save the remnants of the army, and hope the West would pressure Moscow to stop before it was too late. Central Georgia is mainly an open plain with scattered hills—excellent terrain for tanks. The Georgians had no chance of stopping the Russian army with armor and airpower in such terrain. Just northwest of Tbilisi, the road to Gori passes through a steep gorge at the ancient Georgian capital of Mtskheta—perhaps the only natural defense position where a determined foe could stop an advancing force. By August 12 this is where the Georgian command had gathered much of its remaining forces for a possible last stand.

It was a decisive moment in which the future of Georgia was on the line. But the country was not prepared for this kind of fight. There was no plan for the defense of Tbilisi or Mtskheta nor were there any prepared defensive positions for stopping Russian tanks or bunkers in which to hide from Russian air attacks. Back in Tbilisi there was also discussion about trying to fight a guerilla war against the Russian army, and the Interior Ministry had taken some initial steps to prepare for such an event. But Saakashvili knew that even if they could inflict a lot of damage on the Russian army, it would mean the destruction of his country and the end of his vision of Georgia's future. He didn't want Georgia to become another Chechnya. He decided to try to sue for peace, to save the Georgian army, and to turn to the international community to put pressure on Moscow to stop the Russian offensive.

Saakashvili addressed the nation in the evening of August 11 from a session of the National Security Council. At the time, he was still worried that the Russians were planning to take Tbilisi. He warned his citizens that the situation was extremely grave, that Moscow was attempting to occupy and destroy Georgia—to put an end to the existence of the Georgian state.[14] The chairman of parliament, David Bakradze, also issued a statement, hinting at the possibility of popular resistance if the Russians continued their push into western Georgia. It was another last-ditch effort to signal to the Russians that Georgia wanted to stop the hostilities and sue for peace, but that if Moscow started ethnic cleansing in Georgia proper, Tbilisi would have no choice but to fight back. In Tbilisi a mild panic had begun as people lined up at ATM machines and gas stations in preparation for leaving the city.

Bryza arrived in Tbilisi later that same day. After a brief press conference at the airport, his security detail told him he had to move because there were rumors that Russian tanks were on their way to the Georgian capital. He met up with Carl Bildt, who had come under the rubric of Sweden's role as rotating chairman of the Council of Europe. Together with Tefft and Semneby, they spent much of the rest of the evening in the president's chancellery, talking to senior Georgian officials and being briefed on breaking events. The Georgian government was in disarray. Information on exactly what was happening and where the Russians were was spotty. One interesting but informal intelligence indicator was the black market behavior of the invading Russian soldiers and their willingness (or lack thereof) to sell surplus gasoline to earn some extra cash. On that Monday they were largely unwilling to do so, explaining to their potential customers that they were waiting to find out if they would be ordered to move on Tbilisi. It was not a good sign.

The Georgian government seemed almost paralyzed and on the edge of disintegration. As they sat camped outside the president's office in the chancellery, trying to be helpful, Bildt, Tefft, Semneby, and Bryza noticed that the pictures had been taken off the walls in the corridors outside the president's office as if in preparation for moving—to where, no one knew. Georgian officials were increasingly distraught, and some were nearly in shock as reports came in of ethnic cleansing and atrocities being committed against Georgian citizens by South Ossetian and other irregular troops with the Russian army in the background and at times playing a facilitating role. At one point, cell phones and BlackBerrys stopped working. Were the circuits simply overloaded or was this the beginning of Russian electronic countermeasures in preparation for an assault? It occurred to Bildt, Bryza, and Tefft that if the Russians did move on Tbilisi, the building they were sitting in was undoubtedly high on Moscow's target list and their lives could be at risk, too.

David Bakradze came rushing into the chancellery to see Saakashvili and ran into Bryza sitting in his waiting room. Bakradze was known as one of the calmer personalities in the Georgian leadership, but he was clearly emotional and angry—and disappointed in the Western response in general and in the United States in particular. He turned to Bryza and said, "We were warning you that this would happen! Where were you guys? Why didn't you do more to help us to prevent this? What are you going to do now?" Bryza pointed out that Georgia was not part of NATO, that Washington had no obligation to defend it and that Washington and he personally had repeatedly warned Tbilisi not to get into a fight with Russia and had told the Georgian leadership clearly that if it did so, Washington would not come to its defense. His presence in Tbilisi was evidence that Washington was trying to help Georgia diplomatically, he said. Humanitarian help was arriving and he was heading out to the airport shortly to welcome the first American C–17 delivering that assistance. Moscow had issued another warning that the U.S. planes on the tarmac should leave lest they be bombed, but such flights were still coming and the C–17 was there.

Bakradze then shouted, "What? Don't you understand that if you remove this plane it will be seen by the Russians as a green light to attack us? What do we need your humanitarian assistance for if Russian tanks may be in Tbilisi tonight?" He went on to say, "We have decided to stay and fight to defend the city! Before I came here, I said good-bye to my wife and family. I may never see them alive again—and you are talking about humanitarian assistance?" Bryza was taken aback. At President Saakashvili's request, he had traveled to the focal point of a potential Russian attack in order to show American solidarity and political backing. The fact that his life might also be at risk had not escaped him. But there was a huge gap between what the Georgians wanted from Washington and what the United States was doing— and he felt it. The Western diplomats returned to the Tbilisi Marriott where they found a number of other diplomats and leading Georgians had gathered to exchange gossip—but also in the hope that a Western hotel might be somewhat safer if the Russian army did indeed try to take Tbilisi.

With the Georgian government in danger of crumbling and Russian troops only hours away from Tbilisi, the debate in Washington over what to do to save Georgia was also reaching a climax. Bush was talking to Saakashvili regularly, trying to buck him up. The Americans had flown Georgian forces back from Iraq to Tbilisi starting on August 10. But the Georgian leader was increasingly desperate and in several phone calls pleaded for more tangible U.S. military assistance, such as Stingers or some kind of symbolic, deterrent U.S. presence, to save his country. The sheer scale of the Russian attack did lead several senior White House staffers to push for at least some consideration of limited military options to stem the Russian advance. The menu of options under discussion foresaw the possibility of bombardment and sealing of the Roki Tunnel as well as other surgical strikes to reduce Russian military pressure on the Georgian government.

Such discussions took place in conjunction with a broader debate over whether Moscow's move in Georgia was just the first part of a broader offensive that could eventually envelop Crimea in Ukraine and perhaps even the Baltic states. If it was, where and how should the United States take a strong stand and draw its own line? National Security Advisor Hadley, however, thought Russia was focused only on Georgia. He was a strong supporter of Georgia but belonged to the administration's skeptics on Saakashvili and suspected that the war's origin lay more in the specifics of a bad Russo-Georgian relationship than in a broader geopolitical offensive by Moscow. But no one knew for sure. And Hadley knew that others, including Vice President Cheney, had a different and harder-edged view of Moscow's goals. Both Hadley's and Cheney's staffs had also raised the question of considering limited military options. Hadley had pushed them to think hard about the consequences of any proposed military steps and where they could lead. He was convinced they would lead quickly to a U.S.-Russian military confrontation.

But he concluded that it was necessary for Bush to know what his closest advisors, Cheney in particular, thought and for the president to have an open discussion with his key cabinet members for the record on whether the United States should consider using its military power to help the Georgians. At a meeting of the Principals Committee on Monday, August 11, Hadley therefore put the military option on the table to see whether there was any support for such steps to help the Georgians repel the Russians. There was not. The president recognized that if the United States started down the path of anything military, they had to be prepared for an escalation and thus, in the end, for fighting Russia. There was a clear sense around the table that almost any military steps could lead to a confrontation with Moscow, the outcome of which no one could predict, and which was not in the U.S. interest. Bush did decide that the U.S. military should take over the role of providing humanitarian assistance, an indirect way of showing American military power and thus have a deterrent affect, but he insisted that they do so in a transparent way to avoid any chance of escalation.

The United States had taken a considered look at the military option—and decided against it. Instead, the Principals asked the White House to start exploring the option of evacuating Saakashvili and his leadership team if the situation continued to deteriorate. Speaking in the Rose Garden later that same day, President Bush delivered a stern statement in which he said he was deeply disturbed by reports that Russia was threatening Tbilisi. "It now appears," the president said, "that an effort may be underway to depose Georgia's duly elected government." Such an action, he continued, was "unacceptable," and he urged Moscow to reverse course. "These actions," he concluded, had "substantially damaged" Russia's standing in the world, and if they were not halted, they would jeopardize Moscow's future relations with the United States and Europe.[15] But the United States was relying on diplomacy and the bully pulpit to stop Moscow.

The war was essentially over. The Georgian army had been defeated and the nation effectively cut in half by the Russian army. The Georgian government was in danger of crumbling, and the road to Tbilisi was open. The question was how this drama would end and whether the Georgian government would still be standing. In Washington as well as in European capitals, diplomats were scrambling to send messages to Moscow to stop its offensive. When they headed back to the U.S. embassy later that night, Tefft and Bryza had a hard time getting through traffic because people were lining up at gas stations and seeking to leave the city. They passed truckloads of Georgian soldiers streaming back into the city. It looked like a defeated army, they thought to themselves.

Tefft, who had been in Jerusalem as a young diplomat during the 1973 Yom Kippur War, debated whether he should evacuate the remaining American diplomatic personnel. The embassy was located on a major route north of the city that was likely to be an attack route if the Russians did try to take Tbilisi. On the other hand, if the Americans were evacuated, it was likely to trigger a mass exodus of the diplomatic community and would be seen as the Georgians' closest ally cutting and running. In the middle of that night, Tefft received a phone call from Georgia's deputy foreign minister, Giga Bokeria, saying that the expected Russian assault was apparently not coming after all.

CHAPTER 7

CEASEFIRE

President Saakashvili had ordered his army into action on the evening of August 7 to defend Georgian villages, to preempt what he feared was a larger Russian move, and to hopefully buy some time—time to evacuate Georgians at risk in South Ossetia and time for the world to respond. But he had set into motion a broader war that Georgia could not win and a set of dynamics that he would end up being almost powerless to control. There is an old saying among generals that starting a war is the easy part of the battle. Ending one is far more difficult. From the outset, Tbilisi placed its hopes on the diplomatic and political intervention of its allies and friends in the West to end the war. Georgia could not end this war on its own. Its fate was tied to the willingness and ability of the West to rescue it.

President Bush had been in Beijing for the Olympics when the war broke out. He was getting ready to enter the Great Hall for the opening reception when the first intelligence reports of Russian missiles hitting Georgia reached aides traveling with him. They scrambled to find out what was happening as the president entered the reception. Bush spoke to Prime Minister Putin there, but only briefly. It was still unclear what was happening, as U.S. intelligence was spotty. Bush and Putin spoke a second time the next day. While there is no official record of the conversation, it was a tough one, and Bush came away with no illusions about Putin's determination to punish Saakashvili. He returned to Washington from the Beijing Olympics on August 13 and immediately convened a meeting to discuss the situation and issue a White House statement on the war from the Rose Garden.

By the time he returned to Washington, however, Bush had made a decision that the United States should not take the lead in seeking to mobilize a Western effort to help Georgia and bring this war to an end. The president was determined not to run the risk that the Russo-Georgian war would escalate into a U.S.-Russian confrontation and a new cold war. That was his clear imperative to his national security team throughout the crisis. He wanted the international community, and above all, the European Union, to take the lead in stopping it. He decided the United States would play an active role—but a supporting one, from behind the scenes.

It was a big moment and a turning point in the way the diplomacy of the Russo-Georgia war would play itself out. A long-standing assumption of U.S. policy had been that Europe was not yet strong or coherent enough to stand up to Moscow on its own. While the Cold War had ended and Moscow was no longer considered an adversary, Washington had still felt it necessary in the 1990s to take the lead when it came to managing Moscow on big and controversial strategic issues. Washington also knew that Europe was far less supportive of Georgia. But Bush was now setting aside that assumption and those concerns. He turned over the lead in ending this war to the old continent and to France, which held the rotating presidency of the European Union that summer.

Senior Bush Administration officials insist that this was an enlightened move on their part, that a major American role would only have allowed Moscow to escalate this into a U.S.-Russian showdown and thus make it too easy for European allies to stay on the sidelines and duck their responsibility. They wanted to demonstrate to Russia that the international community and not just the United States was against them. France's warming relationship with the United States under Nicolas Sarkozy made Washington comfortable with Paris taking on this role—something senior Bush officials admitted would have been inconceivable had Jacques Chirac still been in the Élysée.

Administration critics as well as most European governments had a different explanation. A lame-duck American president in his final months in office was simply too weak; relations with the allies had never been fully repaired after the acrimony over the Iraq war; Washington also no longer enjoyed the kind of leverage with Russia that could have allowed it to either lead the West or face down Moscow. While Bush's own relationship with Putin was cordial, U.S.-Russian relations had become increasingly hollow. Nor did Bush's national security team necessarily have the kind of relationships with their Russian counterparts that would have given them leverage and enabled them to effectively deal with Moscow. Rice's relationship with Foreign Minister Lavrov, for example, was contentious and essentially broken. A decade earlier, when the West and Russia had nearly come to blows over Kosovo, senior U.S. officials were not only in regular contact with their Russian counterparts by phone, but also went to Moscow to deal with them face-to-face to keep things from spinning out of control. A decade later, Washington did not have the same relationships or influence—and American officials knew it.

Whatever Washington's motives were, the consequences of Bush's decision were far-reaching. It meant that Georgia's strongest supporter and ally would not be out front in trying to mobilize a common Western response or negotiating with Moscow. It meant that NATO would not assume a major role in the crisis. It meant that any kind of military response was taken off the table, as the United States was the only country that had the military capability of deterring Moscow from further moves. It meant Tbilisi would have to rely on a European Union openly divided in its views on and support for Georgia's aspirations to go West. Given those divisions, was the European Union was capable of standing up to Moscow, let alone pushing it to reverse what it had already gained militarily on the ground?

That the United States would not be at the fore of efforts to influence Moscow to cease its attack also meant Georgia had to rely on France, which held the rotating chair of the Presidency of the European Union that summer. The good news was that France was a powerful country in the EU and, if it focused its efforts, could lead and get things done. It was also led by Nikolas Sarkozy. The French president had a love for the limelight and a yearning to put France, the European Union, and above all himself on the world stage. The less good news was that France was not focused on the Georgian issue. The wider Black Sea region was hardly among France's priorities when it took over the EU presidency earlier in the summer. In June, one senior French Foreign Ministry official privately described where Georgia and the Southern Caucasus stood in his country's list of priorities for the presidency as follows: "Georgia is not, has never been, and will never be a French national priority.

But it is our goal to make sure that Georgia does not become a source of conflict within the Union. Our priority will therefore be to find the middle ground between the positions of those who want to do more to help Georgia and those who do not."

Sarkozy, too, was somewhere in the middle of this European spectrum on Georgia. He was more open and sympathetic to countries like Ukraine and Georgia than his recent predecessors in the Élysée had been. Unlike Angela Merkel, the French president did not personally dislike Saakashvili. More than one commentator noted similarities in their personalities—their at times exaggerated styles and a certain penchant for bold and not always fully considered decisions and actions. While Sarkozy was also more open in his criticism of Putin and of Russia's fall back into autocracy, maintaining a close relationship with Russia was a central part of the French diplomatic tradition as a way of maximizing French influence in Europe and beyond.

Like others in the West, Paris had not seen this war coming. With the war having broken out on its watch, however, it was responsible for shaping Europe's response whether it wanted to be or not. Many Europeans still remembered Europe's failure to initially stop the bloodshed in the Balkans in the early and mid-1990s. If the European Union stood by and did little or nothing while Georgia was invaded and crushed, it would be a disaster for European foreign policy and for France. If the European Union succeeded, it would be a French success as well. In reality, Sarkozy had little choice but to be engaged—the European Union's and his own credibility were on the line—but it was not a decision without risks.

Sarkozy had also approached Putin in Beijing on August 8 during the opening of the Olympic Games. Like Bush, he had been rebuffed by the Russian leader. The French president had asked Putin to give him two days to mediate a peaceful end to the conflict. Putin had refused. Sarkozy then asked for at least one day to try to stop the fighting. Putin refused a second time. Sarkozy concluded that the Russian leader had no desire to nip this fight in the bud but was determined to teach Saakashvili a lesson. Paris was worried that Putin was determined to take advantage of the conflict to crush Georgia once and for all. Sarkozy flew home to France to decide what to do.

The normal course of action for an EU presidency would have been to consult carefully within the ranks of the Union, assemble some degree of consensus on next steps, and then move forward cautiously with an initiative. But there was no time, and this was hardly Sarkozy's modus operandi. Sarkozy understood that the situation was dangerous not only for Georgia but for Europe. Paris was furious at the Georgian move, and many blamed Saakashvili for having launched the war. After the war was over, the French president summed up his interpretation of what had happened by saying, "There was a military intervention by Georgian forces, which was an error. The reaction of the Russian army was disproportionate to the Georgian military intervention."[1]

That interpretation of cause and effect may be narrow or even wrong. But when the situation was handed to them, Paris had little time to debate or investigate how the war had started and who was to blame. A war was underway and it needed to be stopped. There is nevertheless little doubt that France's thinking and diplomacy during the crisis were shaped, if only directly, by a sense that Georgia had been in the wrong. Tbilisi was fortunate to have a strong leader like Sarkozy heading the EU. But Paris was also a skeptical leader. It had not been a major player on these issues, and Sarkozy knew little about Georgia and often cared less. He was afraid that this war could lead not only to Georgia's demise but to a long-term divorce between Europe and Russia. The important thing was to bring this war to a quick end—period. France wanted to prevent a Georgian defeat and occupation. But for Paris, it was also about ensuring that this war did not plunge the West and Russia into a new cold war. Europe's interest in and relationship with Russia were at stake.

Having been rebuffed by Putin in Beijing, Sarkozy focused on opening a channel to Medvedev. The previous spring Foreign Minister Bernard Kouchner had returned from Moscow telling him that Medvedev was different from Putin, that he was the representative of a new generation in Russia and potentially a man you could do business with. In a series of breakfast meetings with French intellectuals and journalists in the spring and summer of 2008, Sarkozy had described how in dealing with Russia he wanted to focus his attention on Medvedev as opposed to Putin. It was Sarkozy's way of squaring the anti-Putin side he had shown during his presidential campaign with his desire to be a leader who could deal with Russia.[2]

When Paris suggested Sarkozy might be willing to come to Moscow to negotiate a ceasefire, Medvedev's response was immediately positive. The situation was risky, however. The Georgian army was disintegrating, and Russian armed forces were only a few hours' drive from Tbilisi. Medvedev's demands to end the war thus far had not included regime change, and the Russian president had suggested he might be prepared to return to the status quo that existed before hostilities broke out. But French intelligence had intercepted communications between Moscow and Russian generals on the ground in Georgia saying that the road to Tbilisi was open and requesting permission to move on the capital. There appeared to be different views in Moscow over whether or not to let them do so. Like Washington, Paris was not sure what Moscow's real goals were. If the French president were to travel to Moscow only to be confronted with a Russian takeover of the Georgian capital, it would be a disaster. But to not go and to let Tbilisi fall without the European Union doing anything was also dangerous. French national security advisor Jean-David Levitte, for example, initially advised the president not to go because of the risk of being confronted with a fait accompli.

Paris went back to Moscow with the following message: The French president was prepared to come but not to bless what Russia had done. Sarkozy would be coming to find a solution to the conflict and to put an end to the war on terms that were also acceptable to Europe. Sarkozy and Medvedev spoke on the phone four times, and their key advisors spoke even more often. Sarkozy insisted on two conditions. The first was that a ceasefire would be in place by the time he arrived. The second was that Moscow would not move on Tbilisi. Medvedev assured the French president that he was not inviting him to Moscow to put him in an embarrassing situation. He promised that both conditions would be met. But who was calling the shots in Moscow—Medvedev, Putin, or the Russian military? As Sarkozy left the Côte d'Azur for Moscow early on the morning of August 12, there was a sense of uncertainty about whether those pledges would really be met.

Bernard Kouchner had in the meantime headed to Georgia to see the situation at firsthand. Kouchner's background in dealing with humanitarian crises and refugees made him eager to get a feel for what was happening on the ground. With him on the plane was Finnish foreign minister Alex Stubb, representing the OSCE. Stubb was young and charismatic and a self-described "EU nerd," perhaps best known for his blog. But it was the OSCE, not France, that led the monitoring mission on the ground in South Ossetia—it knew the terrain and had armored cars and staff that would come in handy. On the evening of August 7, Stubb had written on his blog, "I am afraid of the worst." The next morning war broke out. Stubb reached out to Kouchner and the two agreed to travel to Tbilisi as representatives of the European Union and the OSCE. By the time they arrived, late on August 9, Russia was bombing targets across the country—having dropped several bombs close to the international airport in Tbilisi less than an hour before the ministers' plane landed.

Upon arrival, Kouchner and Stubb were whisked off to a meeting and then to dinner with Saakashvili. Sitting at the rooftop restaurant Kopola, they and their advisors discussed the need for an immediate ceasefire. The whole scene seemed somewhat surreal—there was a war going on, but Tbilisi still seemed untouched by it, with people still partying and enjoying themselves. When Kouchner and Stubb mentioned that, Saakashvili suggested they drive to Gori to get a close-up look at the real war. It was 0100, so the two men decided to wait. The next morning the French- and Finnish-led OSCE teams drafted a ceasefire. Shortly after 1000 they reached an agreement on the text with Foreign Minister Ekaterine Tkeshelashvili, who had assumed that position from Gela Bezhuashvili in the spring.

But there was a problem. They wanted Saakashvili's signature before heading to Moscow. A notorious night owl, Saakashvili had been up all night and was sound asleep. His staff did not dare wake him, even for this. The Georgian president was awoken a couple of hours later and signed the draft at 1214. Kouchner and Stubb toured Gori, where they saw the damage that Russian bombing raids had caused. At this point the damage to Gori was still modest, but that did not prevent the Georgians from exploiting the OSCE visit to maximum effect before the cameras in what was rapidly becoming a public relations war with Moscow.

Kouchner and Stubb had planned to meet again in Moscow to present the ceasefire agreement to the Russians. During their talks, however, Kouchner had a rather stormy call with Paris after which he somewhat sheepishly admitted to Stubb that he had an "administrative problem" back home. It turned out that the Élysée had wanted Kouchner to undertake a fact-finding mission. It also did not want to be limited by a ceasefire negotiated with the Georgian side. Sarkozy had decided to go to Moscow himself to negotiate and didn't want his hands tied by a paper negotiated in Tbilisi without his input and with someone the Russians hated. Stubb immediately understood that the OSCE's and Finland's role had come to an end. He nonetheless felt that Finland had played a useful role in helping draft a ceasefire. Little did he know that a second draft was being prepared in Paris by Jean-David Levitte, Sarkozy's national security advisor.

But the real problem was going to be getting Moscow to agree to any draft. Kouchner left Tbilisi to travel separately to Vladikavkaz, North Ossetia's capital and the historic Russian military fortress from which Moscow had launched its original conquest of the Southern Caucasus. Having visited Georgian war refugees in Gori, Kouchner also wanted to see South Ossetian war refugees who had fled across the border into Russia. He heard harrowing stories of the Georgian midnight artillery shelling and the subsequent Georgian offensive, including stories of hand grenades being thrown into cellars where refugees were hiding. He found their stories compelling and had no reason not to believe them. They were also part of the truth of this war. It reinforced his sense that Georgia had launched a foolish attack and had lost the moral high ground.

En route to the refugee camps, the French delegation saw long columns of Russian armor and troops moving south in the direction of the Roki Tunnel and Georgia. It was an impressive sight. As the French delegation sat in Vladikavkaz, the French ambassador to Georgia, Eric Fournier, called with the latest military update. He suggested they take out a map of Georgia, find two small towns on the map, and draw a line between them. It was the forward position of the Russian army—and it clearly showed how Georgia had now been cut in half. Coupled with the sight of kilometers of additional Russian tanks and troops rumbling down the military road outside their window in the direction of Georgia, it was a graphic reminder of Russian military power and of what Georgia was up against. If Russia decided to deploy that power, Georgia was finished.

Two factors would help shape French thinking later that afternoon as Sarkozy went head-to-head with Medvedev and Putin. Georgia was clearly at great risk and needed to be saved. But Paris was also convinced that

Saakashvili had blundered into this war of his own accord and had shown himself to be the hothead many feared. As far as Paris was concerned, Tbilisi bore partial responsibility for the situation. Their task was not, in French eyes, to win back for him what he had lost on the battlefield but to stop the war, to save Georgia, and to prevent the eruption of a new cold war between the West and Russia over Georgia. That understanding of French objectives is critical for understanding what happened in Moscow that afternoon.

Prior to Sarkozy's departure, Paris had, of course, been in close contact with its fellow EU partners as well as with Washington. The key issue was what objectives Sarkozy would pursue and what the West's bottom line should include in terms of a ceasefire. No one knew exactly what Russia's war goals were, but the farther the Russian army advanced, the greater the risk that Moscow's ambitions would grow. There was Western agreement on the need to prevent regime change. There was also agreement on the desirability of getting Russia to return to the military status quo ante. In spite of his harsh criticism of Saakashvili, Medvedev had told both Sarkozy and Bush that he was in principle prepared to agree to that. The question was how to lock him in to such a commitment and execute it on the ground before it was too late. The third and final goal was to prevent the crisis from escalating into a broader confrontation and to convince Russia it had made a mistake, and thus ensure that this did not become a precursor for moves against other neighbors.

Throughout this period Paris and Washington were in close touch. Having decided that it was best for Europe to take the lead did not mean that Washington did not seek to influence the diplomacy behind the scenes. In a sense, it assumed the role of the bad cop staking out a tough public position vis-à-vis Moscow while Paris assumed a more accommodating stance. The Élysée and the White House were nevertheless coordinating views and agreeing on common principles. Sarkozy and Bush spoke three times to ensure that both sides of the Atlantic had a common view, and senior administration officials insist that the president was fully supportive of Sarkozy's trip. The French president's final words to Bush in their last conversation before leaving for Moscow were, "George, I am glad we have had this conversation. There is no daylight between us."[3]

But there is an old rule in diplomacy. He who controls the typewriter or conducts the actual negotiation has the final say. In reality, Washington was playing the role of backseat driver—with all the limitations that implies. The heavy lifting of getting the Russians to actually agree to the terms of a ceasefire and remove their troops would have to be done by Paris, head-to-head with the Russians in Moscow—and Washington and American power would not be present. The United States had outsourced the diplomatic lead in this crisis to France, representing the European Union. As Sarkozy left for Moscow, the White House thought it was as closely coordinated with Paris as was possible. It knew that Sarkozy could be a strong and effective leader. It also knew he could be a showman who at times let his sense of grandeur take precedence over the finer points of diplomacy. And it was worried that the Élysée and the French Foreign Ministry did not always seem to be on the same page.

President Sarkozy arrived in Moscow shortly before midday on August 12. Not long before his plane touched down, Moscow publicly announced a ceasefire for its forces. Tbilisi was still standing as well. Moscow had technically kept its word on both issues although the French delegation soon heard that some Russian units on the ground were still advancing. Sarkozy initially met with President Medvedev for talks. As president of Russia, Medvedev was officially the commander in chief of the Russian armed forces and Sarkozy's counterpart in terms of protocol.

Medvedev was the person Sarkozy wanted to negotiate with, but everyone understood that Putin was the power behind the throne. The French delegation was informed that the Russian prime minister would soon join the talks, adding an element of drama. Sarkozy knew from Beijing that Putin wanted Saakashvili out, and he knew that Lavrov had made the president's departure a condition in their talks. The danger of regime change was still in the air. Later that day the Kremlin spin doctor Gleb Pavlovsky told the radio station Ekho Moskvy that at "an important meeting" that day there had been calls not to accept a ceasefire, to march on Tbilisi, and—as he put it "maybe further than Tbilisi." He went on to criticize those calls saying that such a move could permanently ruin Russia's relations with the West and wreck President Medvedev's hopes to modernize and Westernize Russia.[4]

As the talks started, Kouchner discovered to his surprise that the draft he and Stubb had produced in Tbilisi was nowhere to be seen. Although he had sent it back to Paris, National Security Advisor Levitte had concluded that this draft was a nonstarter for the Russians and that it was a mistake to present Moscow with a text first negotiated with Saakashvili. The French National Security Council had produced a second alternative draft but it, too, had been rejected as unacceptable. Instead, the conversation started with the Russians setting out a large map on the table on which they sketched out the security zone they wanted to establish around South Ossetia—ostensibly to protect it from further Georgian attacks.

That security zone initially demanded by the Russians would have given Russia control over the major east-west highways that led from the west to the Tbilisi border and could have in effect given Moscow a veto over Georgia's chances at economic recovery. It included the same highway from the Russian border to Tbilisi that Moscow had used to invade when Georgia lost its independence in 1921. The Russians had kept their word in the sense that Tbilisi was spared, but Moscow was clearly still positioned to pounce and determined to dominate Georgia in a way that would bring the country and its economy to its knees—and would in all likelihood lead to the end of the Georgian government and to regime change through political and economic, as opposed to military, means. During the talks, the French side continued to receive updates that Russian forces on the ground were still on the move. The danger to Tbilisi was not over. And then Putin joined the meeting. He had apparently just come from the dentist and was in a foul mood. How much of that anger was from the dentist and how much was over Georgia was not clear.

What was clear was that the Russian prime minister was determined to oust Saakashvili one way or the other. Sarkozy and Putin had the following brutal exchange, which was subsequently revealed in the French press:

Putin said: "I want to hang Saakashvili by the balls."

"Hang him?" a startled Mr. Sarkozy interjected.

"Why not?" Mr. Putin replied. "The Americans hanged Saddam Hussein."

"But do you want to end up like Bush?" Mr. Sarkozy asked.

Mr. Putin apparently paused and said: "Ah, there you have a point."[5]

Sarkozy then responded, "Let the Georgian people decide for themselves who they want as a leader. It is a democracy, they will decide. That is none of your business. If you have security concerns because of the attack, then let's discuss those issues. That is why I have come."

The three leaders had lunch while their foreign minister and national security advisors worked on a new draft. But the differences were so large the advisors could not even produce a working text for the presidents to review. After the lunch, they reported back to their leaders that they had failed to produce a new document. The talks had reached an impasse. At this point, Sarkozy and the French delegation had to make a crucial decision—threaten to leave with all the risks that entailed or redouble their efforts to find a compromise even if it did not meet all of the West's conditions.

Paris knew full well that Moscow had broken the cardinal rule of post–Cold War European peace—they had overrun a border in Europe by force. In French eyes, that was not acceptable. But Paris concluded that it was impossible to reverse it then and there. France and the European Union did not have the power or the leverage to compel Moscow to accept a ceasefire that included all of the key Western or Georgian demands. With its troops poised to take the Georgian capital, Moscow had the stronger hand. So Sarkozy and his team decided to focus on the immediate—stopping the advance of the Russian army and saving Tbilisi—and not let perfection become the enemy of the good. What was critical was to save Tbilisi from total defeat and occupation. As Kouchner subsequently put it, "We wanted to stop their Army. That was our purpose, our goal. And in order to stop the [Russian] Army, we had to accept that they [Russia] are the winners in Abkhazia and South Ossetia but then [ask them to] stop the movement of their armed forces."[6]

At this point, Sarkozy said to Medvedev: "Okay, let's try to do it ourselves." He took out a pen and drafted a text in longhand, listing a set of principles. There was no mention of Georgia's territorial integrity, as there had been in the original ceasefire draft. The four points from the initial Kouchner-Stubb draft now reappeared in a slightly altered form. But two new ones were added. They addressed Moscow's insistence on so-called additional security measures around the conflict zones as well as a pledge for talks on the future status of Abkhazia and South Ossetia. This Sarkozy draft was taken down to the presidential secretariat by Jean-David Levitte and Sergei Prihodko, Sarkozy's and Medvedev's national security advisors, typed up, and translated into Russian. Unfortunately, no one checked the final French and Russian texts to make sure they were identical.

At the end of some four hours, the two leaders finally had an agreed-on text based on six principles for a ceasefire. Sarkozy and Medvedev subsequently announced those principles at a press conference. The points read, verbatim:

- do not resort to the use of force
- the absolute cessation of all hostilities
- free access to humanitarian assistance
- the armed forces of Georgia must withdraw to their permanent positions
- the armed forces of the Russian Federation must withdraw to the line where they were stationed prior to the beginning of hostilities; prior to the establishment of international mechanisms the Russian peacekeeping forces will take additional security measures
- an international debate on the future status of South Ossetia and Abkhazia and ways to ensure their lasting security will take place

This language was poorly written and ambiguous on a number of points even to an untrained diplomatic eye. It masked the divide between what Russia and France were seeking. In his opening remarks at the press conference, Medvedev had avoided mentioning Georgia's independence and sovereignty—let alone its territorial integrity. Sarkozy jumped in to underscore his support for the first two principles—and invited Medvedev to say he shared that view. He wanted the Russian leader to go on record supporting both. Both leaders were immediately asked why territorial integrity was not mentioned in the statement. Medvedev ducked the question. Sarkozy responded that his goal was not to resolve all outstanding issues but to achieve a ceasefire. "There are two options," he said. "We can try to resolve all the issues now and end up achieving no result at all, or we can try to restore peace and attempt through dialogue to find a long-term solution and that is what we have tried to do."[7]

Medvedev finally and grudgingly affirmed that he, too, recognized Georgia's independence and sovereignty. But he quickly added, "This does not mean that a sovereign state has the right to do whatever it pleases." On the issue of whether Georgians and Ossetians and Abkhaz could ever again live together, he stated, "This is a question for them to ask of themselves and it is they who will give their own clear answer. It is not for Russia or any other country to answer for them." He then went on, "Over these last years international law has given us numerous very complicated cases of people exercising their right to self-determination and the emergence of new states on the map. Just look at the example of Kosovo." Moscow was now playing back to the West its own arguments on the Balkans. It was the diplomatic equivalent of blowback.

Sarkozy and Kouchner left Moscow believing they had succeeded. They had stopped the war and the Russian military advance. They believed that Saakashvili was wrong to have launched his military offensive and that Georgia had in essence lost the war. Their goal all along was not to accuse Russia of being the aggressor. Nor had they intended to try to win back for Georgia what it had lost on the battlefield. They were keenly aware of the limits of their influence, given Russia's military power. They wanted to bring the war to a close while preventing a chasm from opening up in relations between Moscow and the West. They had saved Georgia, preserved Europe's relationship with Russia, and shown that the European Union could manage a crisis of this magnitude on Europe's periphery under French leadership. That was success in their eyes. On the plane from Moscow to Tbilisi, they celebrated.

Others were far less sure. When senior American officials saw the text, they were—in the words of one senior official—"appalled." A ceasefire was supposed to have specific dates and locations. This document had neither. The text was vague and open to various interpretations. It spoke about Russian forces without distinguishing between the Russian peacekeepers and the invading forces. What did "additional security measures" mean in practice? If that were left for the Russians to define, they might be roaming across the country doing whatever they pleased. What kind of new "international mechanisms" were envisioned—and how long would it take to set them up? There were huge loopholes that Moscow could exploit to leave its forces in strategically critical areas.

But Washington had placed its bet on Paris. It had not been in the room during the negotiations and could hardly judge what was or was not possible. There was no other option at that point. France had to succeed if Washington hoped to reach its own objectives. The administration was willing to accept the criticism that it was not active enough or doing enough. It believed that Europe had to be in the lead and that it had a French partner who fundamentally shared the same objectives. And when the result came up short of America's expectations, it had little choice but to swallow hard and refrain from criticizing.

To this day, there is debate over how to assess the Sarkozy-Medvedev ceasefire agreement. Was the French president courageous to go to Moscow, and did he achieve the best result possible? Or did he fail to push hard enough in Moscow and therefore produce a poorly drafted document whose weaknesses continue to haunt us today? Did Paris do the best it could in a difficult situation, or did Sarkozy, focused on getting a deal under any circumstances, agree to a flawed and vague text? Did France and the European Union lack the heft by themselves to get Moscow to agree to a more balanced agreement? Would closer transatlantic cooperation and a more visible American political and diplomatic role have made a difference—or would it have lead to precisely the kind of U.S.-Russian confrontation everyone was eager to avoid? Historians are likely to debate such questions for some time to come.

For their part, French officials insist they did the best they could with a difficult hand. While Washington insists it was in close touch with Paris, some French officials are less charitable and instead contend that the United States was "out of the game" and that Europe was on its own in dealing with Moscow. In the words of Foreign Minister Kouchner, "The Americans were out. They were nowhere. The Americans were phoning to us and we were phoning back. They were sending a navy ship to the Black Sea, but so what? Nothing! So we had to stop the Red Army ourselves and it was our main and unique purpose—not to let the Russians take the capital [of Georgia]."

What France considered a success, however, was viewed quite differently in Tbilisi. Saakashvili and his team had initially been dismayed when Bush told him that the United States was not going to take the lead but instead rely on France. It nevertheless welcomed President Sarkozy's mission to Moscow. Saakashvili knew he needed someone had to engage the Russians to end the war. If Washington was not prepared to do it, then the European Union was the only alternative. But as the Georgians watched the Medvedev-Sarkozy press conference, they were stunned. Saakashvili had signed a draft ceasefire a day earlier that had included their bottom line—a mention of Georgia's territorial integrity. Now they were confronted with a new draft from which it had disappeared and had been replaced by two new and ominous conditions. The fact that the draft was being announced publicly in Moscow meant it would be almost impossible to change.

While the French delegation was celebrating on the plane en route to Tbilisi, Saakashvili phoned several diplomats to test their reactions. He was furious about the new language and asked for advice on how to interpret it as he waited for the French president's arrival. From Tbilisi's perspective, Georgia had just been invaded after a long series of aggressive Russian steps against which the West had done too little. The West's reaction to the war had been, in Georgian eyes, a waffle. As opposed to issuing an outright condemnation, it had criticized Russia for the "disproportionate use of force," implying that some degree of Russian force was acceptable. While disappointed in Washington, they knew the United States was the best friend they had. It was Europe that they were most disappointed in. And it was now Europe, led by France, whose help they depended on to survive.

The previous day Saakashvili had called for a rally of national unity in front of the Georgian parliament building. It was his attempt to boost public morale. Sarkozy arrived in Tbilisi as the rally was taking place. His motorcade headed to the parliament, where Saakashvili was speaking. When Sarkozy's motorcade pulled up next to the parliament building, the crowd started chanting, "Sar-ko-zy, Sar-ko-zy." Saakashvili had invited Sarkozy to address the crowd, but the French president turned down the offer, telling the Georgians that he had come not to give a speech but to end a war. The French delegation was worried that Saakashvili was trying to manipulate them. They knew anything Sarkozy said in public would be watched closely, especially in Moscow.

Things got worse as both sides looked for a room where the two delegations could meet. The meeting had initially been scheduled to take place in the chancellery, but the rally and the late arrival of the French president forced a change of plans. Nothing was set up for the meeting. The Georgian president had a suite reserved for his use in the parliament building, and they decided to use that. It lacked air conditioning and was therefore hot, and refreshments had to be fetched. In addition, no one had bothered to translate the French and Russian texts into English. While Saakashvili himself spoke decent French, many of his key pro-American lieutenants did not.

Shortly after the meeting started, Polish president Lech Kaczyński, Estonian president Toomas Ilves, Lithuanian president Valdas Adamkus, and Latvian prime minister Ivars Godmanis also arrived. They had come to demonstrate their solidarity. Although the Russian air force had allowed Sarkozy to fly to Tbilisi, it denied the Polish jet safe passage through Georgian air space, so the officials had been forced to journey via Azerbaijan and then travel overland by car to Tbilisi. Saakashvili dashed out of the Sarkozy meeting to greet them and take them to the rally, where they were invited to address the crowd. He then literally ran back to see the French president, leaving his guests standing somewhat bewildered in front of a crowd of some 100,000 Georgians. The visit was not off to a great start.

The Georgian side saw, or wanted to see, in Sarkozy and Kouchner friends who had come to help them in their moment of national peril. They wanted to understand what had happened in Moscow, how and why the document they had signed two days earlier had changed so radically. They were hoping for a dialogue and some give-and-take on how to fix or mitigate its flaws. For France, the task was a different one. Sarkozy did not want to engage in further give-and-take. He needed to convince the Georgian leadership that it had no choice but to accept a document achieved under difficult circumstances and through tough negotiations. Having just come from Moscow, he did not know if the ceasefire would hold or if the Russian generals might still attack. France's and his own reputations were on the line. If the ceasefire fell apart, he would look bad, too.

In short, Sarkozy wanted Tbilisi to sign on the dotted line in order to ensure Georgia's own survival as well as to underscore his own role as peacemaker. The psychological gap between the two sides and how they looked at the document quickly became evident. Sarkozy's message was crystal clear: you need to sign this document or else Russian tanks will be in Tbilisi in a matter of hours. While the document was imperfect and vague in places, it was the only way to end the war and save the Georgian state. They could sort out all the other issues later. The Georgians, on the other hand, wanted to ask questions, to push for clarifications of wording, and explore possible changes. By this time, Sarkozy was exhausted after a grueling day. Impatient and short-tempered, he kept jumping up and insisting in a loud voice that the Georgians had to sign. "Where is Bush? Where are the Americans?" he asked the Georgian delegation. "They are not coming to save you. No Europeans are coming either. You are alone. If you don't sign, the Russian tanks will be here soon."

The Georgians were scared because they knew Sarkozy might be right. Their intelligence told them that the Russians were still prepared to strike, but they also thought the French president was grandstanding. It was obvious to them that he wanted to declare victory and go home, but there were too many unanswered questions. They were not sure Paris fully understood the different kinds of borders in South Ossetia. No one could say with any confidence how this document would be applied on the ground. At the same time, the Georgians knew they had little leverage. They were afraid that if they pushed too hard, Sarkozy would go ballistic, side with the Russians, and say that they would be portrayed as the ones who were being uncooperative.

Tbilisi had three specific problems with the document. The first was that any mention of territorial integrity had disappeared. The French told them it was impossible to reopen that issue. The second problem was point five, the security of the buffer zone. It was vaguely worded, and the Georgians feared Russia could exploit it to occupy parts of Georgia well beyond the conflict zones. Sarkozy offered to write a side letter clarifying the spirit of what was intended, but he refused to change the wording of the document itself. Tbilisi decided it could live with that. The third and biggest problem with the text was point six, future talks regarding the final status of Abkhazia and South Ossetia.

Tbilisi immediately saw the parallel with Kosovo and interpreted this as a Russian trick. If they agreed to that language, it would be the first time they had ever accepted a document that questioned Georgia's territorial integrity. It was, in their view, a complete nonstarter. The French argued that, on the contrary, committing the Russians to address the status of Abkhazia and South Ossetia through international discussions was the best and perhaps only way to keep the future of these provinces open and to prevent Moscow from unilaterally recognizing their independence. The word "status" was an invitation to an open-ended negotiating process with the international community that could even help the Georgians. Sarkozy was very clear: "We are sitting here now and you are trying to negotiate this single word out of this agreement. But I can tell you that if you do not accept this agreement, the Russians will be here in a couple of hours. I know that," said the French president. "So your choice is whether they take Tbilisi or whether you sign this agreement, forget about that word which we can interpret however we want later. We will never recognize Abkhazia and South Ossetia."

But the Georgians would not budge. In their minds, it was tantamount to capitulation. Finally, Sarkozy conceded, "Okay, I will speak to Medvedev and maybe we can change this one word." Bakradze, the chairman of the Georgian Parliament, had a special communications line in his office that he used to try to place a call to the Kremlin. It was after midnight. He first reached an operator, told her who he was, and asked to be put through to Medvedev. She responded, "Are you crazy?" He made it clear that it was not he but President Sarkozy who wanted to speak to the Russian president. The answer was still no—the president was asleep and could not be disturbed—not even to end a war.

At this point the Georgian and French delegations decided to take a break. Saakashvili went out to address the crowd at the rally that was still going on outside the parliament building. During the break, the French delegation tried to call Moscow using their own contacts and communications. They got through immediately. Sarkozy spoke to Medvedev, and he agreed to delete the word "status." The French delegation informed the Georgians of this good news—but for the Georgians it was simply a further sign of how the Russians tried to deal behind their backs. Sarkozy and Saakashvili held a brief and hastily improvised press conference, and the French president departed.

After the French delegation had departed, the Georgian side had an uneasy feeling that this agreement would come back to haunt them. Saakashvili finally caught up with the presidents of Estonia, Lithuania, and Poland for a late dinner and to brief them on what had happened. The three EU presidents, along with Ukrainian president Viktor Yushchenko, had waited for hours in a room next to the one where the Franco-Georgian talks were taking place in the parliament building. Sarkozy at one point came out to briefly shake hands with the other presidents but would not meet with them as a group. It was not the greatest demonstration of EU solidarity. When the presidents heard the details of the talks and the ceasefire, it only reinforced the Georgian concerns.

The next day President Bush put the full weight of the United States behind the ceasefire effort. He underscored his concern about reports that Russian forces continued to advance and about the danger of an attack on Tbilisi. "Russia has stated that changing the government of Georgia is not its goal," he proclaimed. "The United States and the world expect Russia to honor that commitment." He announced that the U.S. military was launching a humanitarian assistance effort and issued an explicit warning that Russia's future relations with Washington were now at stake. Noting that Moscow had sought to become a closer partner with key Western institutions like NATO and the European Union in recent years, Bush warned that Russia was "putting its aspirations at risk by taking actions inconsistent with the principles of those institutions." Moscow needed to keep what Bush felt Medvedev had promised him. "To begin to repair the damage to its relations with the United States, Europe, and other nations," the president concluded, "Russia must keep its word and act to end this crisis."[8] Secretary of Defense Robert Gates was more direct: "If Russia does not step back from the aggressive posture and actions in Georgia, the U.S.-Russian relationship could be adversely affected for years to come."[9]

The Georgia war almost immediately became a political football in the U.S. election battle between Senators Barack Obama and John McCain as well. A personal friend of Saakashvili, McCain was on the phone with the Georgian president getting briefed by him firsthand. He felt the initial White House response was too weak and behind the curve. On the campaign he declared that he had spoken to the Georgian president and told him, "Today we are all Georgians," a plea he repeated in an editorial two days later.[10] An editorial in the *Wall Street Journal* went further and criticized the White House for what it called "a Carteresque note of weakness."[11] Senator Obama's initial response—based on a cautious initial White House briefing—had been subdued, as he had called on both sides to show restraint. But he too quickly toughened his message as it became clear what was happening on the ground. For a brief moment, Georgia became a political flash-point and virtual test of each man's potential skills as the next commander-in-chief on the road to the White House.

Saakashvili had not actually signed the agreement during Sarkozy's visit. He was too worried about the ambiguities and flaws, and the Georgian side felt they were being browbeaten into an unjust peace. They had asked for time to reflect, but Russian troops were still only a few hours away and the threat of a Russian assault on the capital still hung over Georgia's head. Both the Georgians and the French now turned to Washington for help in closing the deal. One idea that had been floated while Sarkozy was in Tbil-isi was issuing a side letter to the ceasefire that would clarify some of the am-biguities. Secretary of State Rice was on her way to Tbilisi, and she stopped over to meet with Sarkozy in southern France on August 15 to confer on the language of the ceasefire agreement and possible improvements.

Both sides understood that the draft ceasefire had helped prevent Moscow from taking Tbilisi. But the language about where Russian troops could or could not deploy was too loose. It left open the option of Russia using its troop deployments to try to strangle Georgia economically and thus pursue regime change though different means. The two sides produced a draft side letter giving the Georgians additional clarifications that Rice agreed to take with her to Tbilisi while Paris ensured that the language was acceptable to the Russians. When Rice arrived in Tbilisi later that day with the draft letter, the first thing the Georgians asked was how much time they had to study the letter before they had to decide. They were still feeling bruised from their meeting with Sarkozy.

Rice told them they could have all the time they needed. The American and Georgian sides spent eight hours patiently working through all the is-sues, the Georgians asking questions about the exact demarcation lines, and making edits with Rice on the phone with Levitte in Paris to finalize the let-ter. At this point, Rice saw her role as convincing the Georgians to agree to a ceasefire that was flawed but necessary, but it had to be done in terms that were not demeaning to the Georgians. Walking to the press conference after they had completed the document, the secretary of state suggested to Saakashvili that he let her take the lead in answering the tough questions in front of the press and that he hang back and be restrained.

Saakashvili's first few answers were fine. But it was not long before his frustration and his anger at Europe and at being perceived as the one who had started the war boiled over. The Georgian leader accused Europe of having asked for trouble by denying Georgia MAP and termed the Bucharest summit "a new Munich." He recalled the aggressive steps Russia had taken in the spring and summer and how the West had not responded, and concluded:

> So who invited the trouble here? Who invited this arrogance? Who invited these innocent deaths? Who is—not only those people who perpetrate them are responsible but also those people who failed to stop it. And who is now trying to look for every excuse, saying, oh, you know, Georgians might have started it. Excuse me? Twelve hundred tanks came into Georgia within few hours. There is no way you can mobilize those tanks in such a fast period unless you were ready. There were Russian pensioners taken off the streets of Moscow to fly the planes several days before the invasion. There was no way they were not preparing the invasion. . . .
>
> And unfortunately, today we are looking evil directly in the eye. And today this evil is very strong, very nasty, and very dangerous—for everybody, not only for us. . . . I want the world to know, never, ever will Georgia reconcile with occupation of even one square kilometer of its sovereign territory. Never, ever.[12]

In the car after the press conference was over, Rice turned to Bryza in dismay and noted how disastrous the Georgian president's performance had been. Georgia and Saakashvili needed European support. They needed the European Union to hold Russia to the terms of the ceasefire, and the French deserved credit for stopping the war in spite of all the shortcomings in the text. How shortsighted it was for Saakashvili, she continued, to treat the allies he needed most that way. Looking back months later, Rice would say that this had been the second most difficult press conference of her tenure as secretary of state.[13] Rice's trip was followed by a visit by Senator Joseph Biden, who launched the idea of a billion-dollar U.S. assistance package to help Georgia recover from the war.

But the saga was not over yet. The principles of the Sarkozy-Medvedev agreement needed to be translated into a more detailed implementation plan. This was supposed to entail a phased withdrawal of Russian forces back to their positions prior to the outbreak of hostilities, coupled with the deployment of EU observers. In the weeks that followed, however, the Russian army continued to use the loosely drafted language of point five in the agreement to open multiple new checkpoints deep in Georgian territory, often near economic infrastructure like ports, thus dramatically increasing the costs of shipping insurance and of doing business. The longer Russian troops lingered, the greater the financial costs to Georgia and the slower its political and economic recovery. It was becoming obvious that Moscow was indeed still hoping for regime change through economic collapse.[14]

Moscow moved quickly to exploit the situation on the ground in other ways as well. Paris had originally hoped to go back to the UN and try to reaffirm past resolutions on Georgia's territorial integrity. But the Kremlin preempted that move. On August 26, President Medvedev recognized Abkhazia and South Ossetia as independent states. In justifying his move, he returned to the false accusation that Georgia had sought to perpetrate genocide in these two provinces and against their peoples.[15] Writing in the August 27 *Financial Times*, Medvedev justified his decision by invoking the region's history, the desire of these peoples for independence, and the events of early August as well as the example of Kosovo.[16] In an interview on August 31, he took the next step in rationalizing his country's invasion of Georgia by laying out five basic principles guiding Russian foreign policy. The first three were nothing new. The fourth one pledged to protect the lives of Russian citizens "wherever they may be."

The fifth, however, was an unabashed claim to a renewal of a Russian sphere of influence on its borders. "Russia," according to Medvedev, "like other countries in the world, has regions where it has privileged interests. These are regions where countries with which we have friendly relations are located." Asked if this sphere of influence encompassed those states bordering Russia, he responded, "It is the border region but not only."[17] Georgia was clearly part of that definition whether it wanted to be or not. Two days later Medvedev said Russia considered President Saakashvili to be persona non grata: "For us, the present Georgian regime has collapsed. President Saakashvili no longer exists in our eyes. He is a political corpse."[18] It was virtual regime change—Moscow would simply ignore official Tbilisi while still working to topple the regime.

This set the stage for a second and equally dramatic visit by Sarkozy to Moscow for talks with Medvedev on September 8. By now it was nearly a month since the original ceasefire had been signed, and there was little sign of progress on the ground. The French had hoped to go back to the UN and reaffirm past resolutions that spoke of Georgia's territorial integrity, but that plan had collapsed with Moscow's recognition of Abkhazia and South Ossetia. That recognition and Moscow's ostentatious expansion of new checkpoints deep in Georgian territory had produced the first calls for sanctions against Moscow and a possible suspension of talks on a new EU-Russia treaty. The goal of getting back to the status quo ante either politically or militarily was going nowhere fast—and there was an EU-Russia summit scheduled for mid-November. Speaking at a press conference on September 6, referring to the ceasefire agreement, Kouchner warned, "Of the six points, only two or let's say two and a half, perhaps three, have been implemented."[19]

French prestige was now on the line to ensure that Sarkozy's first agreement would be successfully implemented. Washington's advice was to name and shame—to simply call the Russians on their nonfulfillment of the terms of the ceasefire in front of the international community. In American eyes, the Russians needed France and Europe more than the other way around. But Paris's priority was to resolve these disputes without torpedoing the European Union's relations with Russia. The Georgia problem needed to be fixed—and soon—if EU-Russian relations were to stay on track. Moscow had initially wanted Sarkozy to again come by himself and not with a full EU entourage. But Paris insisted that the European Union be fully represented, and the French president was accompanied by EU commission president José Manuel Barroso and EU high representative Javier Solana.

After four hours of talks at the Maiendorf Castle outside Moscow, the French leader emerged to proclaim what he described as a "momentous" agreement in which Moscow promised to scrap its checkpoints in Georgia within a week, remove Russian forces from areas adjacent to South Ossetia and Abkhazia in a month, allow the deployment of a 200-member-strong EU observer mission, and start international talks on the future of South Ossetia and Abkhazia within a month. French officials let it be known that, in order to get the deal done, Sarkozy had at one point when they reached an impasse threatened to storm out of the talks and go home. "All has not been resolved. We are aware of that. But what has been resolved has been considerable," Sarkozy said, adding that the European Union and Russia had avoided "a cold war that we don't need."[20]

Speaking at a press conference in Tbilisi later the same day, the French leader was even more emphatic in insisting that Russia had agreed to his terms. Asked whether he was sure the Russians would keep their commitment to withdraw to the lines their forces had held prior to August 7, Sarkozy said:

> There's a commitment, there's a date, there are deadlines. As one of the text's negotiators, I can just tell you it's absolutely mathematically precise. On October fifteenth there must no longer be a single Russian soldier anywhere other than where he was before August seventh. It's clear and simple. Either it's done, and in that case everyone has honored their word, or it isn't done and then, five days later, Europe will draw the appropriate conclusions.[21]

Asked whether the EU observers would have access to the conflict zones, he also pledged that they would be able to enter the separatist provinces and assist refuges in returning home. Emphasizing that no deal was perfect, the French president still expressed his pride that Europe had been able to stop a war in less than ten days and get agreement on the withdrawal of Russian forces in a month. "No political force other than the European Union," he proclaimed, "could have done it."[22]

France had indeed succeeded in achieving two key goals. The war in Georgia was ended with the government of President Saakashvili still standing. A new cold war had also been avoided and EU-Russian relations had stayed on track. The European Union and Russia agreed to resume talks on a new partnership agreement at their summit in Nice in mid-November 2008. Previous discussion of sanctions faded quickly. The European Union continued to uphold the principle of Georgia's territorial integrity and called Russia's recognition of South Ossetia and Abkhazia "unacceptable." International talks on the future of these two entities commenced in Geneva and continue to this day. EU monitors were deployed in less than a month, but they were not given access to either Abkhazia or South Ossetia as originally envisioned.

On several other key points Western policy also failed to meet its objectives—or even the terms of the Sarkozy-Medvedev ceasefire. Russian troops withdrew within the agreed timeframe from the areas adjacent to Abkhazia and Ossetia but not to the lines where Russian peacekeepers had been stationed before the conflict. The West never came close to convincing Moscow to return to the political or military status quo ante. Several key valleys in both South Ossetia and Abkhazia previously Georgian populated and controlled were ethnically cleansed and were now dominated by Russian and South Ossetian and Abkhaz forces. Very few Georgian refugees have been allowed to return—and there is almost no prospect of return for those from the Georgian villages north of Tskhinvali that were flattened and burned to the ground. The reality is that Russia unilaterally changed the borders of a sovereign member of the OSCE by force, allowed the ethnic cleansing of Georgian citizens from parts of Abkhazia and South Ossetia to create ethnically more homogenous entities, has not fully complied with the terms of a ceasefire bearing the name of its president—and has gotten away with it.

To this day, Russian forces hold swaths of territory that were previously under control of the Georgian government in Abkhazia and South Ossetia. Those same forces show no intention of going back—in the words of the Sarkozy-Medvedev ceasefire—"to the line where they were stationed prior to the beginning of hostilities." The number of Russian forces in Georgia today is significantly higher than before the war, possibly posing an ongoing offensive threat. Whether Russia has abandoned its goals of regime change in Georgia is an open question. The war is over, but the struggle over Georgia's future and its place in the world is not. Whether Western diplomacy had indeed made Moscow pay a price, convinced it that this invasion was a mistake, and removed any temptation for additional aggressive steps vis-à-vis other neighbors—another key Western objective—remains to be seen.

CHAPTER 8

GEORGIA, RUSSIA, AND THE FUTURE OF THE WEST

The Russo-Georgian war of August 2008 was a little war that shook the world. It shocked a West that had become complacent in its belief that war in Europe had become a thing of the past and thus ignored the warning signs that conflict was brewing between Moscow and Tbilisi. It also called into question the West's relationship with Russia, a country many knew was becoming more difficult but a country few believed would actually resort to military force to attack one of its neighbors. Perhaps most importantly, this war violated several core principles of what was supposed to be a new European security order, thus raising questions about its future. As a result, this little war shook the belief that a democratic and cooperative peace had triumphed in Europe twenty years after the Iron Curtain fell and that the kind of geopolitical competition and spheres of influence thinking that had produced so much conflict and bloodshed in the continent's past had been banished.

My core argument in this book has been twofold. First, the origins of this war do not lie in the details of local ethnic rivalries between Georgians on the one hand and Abkhaz and South Ossetians on the other, or even the future status of these provinces. Those problems were real. They were certainly capable of producing conflict and bloodshed—as they did in the early 1990s, following the breakup of the USSR. But they were no more and no less insoluble than the problems the West faced in the Balkans, for example. The South Ossetian conflict could, in my view, have been resolved with appropriate guarantees of power sharing, minority rights, and cross-border cooperation and contacts. Many of those elements were contained in the secret proposal Tbilisi tabled with Moscow in 2007 but which was never fully explored as some in Russia sabotaged the proposal before it could even get a fair hearing.

Abkhazia was a tougher case. The wounds of war ran much deeper and the final result was less apparent. Whether a final solution might have entailed some kind of loose autonomy with Georgia, some variant of partition, or some kind of conditional independence is harder to say. A serious discussion about these alternatives never even got started, however, as too many actors, above all, Russia, had an interest in keeping the conflict unresolved. And the West was unwilling to engage in the kind of heavy lifting that would have been required to launch the kind of authentic and internationally sanctioned peace process that might have changed the status quo. Had the international community applied the same political will, strategic imagination, and resources to this region and created an international process to resolve these status issues as it did in the Balkans, I nonetheless believe progress could have been made there as well.

The unresolved status of Abkhazia and South Ossetia were, however, only the superficial causes for this war. The real reason was the core conflict between Russia and Georgia over Tbilisi's desire to break free of what had been a quasi-colonial relationship with Moscow and to become part of a democratic West. This war was fought because Georgia wanted to guarantee its future security and sovereignty and independence by aligning itself with the West, becoming a member of NATO and eventually of the European Union as well—and Moscow was equally determined to prevent it from doing so and to keep it in a Russian sphere of influence. To that end, the Kremlin was willing to manipulate and exploit the conflicts in Abkhazia and South Ossetia to sabotage Georgian aspirations, undercut the democratically elected government of Mikheil Saakashvili to pursue regime change and rollback, and prevent what it saw as the encroachment of Western influence on its southern border.

This brings me to the second part of this book's argument. This war also did not start on August 7, 2008. Nor was Moscow's aggression aimed solely at Georgia. Russia and Georgia had been engaged in a kind of Cold War for many years. We tend to forget how hostile Moscow was to Saakashvili's predecessor, Eduard Shevardnadze, a man still admired in the West but hated in the Kremlin. The attempts to assassinate him and to dominate Georgia even before the Rose Revolution underscore that this was not just a personal grudge between Mikheil Saakashvili and Vladimir Putin. That Russo-Georgian conflict nevertheless reached a new degree of intensity after the Rose Revolution and the election of Saakashvili as president of Georgia. While Saakashvili's own style may at times have inflamed Russo-Georgian tensions, the real reason the conflict escalated was because of his success in turning the country around and starting to transform it into a viable candidate for eventual membership in NATO. The more successful Tbilisi was, the more hostile and worried Moscow became.

Tbilisi was starting to move westward at precisely the time Moscow was deciding to turn its back and abandon the pro-Western course that Yeltsin had adopted in the 1990s, which Putin had initially embraced as well. As Russia moved in a more authoritarian and anti-Western direction, it became even more determined that its neighbors not go West either. Instead, the Kremlin became even more focused on reasserting its control over them to rebuild its own influence in the space of the former USSR. Eurasianism now became the alternative to coming closer to the West. That Russian shift away from the West coincided with the Rose and Orange Revolutions, which brought to power new elites in Tbilisi and Kiev who wanted to take their countries in exactly the opposite direction.

This war was also aimed not only against Georgia but against the West more generally. Georgia was the physical target, but we were in the political crosshairs, too. Tbilisi became the whipping boy for Russian complaints and resentments that had been building for years against the United States, NATO, and those countries Moscow saw as giving encouragement to Georgia. That was clear in everything from how the war was treated in the Russian media, to the way Russian officers described their mission during the brief occupation period, to the graffiti left behind by departing Russian troops. Those resentments started with the United States and NATO but they did not end there. Russian soldiers took pleasure in destroying EU flags as much as they did any symbol of U.S. or NATO presence. Russia's propaganda effort not only blamed the war on the Georgians but directly implicated the United States as having fostered and created this conflict.

Many in the West have tried to step back and pretend that the Russo-Georgian war was a local conflict that they were not party to. But there is little doubt that in Russian eyes this war marked a new Russian policy of rollback and containment—an effort to roll back Western influence and to contain any future expansion of Western institutions to Russia's borders. Moscow was announcing that the days of what it saw as retreat were over. This was its way of saying to the West collectively that Georgia was in its backyard and that we should stay out. It was meant to send a signal that Russia was literally willing to fight back to prevent further Western encroachment on its borders, above all through NATO enlargement. In that sense, this was the first post–Cold War East-West military conflict.

Russia was not only revolting against Georgia's attempt to go West. In laying claim to a new sphere of privileged interest and influence, it was also protesting against the rules of a European security system that, from its perspective, had facilitated and legitimated the enlargement of NATO and the European Union—and that now promised to bring NATO even closer to its southern border. In short, Moscow was rebelling against a European security architecture that in Western eyes has been successful in overcoming the geopolitical division of Europe, but which from the Kremlin's perspective was facilitating a geopolitical shift against it. This was the clash between a twenty-first-century Western world that saw the extension of democratic integration closer to Moscow's borders as a positive step toward greater stability and a Russia that was returning to the habits of nineteenth-century great power thinking and viewed it as a threat.

Moscow had of course signed dozens of key documents and communiqués that had codified these new norms of this European security system. It had again and again recognized the right of every country in Europe to equal security and to choose its own alliance system. But those commitments on paper now seemingly didn't matter. When countries tried to implement these principles and game rules—which the West considered a foundation of the post–Cold War peace—Moscow didn't like it. It was leading the Kremlin to conclude that the European security system as constructed was tilted against its interests. The Russo-Georgia war of August 2008 was also Moscow's way of saying that those rules no longer apply. That is why the war was immediately followed by President Medvedev and other Russian officials calling for radical revisions in how European security was run and which institutions had the lead.

The Russo-Georgian war of 2008 was also a war from which no one emerged looking particularly good. In many ways there were no winners, only losers. The biggest loser was of course Tbilisi. It went to war to defend Georgian citizens who were potentially in the line of fire, to preempt what it feared could be a broader assault aimed at toppling the Saakashvili government, and to avoid the potential political stain at home of losing Abkhazia and South Ossetia without putting up a fight. Those actions found little understanding and almost no support in the West—and were subsequently declared to be without legal foundation by the EU's Tagliavini Report. Georgia lost the war militarily yet survived politically—but barely. It was bloodied but not conquered. President Mikheil Saakashvili still heads the country and is likely to serve out his term despite vocal opposition. But his standing and reputation are tarnished, and Tbilisi's ambitions to go West were set back. Georgia lost its positions in both separatist provinces, and tens of thousands of Georgian citizens were ethnically cleansed by being driven from their homes. Tbilisi today has no influence in or control over South Ossetia or Abkhazia.

Whether Abkhazia and South Ossetia are better off, however, is also an open question. I suspect that when the dust finally settles, they will end up losers as well. Both have been recognized by Moscow as independent states but it is not clear what this means in practice. The international community has condemned that step and refused to follow suit—with the exceptions of Nicaragua and Venezuela, which have recognized the two provinces as this book goes to print. The international community is committed to Georgia's territorial integrity and sovereignty over these regions, even if it is only on paper. That is unlikely to change anytime soon precisely because, unlike in Kosovo, the independence of these two mini-states was not the result of a

UN-led international process to determine and legitimize their status but a unilateral military act by Moscow.

While local separatist leaders rejoice in their newly won independence, the future legitimacy and viability of these isolated separatist provinces as independent states is questionable. Whether Abkhaz or South Ossetian citizens will be better off as a result of this war remains to be seen. The track record of small nations living under Moscow's domination—either as nominally independent satellites or eventually as part of the Russian Federation—is also not an enviable one. Moscow may rue the day in August 2008 when it decided to support separatism in these Georgian provinces if and when those same separatist forces raise their ugly heads inside Russia, and in the Northern Caucasus in particular. The long-term affect of Moscow's war in August 2008 may well be to encourage separatist pressures within Russia's own borders. It is a safe bet that the Southern Caucasus—and the Northern Caucasus as well—will be less stable now and in the future because of this conflict.

That is one of several reasons why the war's self-proclaimed victor, namely Moscow, should also be considered a loser. Once Moscow decided to commit overwhelming military force, its victory was inevitable. Whether it achieved its political goals is less clear. Moscow did not launch this massive military buildup simply to "deter" any Georgian actions or to consolidate its full control over these two separatist provinces. Rather, its goals were to discredit and destroy the Saakashvili government and what it stood for. That was reflected in the scope of Russia's military campaign as well as in Lavrov's remarks to Rice that "Saakashvili must go" as a condition for halting the Russian offensive. President Medvedev's postwar prediction that Saakashvili was a "political corpse" reflected the ongoing hope that the Georgian president would still be toppled from within after Russian tanks had stopped. But here, too, it has failed.

In Russia itself, the mood of martial triumph created by the Russian army's victory was fleeting as the war sparked an outflow of Western capital soon followed by the global economic crisis that has battered the Russian economy. And while Moscow managed to escape from the war without any Western sanctions for its behavior, its international reputation has clearly been damaged. While the EU's Tagliavini Report on the origins of the war places the blame for the first shot fired in this conflict on Georgia, its findings also undercut Russia's official narrative of the war. The report dismisses Russian allegations of genocide as "neither founded in law nor substantiated by factual evidence." It rejects Moscow's claim of having undertaken a humanitarian intervention. It concludes that Moscow's distribution of passports to Abkhaz and South Ossetians in the years prior to the war—thus creating those Russian citizens Moscow subsequently claimed it was defending—was illegal. It acknowledges the Russian right to defend its so-called peacekeepers on the ground—even though those peacekeepers had de facto ceased to represent the international community and had instead become the extended arm of Russian neo-imperial policy. But it notes that Russia's military response "cannot be regarded as even remotely commensurate with the threat to Russian peacekeepers in South Ossetia." Perhaps most devastating for Moscow, however, is the report's conclusion that neither Abkhazia nor South Ossetia had the right to secede from Georgia and that Moscow's recognition of their independence was contrary to international law.

No one can or should look at Vladimir Putin's Russia in the same way after this conflict as it did before. Its behavior in this crisis is just one more factor slowly but surely tipping the scale in the Western debate over how to deal with Moscow.

Finally, Moscow fought this war as a deterrent. It wanted to deter the West from thinking about further NATO enlargement and the countries in the region from seeking it. In punishing their bête-noire Saakashvili, they were sending the message to leaders in other former Soviet republics about what could happen to them if they, too, tried to turn westward and seek admission to Western institutions. The war was designed to discourage them. However, the invasion may end up providing an object lesson in precisely the opposite, namely, why Russia's neighbors should *want* the protection of membership in Western political, economic, and security institutions. How the West will respond is still an open question. In this respect, Russia's move may also eventually turn out to be counterproductive.

But the West did not emerge from this war looking particularly good either. Much of the debate over the war's origins has understandably focused on the Georgian mistakes, the combustible personality of President Mikheil Saakashvili, the hatred Putin and Russian leaders harbored for him, and Moscow's deeper ambitions. However, Western policymakers should look in the mirror and examine where we went wrong and actually accelerated the path to war. Those mistakes commenced with our unwillingness to invest in the kind of authentic peacekeeping that might have kept the peace and facilitated conflict resolution. They included our push for Kosovo's independence without a plan for mitigating the possible fallout in Georgia. And they included NATO's handling of the debate at the Bucharest summit, which may have provided the trigger for the campaign of escalation that started in the spring and culminated in war in early August.

Georgia also paid a price for the lack of Western purpose and unity. That disunity can be traced back to the breakdown in Western ties over the Iraq war, a rift that was never fully healed during the Bush Administration's second term in spite of efforts to do so. A divided Alliance also emboldened Moscow. Once the war started, France, representing the European Union, intervened diplomatically to save Georgia. But that rescue came late in the game and with a ceasefire whose terms were neither clear nor just. Whether Washington's decision to opt out of a leadership role in this crisis was an act of statesmanship to prevent a U.S.-Russian escalation that could have produced a modern-day Cuban missile crisis, or whether it simply reflected the weakness of an unpopular lame-duck administration in its final months in office is another question historians may ponder. This was not the West's finest hour.

I am often asked what the West could have done differently. Could this war have been avoided? I believe it could have. The best way to have prevented it would have been to have authentic and neutral peacekeeping forces on the ground. Stronger UN and OSCE missions could have provided greater transparency, reduced the potential for mischief by all sides, and changed the dynamics on the ground. That would have given the international community leverage over the separatist leaderships as well as the Georgians and limited Moscow's ability to pursue its military buildup. The idea of more robust international missions was floated by diplomats but always shot down as too hard. After the war the EU deployed several hundred unarmed observers to monitor the Sarkozy-Medvedev ceasefire. Had they been on the ground the previous spring, history could have been different.

Better old-fashioned diplomacy and deterrence might have prevented it as well. During the key spring and summer months when Moscow was clearly testing the Georgians and allied reactions to its buildup, the Western response was too weak. Western statements protesting Russian moves were almost ritualistic in not taking sides and instead calling on all parties to practice restraint. They had no bite and carried no real consequence. And they were not backed up by a clear message to the highest levels in Moscow that a move against Georgia would constitute a fundamental breach of the norms of European security. The West did not have to threaten to go to war to influence Russian behavior. Had the West spoken with a clear and unified voice and told Moscow that a move against Georgia would have very real political and economic consequences, this war might also have been prevented. Russian forces stopped moving toward Tbilisi in August only when that threat of a major rethink of policy was finally made explicit by the United States.

The war may therefore also turn out to mark the end of an era that had commenced almost two decades earlier when Mikhail Gorbachev first spoke of the need to create a new common European home. It was the grand experiment, building a new post–Cold War Europe whose foundation was to be based on common democratic values and mutual interests. It was supposed to be a new community that included Russia in the family of Western democracies. While Moscow had been drifting from those values for some years, the Russo-Georgian war marked a new watershed in Russia's own formal break with the West. After the war one Russian commentator after another announced that such common values no longer existed and that Moscow no longer wanted or needed to be part of the West. Moscow's relationship with the West had seemingly gone full circle in the post–Cold War era from proto-alliance to neutrality to openly and increasingly truculent anti-Westernism.

It is therefore also the culmination of a drama that has played itself out in several acts since the fall of the Iron Curtain two decades ago. That saga is the story of our efforts to build a new post–Cold War democratic peace based on Western integration to overcome the division of the continent. It is intertwined with the story of consolidating democracy in Central and Eastern Europe while also reaching out to Russia and drawing it into an expanding Western community. It is a story of tremendous success and of partial failure. And finally it is the saga of Russia slowly but surely turning its back on the West and adopting its own version of rollback and containment against the West. That saga is ongoing and one in which the Russo-Georgian war is only the latest chapter.

The story began as Communism collapsed in Central and Eastern Europe and in the Soviet Union and a new vision of Europe's future emerged from the peaceful revolutions of 1989. It was the vision of a return to Europe by peoples and nations cut off from the West for half a century by Soviet domination. It was a vision of a continent that overcame its past divisions. It was about creating a new post–Cold War security architecture based on a democratic peace in which the continent's past geopolitical demons would be banished and armed conflict would become inconceivable.

The goal of the architects of the revolutions of 1989 was to secure their newly won freedom and independence by anchoring the eastern half of the continent to the western half. They wanted to enjoy the same security and prosperity the western half enjoyed—and they wanted to join the same institutions that guaranteed it. Achieving that vision of a unified Europe was seen as undoing the legacy of the Second World War's end, when Hitler's megalomaniacal plans of aggression brought the Red Army into the heart of Europe, and the USSR imposed its political will and system on the eastern half of the continent. It was a moral imperative to allow these countries the right to join a Europe to which they should have belonged in the first place. It was a strategic imperative because of the need to ensure that Europe—after two world wars and the Cold War—became a continent that produced peace and not war.

Locking in a new post–Cold War peace in Europe became a central foreign policy imperative of the 1990s—not only for European governments but also for the United States. This debate about Europe's future inevitably became intertwined with the U.S. role in Europe and the future of the Atlantic Alliance and the West. Had that Alliance—forged decades earlier to meet the Soviet threat—fulfilled its purpose? Was it time to retire it with honors? Had the goal been to defeat communism or to make Europe safe and secure once and for all? Could the institutions of the Cold War be transformed to knit together a divided continent? Should—and could—the West as we had known it during the Cold War be reconstituted into a new Alliance for the challenges of a new era?

One of the biggest questions in the debate about the future of the West was what to do about Russia and where it would fit in. The impulse for democratic change had come from opposition movements like Solidarność in Poland or Charter 77 in what was then Czechoslovakia. But it was of course Mikhail Gorbachev's historic decision to allow history to run its course and refrain from using Moscow's massive military power that led to Communism's final implosion in Central and Eastern Europe. And it was Boris Yeltsin's desire to liberate the Russian people too from the yoke of Communism and empire that had fueled his support of the breakup of the Soviet Union itself two years later. The West may have won the Cold War insofar as our Western democratic values prevailed. But it was the courageous decisions of Russian leaders like Gorbachev and Yeltsin that ensured that this epochal conflict ended peacefully and with little loss of life. There was no doubt in American and European eyes that Russia had to somehow be included in any new European security order. The question was how.

Initially the West hoped that Russia, too, could accomplish what Central and Eastern Europe were doing and make the transition to a Western-style democracy, albeit on its own timeline and with its own rhythm. The strategic impulse behind Western strategy was also integrationist—to include rather than exclude Moscow. Those Russians who today insist that Western policy was designed to humiliate Moscow are simply wrong. One can debate lots of issues—whether the West was too timid or inadequate or whether it used the wrong mechanisms and institutions. But there can be no doubt about the West's intent: to support and encourage Russia's democratization and eventual inclusion in Western structures.

How to do so did generate passionate debates—some of which continue to this day. It also led to a set of decisions in the 1990s that laid the foundation for the European security order we have today. The first step was the 1990 Charter of Paris. It built on the Helsinki process and was sort of a bill of rights for a post–Cold War Europe. It was supposed to set the norms and principles that would constitute the foundation of a post–Cold War security order. The cardinal rule was that borders in Europe would never again be changed by military force. Among the other key principles were the right to equal security, the right to choose one's own alliances, and a rejection of the concept of sphere of influence. Moscow's acceptance of these principles was a sign that it, too, wanted to be part of an undivided Europe and part of the West.

The question was how to take this grandiose vision and turn it into reality. Should the OSCE, the European Union, or NATO take the lead in knitting the continent together? The initial impulse to rely on the OSCE faded quickly as it became clear it was incapable of doing so. The European Union also seemed an attractive candidate but it stumbled badly in Bosnia and people realized that it, too, could not move fast enough to answer the pressing security issues of the day. Then and only then did eyes start to turn to NATO. It was of course an irony that NATO—the premier Cold War institution—would play a critical role in shaping the new European security structure. But the new democracies of the East did not only want to return to Europe. They also wanted a link to the United States, which they believed was needed to secure their independence. NATO provided that.

The West took that Central and East European desire to be embraced and made it part of a much larger transformation and reinvention of the Atlantic Alliance and the European Union. That transformation consisted of three historic steps: NATO opened its door to the inclusion of new members from Central and Eastern Europe, which in turn facilitated the enlargement of the European Union; the Alliance also adopted new peacekeeping missions beyond its borders in the Balkans and took on the task of projecting stability across Europe as a whole; and it reached out to and established a new partnership with its former Cold War adversary, Russia, with the NATO-Russia Founding Act of 1997.

The Alliance was not trying to contain Russia as it had during the Cold War but to engage it as a partner and pull it West. When it came to the military aspects of NATO enlargement, the Alliance bent over backward to accommodate Russian sensitivity. The defense component for new members was essentially left hollow when the Alliance decided it did not need to deploy combat forces or nuclear weapons on the territory of new members to carry out its collective defense. Instead, the Alliance decided it could rely on Western integration, infrastructure, and reinforcements to fulfill those obligations and provide that reassurance. It was further evidence that NATO enlargement was about projecting stability and integration and avoiding the creation of a new military threat closer to Russia's borders.

Did we hedge in case Moscow moved in the wrong direction? Of course. No one could predict what the final outcome of this dramatic Russian experiment in post-Communist government would be—and by the mid-1990s things were already starting to look quite shaky. Some feared that Russia wanted to get close to the Alliance in order to undercut it. The goal of Western strategy was to work for the best possible outcome but keep options open if history turned out differently. When NATO agreed not to deploy combat forces or nuclear weapons on the soil of new members, we made sure that it was a unilateral NATO decision that could be reconsidered or reversed down the road if need be. It was diplomatic code for saying we expected that environment to remain peaceful but reserved the right to change our posture if Russia turned hostile.

That strategy was remarkably successful in anchoring democracy in Central and Eastern Europe and in contributing to stability in Europe as a whole. The European continent was arguably more secure than at any time in centuries. Although relations with Russia had been difficult, the two sides had found a compromise on the first round of NATO enlargement. The train wreck in relations with Russia that was so frequently predicted by enlargement critics never happened. New arrangements for cooperation with NATO and the European Union were set up, and a breakdown of relations with Moscow was avoided. It is often forgotten today that Moscow put up even less resistance or opposition to the Alliance's Big Bang second round of enlargement than it had to the first. The Alliance reciprocated by further deepening its offer of cooperation. In short, the strategy seemed to be working.

It was this expanding community that a young democratic government in Georgia aspired to join following the Rose Revolution of 2003. That Revolution was driven largely by domestic factors. Russian conspiracy theories that depict the Rose Revolution and the 2004 Orange Revolution in Ukraine as some sort of alien import of American NGOs ignore the deep yearning in these societies for the kind of freedom, prosperity, and security associated with the transatlantic world. Georgia wanted that Western connection for the same reasons Central and Eastern European nations had sought their Western link a decade earlier. It wanted to shelter a fragile democratic experiment in a region of despots and to obtain the security that came with integration with the West. The successful completion of NATO's and the EU's Big Bang enlargement to Central and Eastern Europe had a powerful demonstration affect.

Tbilisi looked toward the Baltic states in particular as they been at a similar level of development during Soviet times. Georgia's goal was to follow in those footsteps. It wanted to join NATO first because it was easier and because it lived in a dangerous neighborhood with Russia. But Tbilisi's real goal was to connect to Europe and join the European Union as well. When President Mikheil Saakashvili made his first trip to Washington in February 2004, he inquired about the possibility of receiving MAP. It was reminiscent of when Central and European leaders paid their first visit to the White House in the spring of 1993 to announce to the great surprise of then President Bill Clinton that their top priority was joining NATO. In a symbolic step, the Georgian government took to flying the EU flag to show that they shared European values and EU goals.

Three factors would make Georgia's quest to go West infinitely more difficult than that of Central and Eastern Europe—and also help set the stage for the Russo-Georgian war of August 2008. The first and most important change took place within Russia when President Vladimir Putin made his decision to turn his back on the West. Georgian aspirations now clashed with those of a revisionist Russia that was abandoning its own desire to join this Western community, was turning increasingly autocratic at home, and embracing Eurasianism. Moscow started to again cultivate the image of a Western enemy at the gate as part of a broader nationalist reassertion of Russian distinctiveness and foreign policy greatness.

The debate over why this shift in Russian policy took place is a big one. Did enlarging NATO and the European Union to Central and Eastern Europe drive Russia in an anti-Western direction, as some critics suggest? Or did Russia move in that direction for its own reasons, having little to do with the West and instead a lot with Putin's own authoritarian inclinations and his embrace of a new nationalist ideology to preserve his rule? In this debate, I belong to what might be called the "no guilt" school of enlargement. I think the West was fortunate to use a historical window of opportunity to lock in peace and stability in Central and Eastern Europe though NATO and EU enlargement.

It was also the right strategy to try to reach out to Moscow. Russia had ample opportunity to seize the opening to build a new strategic partnership with the West. The West may not have done everything right but the political will to cooperate with Moscow was there—and the doors of our institutions were open for business. That attempt failed because Moscow chose not to take up those opportunities and to go in a different direction. But as Russia went in a more autocratic and nationalistic direction, it increasingly saw Georgia's Western aspirations as a threat. As a result, Moscow's opposition to Georgia was of a completely different magnitude than anything we had seen in Central and Eastern Europe in the 1990s.

Second, Tbilisi was in fact not Prague and the Southern Caucasus was not Central and Eastern Europe. The difference was not only geographic. This was wilder and not wider Europe. Georgia was poorer, its democratic institutions weaker, and it came with a different and deeper set of problems. It was arguably a decade behind in terms of its political and economic development. It had farther to go, and the problems it needed to solve were more complicated. The fact that Georgia was needier than previous candidates did not necessarily mean it deserved less attention. The contrary was true.

Nowhere was this truer than when it came to the "frozen conflicts." In the early 1990s the United States and Sweden made a big push to convince Moscow to peacefully withdraw its troops from the Baltic States. This made their eventual quest to join the West feasible. There was no such push at the time to get Russian forces or bases out of Georgia. Instead, Georgia was left locked into a set of frozen conflicts that it could not solve on its own and that hindered its own efforts to integrate with the West.

The third major difference was that Georgia enjoyed a fraction of the Western support that Central and Eastern Europe had received in their day. Enlargement fatigue was rapidly becoming a major issue in Europe as NATO and the European Union grappled with the implications of a dozen new members. Georgia also had less of a claim on the moral and strategic appeal of reunifying Europe. When Europeans talked about reuniting Europe, they were not thinking of Tbilisi but of Prague, Warsaw, and Budapest. Even if Georgians had little doubt that they were part of Europe and deserved the chance to join the West, many in the West disagreed.

Georgia also had the misfortune of trying to go West at a time when the West was coming apart as opposed to coming together. In the 1990s the United States was popular, and Central and Eastern Europe benefited enormously from Western unity and cohesion. Georgia was seeking to go West at a time when the Alliance had fractured over the war in Iraq, the United States was more unpopular than at any time in recent memory, and Western relations were at a historic low.

In the end, it was a combustible combination of factors and timing. Georgia's push to go West coincided with a turn of Russia away from the West. The breakdown of trans-Atlantic cooperation was followed by the growing estrangement in U.S.-Russian ties. The intersection of growing tensions on the ground in Georgia and the unraveling of these key relationships between the United States, Europe, and Russia was explosive. Although the warning signs were there for everyone to see, the mechanisms designed to contain such tensions and defuse looming conflicts failed or were simply overrun. It was not only Georgia that failed. The failure was much bigger: it was that of the European security system.

That is also why this book is not just about the past but also about the future. What comes next? The reality is that none of the issues that caused the Russo-Georgian war were resolved in August 2008. The potential for future conflict is real. Georgia is still determined to go West, and Russia still wants to stop it. Moscow's ongoing saber-rattling and threats against Tbilisi suggest that it has not given up its wish to destabilize and eventually see regime change take place there. In the meantime, Moscow has also prevented any extension of either the UN or OSCE missions on the ground at a time when such missions needed to be significantly strengthened rather than abandoned. Some 200 EU monitors on the ground as a result of last year's ceasefire agreement constitute a thin red line between Moscow and Tbilisi.

The conflict between Russia and the West is therefore also alive and well, even though diplomats are careful to try to keep it under wraps and out of the public eye. NATO has reaffirmed its commitment to eventually bring Georgia into the Alliance and Moscow protests even the tiniest step in that direction. In the meantime, there is little agreement between Russia and the West over what rights, responsibilities, and game rules should govern relations with these countries. It is as if the rule book from the last two decades has been tossed out the window or disappeared.

Thus, the final chapter in this saga has yet to be written—and what it says will depend not only on what happens next in Tbilisi or in Moscow. What that chapter will say depends on what lessons the West draws from this war. Will we reaffirm our commitment to the core Helsinki principles, including the freedom to choose your alliances? Will we maintain that Georgia's aspirations are legitimate but Moscow's are not? Or will Western leaders decide that Russia's demand for a sphere of influence needs to be accommodated, that NATO enlargement should be halted, and that the rules of European security need to be adjusted to accommodate the concerns of Russia?

For Georgia, there can only be one path forward. As unjust as the ceasefire that ended the war was, in spite of the plight of Georgian refugees, and as inadequate as the border arrangements with Abkhazia and South Ossetia continue to be, Tbilisi must set aside any hope of regaining the lost provinces for the foreseeable future. It must settle on a long-term non-recognition policy coordinated with the international community that can endure for years if not decades. There are precedents it can look to and learn lessons from how the West dealt with other situations that contain some similarities. Western policy toward the Baltic states and the case of eastern Germany come to mind. Georgia should maintain its commitment to the eventual reunification of the country but renounce the use of force and pledge to work toward that goal through peaceful means. It must stop trying to litigate or politically re-fight the war with Russia.

Instead, Tbilisi must focus its energies on regaining its passion for reform and democracy at home that made it so attractive originally. Georgian leaders must take the part of their country they currently do control and again turn it into a democratic and reform tiger, the current economic and financial downturn notwithstanding. It is the only way it can regain the political and moral high ground lost, attract foreign capital, grow economically, and convince the West to embrace it more firmly and keep open the hope of one day convincing Abkhaz and South Ossetians to come back to a unified Georgia peacefully if history reopens their status. Eventually Georgia will also need to come to terms with its northern neighbor Russia. Its geography is not going to change.

In the early 1990s, former Estonian president Lennart Meri surprised Russian president Boris Yeltsin at a meeting by asking for a magic carpet. When Yeltsin asked what in the world Meri was talking about, he responded that the best way to solve their bilateral problems would be to transport Estonia somewhere in the North Atlantic but that, alas, was not an option. Meri's point was that Estonia knew it needed to live next to Russia. Georgia will, too. The task has made more difficult by the war. More Georgians are now anti-Russian and believe Moscow will never accept their true independence and sovereignty. Normalizing relations seems impossible so long as Moscow pursues a strategy of regime change. But new leaders and generations will eventually have to heal those wounds. Georgia will of course find it much easier to have the confidence to eventually normalize relations with Russia if it has a sense of security and an anchor in the West.

This brings me to what we in the West must do. For our part, we must return to our own first principles. We should remember why we wrote into the Charter of Paris the right of all European nations to enjoy equal security, to determine for themselves what alliance they want to belong to and why we rejected spheres of influence as the basis for future European security. We did so because Europe's bloody history had taught us that spheres of influence do not produce real security and that compelling nations to align themselves with others against their will is a recipe for instability and conflict. We wrote those principles to guard small states from the predatory behavior of larger, more powerful ones. Our leaders believed that this was the way to create an enduring foundation for a democratic peace on the continent. We did not just write them for Central and Eastern Europe. They were supposed to be universal and apply from Vancouver to Vladivostok. Russia willingly agreed to them. That is why breaking them cannot be without consequence.

We should also realize that supporting democratic breakthroughs on Russia's borders is not part of the problem but rather part of the solution. Opening the doors of NATO and the EU to Central and Eastern Europe was our response to the legitimate wish of these countries to become part of a Western democratic alliance and to share the benefits and burdens of memberships in those institutions. While that decision was controversial, it turned out to be a triumph of statesmanship that helped create the kind of stability Central and Eastern Europe had not seen in centuries. We should also remember that those policies in the 1990s were successful because they were part a broader renaissance of Western power and purpose. They reflected a bigger vision of Europe and a democratic West. That Western unity was key for success—and its subsequent collapse is no doubt part of the reason why so much consequently went off track.

That is why recreating that unity must be the second step in forging a new strategy. The election of Barack Obama as president has raised hopes that the United States and Europe can come together to again revive the Atlantic Alliance to meet the challenges of a new era. In addition to the challenges the West faces in places like Afghanistan and Pakistan and the wider Middle East or the rise of China in East Asia, this administration needs to repair a fractured Alliance and forge a new agenda. A new strategy for Europe's East must be part of that agenda. The right policy response to the Russo-Georgian war should be to clearly reaffirm the principles laid down in the Charter of Paris and to recommit to the goal of expanding a democratic peace in Europe.

The history of Europe has taught us again and again that the abandonment of liberal democratic values in the hope of accommodating authoritarian powers is not a recipe for long-term stability. Alliance leaders must again summon the political will and strategic imagination to rebuild and expand a democratic West. It is crucial that NATO's door remains open and that the prospect of future enlargement into Eurasia and across the wider Black Sea region be kept alive. This is especially true if, as seems likely, the doors of the EU are starting to close. Such a strategy must, of course, be matched with a new effort to rebuild relations with Russia. But we must be clear which Russian interests we consider legitimate and which we do not. Moscow has a legitimate right to equal security and to ensure that no new threat appears on its borders. It does not have the right to interfere in the affairs of its neighbors, to seek to topple their governments, or to deny them their own foreign policy aspirations.

Today Moscow of course dismisses any desire on its part to be part of the West. It claims to want to go in its own Eurasian direction. But I believe that the day will come when a future Russian leader will realize that this is a dead end. I am enough of a historical optimist to believe that the day will come when Russia will realize that the real partners it has to work with are in the West. Already today one can argue that the only truly stable border Moscow is in the West, a border whose stability was in part created by the democratic peace on the continent that NATO and the EU helped bring about. At some point, Russia will again turn back to the West and seek to deepen its relations with and eventually integrate with us—or it will run the risk of going the way of the USSR. That day may be hard for many to imagine given where Russia is today. A Western strategy must nonetheless work to help bring it about, while remaining true to its principles. We must make it clear that there is room in our community for a Russia that shares our values and plays by the rules. And when the day comes that Russia truly shares our values and wants to become part of our community, we must be prepared to be bold and seize the chance.

That is the challenge that lies ahead of us—for Georgia, Russia, and the West. The most fitting epilogue to the Russo-Georgian war of 2008 would be for the United States and Europe to recommit to building democracy in Georgia and finding new ways to tie Tbilisi and the wider Black Sea region to the West. We need to do so while continuing to work and engage with Russia in ways that eventually lead it to rethink its own interests and role in the region and to see the benefits of a democratic peace. A recommitment to those goals would be proof that the West has learned the right lesson and has drawn the right conclusions from this little war that shook the world.

A NOTE ON
BIBLIOGRAPHY
AND SOURCES

The literature for a western reader on the background to the Russo-Georgian war of August 2008 is unfortunately sparse. An excellent history of the overall region is Neil Ascherson's *Black Sea* (UK: Jonathan Cape Ltd. Publishers, 1995) as are Charles King's *The Ghost of Freedom: A History of the Caucasus* (New York: Oxford University Press, 2008) and his *The Black Sea: A History* (New York: Oxford University Press, 2004). Jack Matlock's *Autopsy of an Empire: The American Ambassador's Account of the Collapse of the Soviet Union* (New York: Random House, 1995) remains a classic on the demise of the USSR and the associated conflicts on the periphery of the former empire, including in Abkhazia and South Ossetia. Thomas Goltz's *Georgia Diary* (New York: M.E. Sharpe, Inc., 2006) offers an up-close look at the reality of war and political chaos in the South Caucasus in the early 1990s.

The evolution of Georgia and Georgian politics since independence are captured in *Statehood and Security: Georgia After the Rose Revolution* (Cambridge, MA: MIT University Press, 2005), edited by Bruno Coppieters and Robert Legvold. Ronald Grigor Suny's *The Making of the Georgian Nation* (Bloomington: Indiana University Press, 1994) is very much worthwhile reading, as is Edmund Herzig's *The New Caucasus* (London: Royal Institute of International Affairs, 1999). The two volumes of essays edited by the author for the German Marshall Fund—*A New Euro-Atlantic Strategy for the Black Sea Region* (Washington, DC: German Marshall Fund, 2004) and *Next Steps in Forging a Euro-Atlantic Strategy for the Wider Black Sea* (Washington, DC: German Marshall Fund, 2006)—help provide insights into the policy debates of the past few years surrounding Georgia and a transatlantic wider Black Sea strategy. Shortly before I finished my initial manuscript, Svante Cornell and S. Frederick Starr published their excellent edited volume on the war entitled *The Guns of August: Russia's War in Georgia* (Armonk, New York and London: M.E. Sharpe, 2009). As this book went to print, the European Union issued the report of the Independent International Fact-Finding Mission on the Conflict in Georgia (IIFFMCG), headed by Ambassador Heidi Tagliavini. That report, along with the accompanying documents and analysis, will provide a treasure trove for future historians.

Most of the research for this book is based on open sources. Sections of it are based on extended interviews with senior officials in the United States, Europe, and

Georgia. In most cases, these interviews were conducted on the record. In some cases, however, officials asked not to be named or identified. Often there were multiple interviews with the same individuals. Many interviews were conducted with the interviewee having first had the opportunity to refresh their memory by reviewing e-mails, memos, letters, or critical memoranda of conversations. This has allowed me to recreate several key conversations and exchanges better than I could have otherwise. Wherever possible, I have crosschecked the details to ensure historical accuracy.

In the United States, interviews were conducted with Judy Ainsley, Matt Bryza, Daniel Fata, Daniel Fried, Stephen Hadley, Jim Jeffries, Condoleezza Rice, Mark Simakovsky, Damon Wilson, and Joseph Wood. In Europe, interviews were conducted with Carl Bildt, Sorin Ducaru, Martin Erdmann, Terri Hakala, Christoph Heusgen, Bernard Kouchner, Jean-David Levitte, Hans-Dieter Lucas, Rolf Nikel, Henne Schuwer, Peter Semneby, Alex Stubb, and Heidi Tagliavini. In Georgia, interviews were conducted with Irakli Alasania, David Bakradze, Gela Bezhuashvili, Batu Kutelia, Ivane Merabishvili, Irakli Okruashvili, Mikheil Saakashvili, Ekaterine Tkeshelashvili, Shota Utiashvili, Grigol Vashadze, and Temuri Yakobashvili.

Numerous American and European officials reviewed different chapters of this book to check on accuracy. A special thanks nonetheless goes to Matt Bryza, Dan Fried, John Tefft, and Damon Wilson, as well as to Carl Bildt, Radek Sikorski, and Jean-David Levitte for reviewing specific sections of the manuscript. Mariusz Handzlik and President Lech Kaczyński were kind enough to review those pages of the chapter on the NATO Bucharest summit describing the president's involvement.

This book has also benefited from a number of additional resources. In Georgia the parliament conducted its own investigation into the origins of the war. The transcripts of the testimony of senior Georgian officials before the Temporary Parliamentary Commission on the Military Aggression and Other Acts of Russia Against the Territorial Integrity of Georgia are a valuable source and are available online in Georgian, Russian, and English. The same is true for the Georgian government's own official report on the war entitled Report by the Government of Georgia on the Aggression by the Russian Federation against Georgia. Much of the information that the Georgian government has provided to the EU Independent International Fact-Finding Mission on the Conflict in Georgia (IIFFMCG) investigating the war's origins has also been made available to the author as well.

These resources also point to the asymmetry that exists in how Georgia and Russia have handled the debate over the war's origins and scholarly and other attempts to understand its roots. The Georgian government has shown a degree of transparency at home and vis-à-vis the international community that has not been reciprocated in Russia. This author has experienced that asymmetry firsthand. It unfortunately proved impossible to conduct interviews with Russian officials. Efforts to arrange for interviews with senior Russian officials to give them the chance to put their version of events on the record or to comment on the American, European, or Georgian versions of key conversations were turned down. Several independent Russian analysts did agree to read and comment on the draft or individual chapters.

Many of the unanswered questions surrounding the Russo-Georgian war concern Moscow's policy, and this book would have benefited from a better understanding of the Kremlin's perspectives. Russia needs its own open and honest debate about the origins of this war. While my book was unable to benefit from access to these Russian sources, perhaps it will encourage Russians themselves to ask for greater transparency about what happened and why in the run-up to August 7, 2008. That is a story that still needs to be told.

NOTES

CHAPTER 1

1. On the Georgian intelligence intercepts see "Georgia Offers Fresh Evidence on War's Start," by Dan Bileffsky, C. J. Chivers, Thom Shanker, and Michael Schwirtz, *New York Times,* September 16, 2008. The transcripts of the calls can be found at http://graphics8.nytimes.com/packages/pdf/world/2008/09/20080916_Georgia_Transcript.pdf.
2. In the Russian army, an infantry regiment consist of three battalions as well as artillery, intelligence, and logistics units. It is sometimes reinforced with a tank battalion. A Russian infantry battalion consists of three companies for a total of some 550 men.
3. These calls took place at 0343 and 0347. The author has been provided with a copy of the intercepts. The first one took place between the Russian peace-keeping commander Major General Marat Kulakhmetov and his Georgian subordinate Brigadier General Mamuka Kurashvili. A second one took place between Kulakhmetov and Kurashvili's deputy Mamuka Tomashvili.
4. The materials consisted of one page of primary information about the Georgian military forces—how many people, the size of the defense budget, where Georgia's five brigades were located and what type of equipment they had, and so on. It also identified the alleged strengths and weaknesses of the Georgian armed forces. The "strengths" included the fact that many soldiers had been trained by NATO instructors; had modern equipment from the United States, France, and Turkey; and that the Second and Third Brigades had field experience with NATO forces in Iraq and Kosovo. The "weaknesses" listed included low levels of discipline; uneven levels of training where there were no American instructors; the psychological state of military staff/soldiers; and drinking and unconventional relationships. The document suggested that many soldiers preferred to serve in Iraq because of additional pay instead of in Georgia, where they had to carry out the "aggressive-military plans of Saakashvili-ists."
5. The following Russian units were reported to be deployed at the northern end of the tunnel: the 135th and 693rd Regiments of the Nineteenth Division of the Fifty-eighth Army, the 104th and 234th Airborne Assault Regiments of the Seventy-sixth Airborne Division, the 217th Airborne Regiment of the Ninety-sixth Airborne Division, and the Thirty-first Special Airborne Regiment.
6. As quoted in Andrei Illiaronov, "The Russian Leadership's Preparation for War 1999–2008," in Svante E. Cornell and S. Frederick Starr, eds., *The Guns*

of August 2008 (New York and London: M. E. Sharpe, 2009), pp. 49–84. Illiaronov is a former chief economic advisor to the Kremlin turned opposition figure who conducted his own fact-finding mission to the region and has since written widely on the Russo-Georgian war.

7. See the article by Yulia Latynina in which she describes how elements of the 135th and 693rd Motorized Rifle Regiments were in South Ossetia before August 7. Yulia Latynina, "200 km tankov. O rossijsko-gruzinskoi voinje. Chastj 2," November 20, 2008, at http://ej.ru/?a=note&id=8587. See also the paper by Andrei Illiaronov, "Another Look at the August War," presented at the Hudson Institute in Washington, D.C., on October 12, 2008, and also his interview in *Ekho Moskvy,* October 24, 2008, at http://www.echo.msk.ru/programs/razvorot/548457-echo/.

8. This mobilization of so-called volunteers was centrally planned and performed via drafting stations at the regional and district military commissariats across Russia's North Caucasus military district. Most of the volunteers were assigned to the Nineteenth Infantry Division of the Fifty-eighth Army or to the North Ossetian peacekeeping battalion while others signed contracts directly with the Ossetian Ministry of Defense. The latter was also illegal.

9. The original article cites Russian army captain Denis Sidristy, who describes how his unit was camped in South Ossetia near the nature park of Nizhniy Zaramah but received an order to go to Tskhinvali on August 7. Captain Sidristy was subsequently wounded in the fighting in Tskhinvali and was presumably part of the column of Russian forces the Georgians encountered when they entered the city on August 8. The 135th Regiment of the Fifty-eighth Army was not part of the contingent of Russian forces officially allowed to be in South Ossetia as part of the Joint Peacekeeping Force. See the article by Irina Zhirnova, "Zhiznj prodalzhayetsa," *Krasnaya Zvezda,* September 3, 2008.

10. Interview with Gela Bezhuashvili, head of Georgia's Foreign Intelligence Department. These deployments are also mentioned in his testimony before the Georgian Parliamentary Temporary Commission on Military Aggression and Other Acts of Russia against the Territorial Integrity of Georgia at http://www.parliament.ge/index.php?lang_id=ENG&sec_id=1329&info_id=20940.

11. Gleb Pavlovsky, the host of the Moscow-based *Realnaya Politika* television program and a staunch defender of Kremlin policies, had suggested in February 2006 that the Georgian president was a "war-monger" and suggested that the best way to resolve the crisis was to remove Saakashvili. "One bullet is cheaper than war," he said on an NTV program broadcast in February 18, 2006.

12. The intercepts of these phone calls have also been made available to this author.

13. In a subsequent interview in the Russian press, South Ossetian National Security Council secretary Anatoly Barenkevich—himself a Russian—describes how he entered President Koikoty's office during the battle for Tskhinvali after Koikoty had fled and found a special phone and a direct line for the South Ossetian leader to the Kremlin. See the interview with Anatoly Barenkevich "Nje mesto etamu prezidentu v Juzhnoy Osetiyi" in *Kommersant,* December 4, 2008, at http://www.kommersant.ru/doc.aspx?DocsID=1089120.

14. See, for example, the press release published by the Ministry of Press and Mass Media of the Republic of South Ossetia and the Information Agency RES on August 7, 2008. http://cominf.org/node/1166477896.

15. Said Tsarnayev, a Chechen freelance photographer for Reuters news agency, arrived in Tskhinvali on August 7 planning to take photographs of the environment and the surroundings for a project he was working on. As he later recalled, "At the hotel we discovered there were already 49 Russian journalists there. Together with us, there were some 50 people. I was the only one representing a foreign news agency. The rest were from Russian media and they arrived three days before we did, as if they knew something was going to happen." Quoted in Brian Whitmore, "Scene at Russia-Georgia Border Hinted at Scripted Affair," Radio Free Europe/Radio Liberty, August 23, 2008.

16. The initial suspicion that the Russians had probably deployed a battalion the previous evening was also given credence when Abkhaz separatist leader Sergey Bagapsh confirmed on Russian TV that afternoon that a battalion of troops from Russia's North Caucasus military district had entered South Ossetia. His remarks were broadcast by the Russian state channel Rossiya at 1600 on August 7. According to BBC Monitoring, Bagapsh said, "I have spoken to the president of South Ossetia. It [the situation] has more or less stabilized now. A battalion of the North Caucasian [Military] District has entered the area." See "Abkhaz Leader Says Russian Troops Deployed in South Ossetia," BBC Mon Alert FS1 FsuPol gv, August 9, 2008.

17. See the article by Lieutenant Colonel Robert Hamilton in "The Bear Came Through the Tunnel: An Analysis of Georgian Planning and Operations in the Russo-Georgian War" (unpublished manuscript). Lieutenant Colonel Hamilton was chief of the U.S. Office of Defense Cooperation from July 2006 to 2008. He is currently a U.S. Army Fellow in residence at the Center for Strategic and International Studies in Washington.

18. The population of Tskhinvali was officially listed at 30,000, but that figure dated from the breakup of the Soviet Union. By early August 2008, some sources believed the figure was actually closer to 15,000. The estimate of 3,000 to 4,000 residents still being in the city before the fighting broke out was offered by a local South Ossetian authority.

19. Interview with Minister Temuri Yakobashvili. The then chief of the joint staff of the Georgian armed forces, Brigadier General Zaza Gogova, also describes receiving that phone call from President Saakashvili in his subsequent testimony before the Georgian Parliament's special commission of inquiry into the war. See his description of the call at http://www.parliament.ge/index.php?lang_id=ENG&sec_id=1315&info_id=21045.

20. That internal Georgian intelligence report was shared with the author. It is an e-mail that arrived at the National Security Council at 0144 and was taken in to the president immediately. In addition to the report of the sighting of Russian units in Tskhinvali, it also contained a second piece of intelligence—namely that the Russian Twentieth Volgorod Motorized Rifle Division had been placed on alert as of August 1 and had been told to be ready to deploy to South Ossetia on August 11. This is one of several pieces of intelligence that led Tbilisi to include that a broader Russian military action against them was pending. Yulia Latynina also makes the argument that Russian attack was supposed to take place a few days later. See Latynina, "200 km tankov."

21. U.S. secretary of state Condoleezza Rice used the term "premeditated" to describe the Russian invasion in a speech on U.S.-Russian relations at the Mayflower Hotel in Washington, D.C., hosted by the German Marshall Fund of the United States on September 18, 2008. See Rice's speech at http://2001–2009.state.gov/secretary/rm/2008/09/109954.htm. In his testimony before the U.S. House of Representatives, U.S. assistant secretary of state Dan Fried stated, "The causes of this conflict—particularly the dispute between Georgia

and its breakaway regions of South Ossetia and Abkhazia—are complex, and all sides made mistakes and miscalculations." See Fried's testimony before the House Committee on Foreign Affairs September 9, 2008, at http://foreignaffairs.house.gov/110/fri090908.pdf.

22. For a good example of the official Russian and South Ossetian interpretation of the war and its origins see the pamphlet *Operation "Tsminda Veli": Genocide of Ossetians*. That pamphlet was supplied to the author by the Russian Mission to the European Union in Brussels, but is officially published by the Independent Journalists Association of Caucasus to Support Victims of Genocide.

23. The first attempt to destroy the Gupta bridge involved the sole air sortie flown by the tiny Georgian air force early on August 8. The bridge was subsequently attacked a second time by Georgian 203 mm PION self-propelled artillery. It was attacked a third time by Israeli-built GRADLAR artillery with cluster munitions as a Russian armored convoy crossed it early in the battle.

24. The claim that the Georgians had killed 2,000 Tskhinvali residents was first made by South Ossetian president Eduard Koikoty on August 9, 2008, when he stated, "We appeal to all international organizations to recognize the fact of genocide," claiming that more than 2,000 residents of Tskhinvali had been killed. "Such huge losses are irreparable for the small people of South Ossetia." The claim is also contained in a statement from August 10, 2008, found on the Web page of the official information agency of South Ossetia "RES" at http://cominf.org/en/node/1166477989. On August 9, 2008, the Russian ambassador to Georgia Vyacheslav Kovalenko also said that "at least 2,000 residents of Tskhinvali have died." See for example http://www.russiatoday.com/Top_News/2008–08–09/The_Georgian_war__minute_by_minute_August_9.html.

25. In subsequent interviews by Human Rights Watch, South Ossetian residents justified the torching and looting of Georgian villages as revenge, referring to the thousands of Ossetians that were said to have been killed by the Georgian attack as reported by Russian media.

26. For data from the Investigative Committee of the Russian Federation Prosecutor's Office see "Identities of 162 People Killed in South Ossetia have been established," *RIA Novosti*, December 23, 2008, http://www.rian.ru/society/20081223/157895855.html. For the Memorial data see "Special Press-release by Memorial Human Rights Centre," from September 11, 2008, that can be found at http://www.memo.ru/2008/09/19/1909082.htm. The South Ossetian data is published by the Public Commission for investigating war crimes in South Ossetia on "List of the Killed Residents of South Ossetia" at http://www.osetinfo.ru/spisok.

27. http://www.sweden.gov.se/sb/d/587/a/109203.

28. That confirmation took place during an OSCE mission briefing mid-day on August 8 when several participants insisted that the OSCE briefer Ryan Grist phone the spokesperson at the Russian peacekeeping headquarters to check whether any peacekeepers had been killed given the Georgian claims that they had avoided shelling Russian peacekeeping positions. The Russian spokesperson confirmed that no Russian peacekeepers had been killed during the initial Georgian shelling.

29. Private correspondence between the author and Brigadier General Kurashvili.

30. That phone call took place at 0023, shortly after midnight, on the morning of August 8. The author has been provided with a transcript of that call.

31. See the blog entry of Alexander Viktorov at http://kqrr.livejournal.com/23331.html.

32. See the obituary of Lieutenant Oleg Galavanov, which states, "On August 7th Lieutenant O. Galavanov was fulfilling the military order to define targeting and alteration of artillery fire. His observation post was located on the roof of the Russian Peacemaking Battalion in the southern outskirts of the town. At that moment, at the night from the 7th to 8th of August this was the most dangerous spot in town because the Georgian army first of all tried to destroy the peacekeepers." See http://www.osradio.ru/news/genocid/eid/14326.html.

33. In his interview "Nje mesto etomu prezidentu v Juzhnoy Osetiy" in *Kommersant,* December 4, 2008, Anatoly Barenkevich describes how he first found refuge in the peacekeeping headquarters and then, using the headquarters as a safe haven, set up defensive positions in civilian buildings to attack Georgian forces passing by. He describes how he and his men blew up at least three Georgian tanks that were passing by and had not fired at him or the JPKF headquarters. http://www.kommersant.ru/doc.aspx?DocsID=1089120.

34. See C. J. Chivers and E. Barry, "Accounts Undercut Claims by Georgia on Russia War," *New York Times,* November 7, 2008.

35. Georgia has a network of seismic monitoring centers, including one in Kekhvi, located at the northern border of the ethnic Georgian enclave about seven kilometers from Tskhinvali. Connectivity with the satellite stations was cut off at 2400 on August 7 by the Russian side—another indication suggesting that Moscow's attack was preplanned and well organized. However, the data collected were stored and subsequently analyzed. The seismic recording confirmed that the Georgian villages around the Kekhiv monitoring station were heavily shelled during the course of August 7, including during the key hours after the ceasefire had been announced. That shelling became more intense later in the evening and in the run-up to 2335 when the Georgian offensive commenced. Further analysis of the data should be able to confirm exactly what kind of artillery was used in the shelling of Georgian villages. The author is in possession of a letter from Dr. Zurab Javakhishvili, director of the Seismic Monitoring Center of Georgia, dated April 25, 2009, confirming this.

36. See the testimony of then Georgian defense minister David Kezerashvili before the Georgian Parliament's Temporary Commission on Military Aggression and Other Acts of Russia against the Territorial Integrity of Georgia at http://www.parliament.ge/index.php?lang_id=ENG&sec_id=1315&info_id=21693.

37. In mid-October 2008, Human Rights Watch (HRW) published a report investigating the use of cluster munitions by both Russian and Georgian forces. While Moscow has officially denied using such weapons, HRW found overwhelming evidence of their use by Russian forces, including the indiscriminate use in populated areas in violation of international humanitarian law. It also found evidence that Georgia used its cluster munitions in some populated areas, including those adjacent to Tskhinvali like Verkhniy Gorodok. But HRW concluded it was not clear to what degree the Georgian use of cluster munitions in such areas was intentional or whether the weapons had simply malfunctioned as large numbers of unexploded cluster munitions were found. Tbilisi cooperated fully with the study whereas Moscow refused to do so. See "Georgia: More Cluster Bomb Damage Than Reported," Human Rights Watch, November 4, 2008.

38. The satellite images can be found on the UNOSAT web page at http://unosat.web.cern.ch/unosat/asp/prod_free.asp?id=101&All=on.

39. Some 130,000 Georgians fled their villages during the course of the war. A majority lived in villages in the regions bordering South Ossetia and were able to return home after the war. An estimated 25,000 Georgians from South

Ossetia could not return. The ethnic cleansing, looting, and torching of Georgian villages have been documented by HRW. For example, on August 12, 2008, HRW researchers witnessed massive looting by Ossetian militias and photographed the still-smoldering torched homes in the Tamarasheni region and surrounding Georgian villages. They interviewed local villagers who confirmed the systematic looting as well as the Ossetian militia members who openly admitted they had burned down homes and villages to ensure that the Georgians would never return. In the words of Rachel Denber, deputy director of the Europe and Central Asia division of HRW, "All of this adds up to compelling evidence of war crimes and grave human rights abuses. This should persuade the Russian government it needs to prosecute those responsible for these crimes." Publicly available satellite photographs from UNOSAT show fires burning well after active hostilities had ended in ethnic Georgian villages on August 10, 12, 13, 17, 19, and 22. See "Georgia: Satellite Images Show Destruction, Ethnic Attacks" at http://www.hrw.org/en/news/2008/08/27/georgia-satellite-images-show-destruction-ethnic-attacks.

40.   See Richard C. Holbrooke, "David and Goliath: Putin Tries to Depose a Neighbor," *Washington Post,* November 27, 2007.

41.   See, for example, Alex Rondos, "What Side Are We On?" *International Herald Tribune,* May 8, 2008.

42.   Ronald D. Asmus, "A War the West Must Stop," *Washington Post,* July 15, 2008.

CHAPTER 2

1.   For insightful portraits of Mikheil Saakashvili as a personality see Melik Kaylan, "Georgia in the Time of Misha," *Travel and Leisure,* September 2007, as well as Gideon Rachman, "Lunch with the FT: Mikheil Saakashvili," *Financial Times,* April 26, 2008, at http://blogs.ft.com/rachmanblog/2008/04/lunch-with-the-ft-mikheil-saakashvili. Saakashvili describes his own life and views in a long book-length interview with Raphaël Glucksmann in Mikheil Saakashvili with Raphaël Glucksmann, *Je vous parle de liberté* (Paris: Hachette Literatures, 2008).

2.   For further details on the link between energy, the ability of countries like Georgia to be independent, and the origins of the war, see Svante Cornell, "Pipeline Power: The War in Georgia and the Future of the Caucasian Energy Corridor," *Georgetown Journal of International Affairs* 10, no. 1 (Winter 2009):131–139.

3.   Two excellent sources on the role of Georgia in the collapse of the USSR and the political and ethnic dynamics that led to the initial Abkhaz and South Ossetian wars are Jack F. Matlock Jr., *Autopsy of an Empire: The American Ambassador's Account of the Collapse of the Soviet Union* (New York: Random House, 1995), and Charles King, *The Ghosts of Freedom: A History of the Caucasus* (Oxford: Oxford University Press, 2008).

4.   As Ascherson recalled: "The National Museum was not burned, but it was looted and devastated. . . . Soldiers do this everywhere in occupied cities. But the fate of the State Archives was different. The shell of the building stands down by the sea. Its roof has fallen in, and the interior is a heap of calcined rubble. One day in the winter of 1992, a white Lada without number-plates, containing four men from the Georgian National Guard, drew up outside. The guardsmen shot the doors open and then flung incendiary grenades into the hall and stairwell. A vagrant boy, one of many children who by then were

living on the streets, was rounded up and made to help spread the flames, while a group of Sukhumi citizens tried vainly to break through the cordon and enter the building to rescue burning books and papers. In those archives was most of the scanty, precious written evidence of Abkhazia's past, as well as the recent records of government and administration. . . . As a report compiled later in Athens remarked, 'the history of the region became ashes.'" This excerpt comes from the new and revised edition of Ascherson's book, which contains a chapter on Abkhazia. See *Black Sea: Birthplace of Civilisation and Barbarism* (London: Vintage Books, 2007), pp. 253–254.

5.   For a good overview of Georgia's economic performance during this period see the date and analysis in the article by former prime minister Lado Gurgenidze, "Georgia's Search for Economic Liberty: A Blueprint for Reform in Developing Economics," American Enterprise Institute, No. 2, June 2009.

6.   The full paragraph reads: "Each participating state has a right to equal security. We reaffirm the right of each and every participating state to be free to choose or change its security arrangements, including treaties of alliances, as they evolve. Each state also has the right to neutrality. Each participating state will respect the rights of all others in these regards. They will not strengthen their security at the expense of the security of other states. Within the OSCE, no state, group of states or organizations can have any pre-eminent responsibility for maintaining peace and stability in the OSCE area or can consider any part of the OSCE area its sphere of influence." See the *Charter For European Security* issued by the Istanbul OSCE summit in November 1999 at http://www.osce.org/documents/mcs/1999/11/4050_en.pdf.

7.   For Lord Robertson's statement at the Pratica di Mare air force base outside of Rome see http://www.nato.int/docu/speech/2002/s020528r.htm. For Putin's remarks at his press conference see http://www.nato-russia-council.info/HTM/EN/documents28may02_5.shtml. For Bush's remarks see http://www.nato-russia-council.info/HTM/EN/documents28may02_6.shtml

8.   See Vladimir Putin, "Annual Address to the Federal Assembly of the Russian Federation," April 25, 2005, at http://www.kremlin.ru/eng/speeches/2005/04/25/2031_type70029type82912_87086.shtml.

9.   See Ivan Krastev, "Russia's Post Orange Empire," October 20, 2005, http://www.opendemocracy.net/node/2947. Also see Ivan Krastev and Fyodor Lukyanov, "The EU, Russia, and the Wider Black Sea Region," October 16, 2007, Black Sea Paper Series, No. 4, at http://www.gmfus.org/doc/Black%20Sea%20Paper%20No.%204%2010-26.pdf; Ivan Krastev, "The Crisis of the Post–Cold War European Order: What to Do about Russia's Newfound Taste for Confrontation with the West," March 2008, Brussels Forum Papers at http://www.gmfus.org/brusselsforum/2008/doc/krastev_web.pdf.

10. See the Human Rights Watch report, "Singled Out: Russia's Detention and Expulsion of Georgians," October 2007. http://www.hrw.org/sites/default/files/reports/russia1007webwcover.pdf.

11. Interview with former U.S. secretary of state Condoleezza Rice.

12. See Brian Rohan, "Saakashvilli 'Planned S. Ossetia Invasion': Ex-minister," September 14, 2008, at http://www.alertnet.org/thenews/newsdesk/LD123780.htm.

13. The Lavrov-Bezhuashvili dinner took place on the eve of a Black Sea Economic Council (BSEC) summit in Istanbul in late June 2007. For the leaked *Kommersant* article see "Mezhgosudarstvennij perevarot" by V. Solovjev and V. Novikov, June 25, 2007, at http://www.kommersant.ru/doc.aspx?DocsID=777492.

CHAPTER 3

1. For an excellent account of the complex and multifaceted course of Western diplomacy during the Kosovo conflict with Russia, see John Norris, *Collision Course: NATO, Russia and Kosovo* (Westport: Praeger Publishers, 2005). See also Strobe Talbott's firsthand account of his dealing with Moscow in Strobe Talbott, *The Russia Hand: A Memoir of Presidential Diplomacy* (New York: Random House, 2002).

2. See, for example, Oksana Antonenko, "Russia and the Deadlock over Kosovo," *Survival* 49, no. 3 (Autumn 2007): 91–106.

3. On NATO's intervention in Kosovo, see Ivo H. Daalder and Michael E. O'Hanlon, *Winning Ugly: NATO's War to Save Kosovo* (Washington D.C.: Brookings Institution Press, 2000); and Wesley K. Clark, *Waging Modern War: Bosnia, Kosovo, and the Future of Combat* (New York: Public Affairs, 2002). On Kosovo more generally see Tim Judah, *Kosovo: War and Revenge* (Connecticut: Yale Nota Bene, 2000).

4. For an excellent overview of the debate on the differences between Kosovo and the frozen conflict in Abkhazia, see Zeyno Baran and Thomas de Waal, "Abkhazia-Georgia, Kosovo-Serbia: Parallel Worlds?" published by Open Democracy News Analysis at http://www.opendemocracy.net/democracy-caucasus/abkhazia_serbia_3787.jsp.

5. See Vladimir Putin's press conference for the Russian and foreign media on January 31, 2006, at http://www.kremlin.ru/eng/speeches/2006/01/31/0953 _type82915type82917_100901.shtml.

6. See the *Report of the Special Envoy of the Secretary-General on Kosovo's Future Status* at http://www.unosek.org/docref/report-english.pdf. For an analysis of the Ahtisaari Plan, see The International Crisis Group, "Kosovo: No Good Alternatives to the Ahtisaari Plan," Europe Report No. 182, May 14, 2007.

7. See the article and recollections by German ambassador Wolfgang Ischinger and Matthias Lüttenberg, "Eine Bruecke zwischen Serbien und Kosovo?" at http://www.securityconference.de/medienberichte/kosovo.php. Ambassador Ischinger was the German representative of the troika, and Luettenberg was his assistant.

8. See Vladimir Putin, "Speech at the 43rd Munich Security Conference on Security Policy," February 10, 2007, at http://www.securityconference.de/konferenzen/rede.php?sprache=en&id=179.

9. See "Putin Warns West over Kosovo Dispute," the Associated Press, February 22, 2008, at http://www.thefreelibrary.com/Putin+warns+West+over+Kosovo +dispute-a01611463534.

10. See Marina Perevozkina, "Moskva otvetit NATO Abkhaziey," *Nezavisimaya Gazeta* April 14, 2008. At www.ng.ru/printed/209407.

11. The parallels between Russian thinking and rhetoric in the Georgia and Kosovo wars was immediately noted by Strobe Talbott, who was the Clinton Administration's point person dealing with Moscow during the Kosovo conflict. See Strobe Talbott, "Russia's Ominous New Doctrine?" *Washington Post,* August 15, 2008.

CHAPTER 4

1. For President Bush's Warsaw speech on NATO enlargement from June 2001, see http://edition.cnn.com/2001/ALLPOLITICS/06/15/bush.warsaw.trans/ index.html.

2. For the arguments in favor, see Ronald D. Asmus with Bruce P. Jackson, "The Black Sea and the Frontiers of Freedom," *Policy Review*, No. 125, June /July 2004; Ronald D. Asmus, Konstantin Dimitrov, and Joerg Forbrig, eds., *A New Euro-Atlantic Strategy for the Black Sea Region* (Washington, D.C.: The German Marshall Fund of the United States, 2004); and Ronald D. Asmus, ed., *Next Steps in Forging a Euroatlantic Strategy for the Wider Black Sea* (Washington, D.C.: The German Marshall Fund of the United States, 2006).

3. See Merkel's speech at the annual commander's conference of the German armed forces on March 10, 2008, at http://www.bundeskanzlerin.de/nn_5296/Content/DE/Rede/2008/03/2008–03–10-rede-merkel-kommandeurtagung.html.

4. See "President Bush Meets with President Saakashvili of Georgia," Office of the Press Secretary, March 19, 2008, at http://www.whitehouse.gov/news/releases/2008/03/print.20080319–4.html.

5. See press conference by President Bush and President Putin at the Ljubljana Summit, June 16, 2001, at http://www.ljubljana-summit.gov.si/en/index.html.

6. See "President Bush and President Yushchenko of Ukraine Exchange Luncheon Toasts," Office of the Press Secretary, April 1, 2008, at http://www.whitehouse.gov/news/releases/2008/04/20080402–4.html.

7. Bush's remarks were made after a meeting with de Hoop Scheffer at the Marriott Bucharest Grand Hotel following his arrival. See "President Bush Meets with NATO Secretary General Jaap de Hoop Scheffer," Office of the Press Secretary, April 2, 2008, at http://www.whitehouse.gov/news/releases/2008/04/20080402–4.html.

8. For the Madrid summit, see "Head-to-Head at Madrid?" in Ronald D. Asmus, *Opening NATO's Door: How the Alliance Remade Itself for a New Era* (New York: Columbia University Press, 2002), pp. 212–250.

9. Excerpts of Putin's speech before the NAC in Bucharest, April 2008, can be found at http://www.unian.net/eng/news/news–247251.html.

10. As quoted in Helene Cooper, C. J. Chivers, and Clifford J. Levy, "US Watched as a Squabble Turned into a Showdown," *New York Times*, August 18, 2008.

CHAPTER 5

1. See "Russian Federation Withdraws from Regime of Restrictions Established in 1996 for Abkhazia," Information and Press Department of the Russian Ministry of Foreign Affairs, March 6, 2008, at http://www.mid.ru/brp_4.nsf/e78a48070f128a7b43256999005bcbb3/79c58f476caec4e8c32574040058934c?OpenDocument.

2. See the official document issued by the Russian Duma on March 21, 2008, at www.duma.gov.ru.

3. See "On the Reply of President of Russia Vladimir Putin to the Messages of President of Abkhazia Sergey Bagapsh and President of South Ossetia Eduard Kokoity," Information and Press Department of the Russian Ministry of Foreign Affairs, April 3, 2008, at http://www.mid.ru/brp_4.nsf/e78a48070f128a7b43256999005bcbb3/af03c091ee962106c3257424002c1427?OpenDocument.

4. See remarks by Andrei Illarionov, "Another Look at the August War," Center for Eurasian Policy, Hudson Institute, September 12, 2008, at http://www.hudson.org/files/documents/Andrei%20Illarionov%20speech.pdf.

5. Ibid.

6. See "The Russian President's Instructions to the Russian Federation Government with Regard to Abkhazia and South Ossetia," Information and Press

Department of the Russian Ministry of Foreign Affairs, April 16, 2008, at http://www.mid.ru/brp_4.nsf/e78a48070f128a7b43256999005bcbb3/b75734 bac2796efbc325742d005a6f7c?OpenDocument.

7. See "Report of UNOMIG on the Situation of 20 April Involving the Downing of Georgian Unmanned Aerial Vehicle over the Zone of Conflict," May 26, 2008, at http://www.reliefweb.int/rw/RWFiles2008.nsf/FilesByRWDocUnid Filename/MUMA–7F34PW-full_report.pdf/$File/full_report.pdf.

8. See Andrei Illarionov, "The Russian Leadership's Preparation for War, 1999–2008," in Svante E. Cornell and S. Frederick Starr, eds., *The Guns of August 2008* (New York and London: M. E. Sharpe, 2009), p. 69.

9. Post-election polling showed that jobs and unemployment were considered the most important issues by some 52 percent of Georgians, while Abkhazia and South Ossetia came in as number three, with 25 percent. In other words, one quarter of voters said regaining the territories was one of their two top voting issues. Some 89 percent of Georgians still thought it was extremely important or important to make "progress on re-integrating Georgia's territories" but the number who felt pressure to do so quickly—i.e., in the coming year—was much lower at 44 percent.

10. The NATO-Russia chiefs of defense meeting took place on May 10, 2008. For commentary on the Russian General's "prediction," see John Vinocur, "Georgia is Focal Point of US-NATO-Russia tension," *New York Times*, May 5, 2009.

11. See, for example, "Russian Railroad Troops Enter Abkhazia to Help Rebuild Roads," RIA Novosti, May 31, 2007, at http://en.rian.ru/russia/20080531/ 108953337.html. See also "Russia Sends 300 Troops to Abkhazia," *New York Times*, June 1, 2008.

12. See "Russia Illegally Deploys New Troops in Abkhazia; Georgia Calls for Immediate Withdrawal, Condemns Reckless Escalation," by the Service of the Government of Georgia, May 31, 2008, at www.president.gov.ge.

13. Interview with former assistant secretary of state for European and Eurasian affairs Dan Fried, January 7, 2009.

14. See "Remarks by Secretary Rice with Georgian President Saakashvili," July 10, 2008, at http://www.america.gov/st/texttrans-english/2008/July/200807 10161637gmnanahcub0.3613092.html.

CHAPTER 6

1. See Nikolai Makarov, quoted by Interfax, December 30, 2008, at http://www .interfax.ru/politics/txt.asp?id=54787&sw=%EC%E0%EA%E0%F0%EE% E2&bd=28&bm=12&by=2008&ed=31&em=12&ey=2008&secid=1446& mp=0&p=1.

2. As the authors of Project Grey Goose conclude, "In the case of possible Russian government involvement with the cyber attacks on the Georgian government website in July and August 2008, the available evidence supports a strong likelihood of GRU/FSB planning and direction at a high level while relying on Nashi intermediaries and the phenomenon of crowdsourcing to obfuscate their involvement and implement their strategy." See *Project Grey Goose Phase II Report: The Evolving State of Cyber Warfare*, March 20, 2009. For the legal implications of these attacks for NATO see *Cyber Attacks against Georgia: Legal Lessons Identified*, Cooperative Cyber Defense Center of Excellence (CCDCOE), Tallinn, Estonia, November 2008.

3. For details on the Israeli connection, see Barak Ravid and Amos Harel, "Russia Declares Itself Ready to Make Peace with Georgia," *Haaretz*, August 11, 2008, at www.haaretz.com/hasen/spages/1009946.html.

4. See Pavel Felgenhauer, "The Russian-Georgian War Was Preplanned in Moscow," *Novaya Gazeta*, August 14, 2008, and at www.novayagazeta.ru/data/2008/59/04.html.

5. As quoted in "Did Russia Plan Its War with Georgia?" Radio Free Europe/Radio Liberty, August 16, 2008.

6. See Gela Bezhuashvili's testimony before the Parliamentary Temporary Commission on Military Aggression and Other Acts of Russia against the Territorial Integrity of Georgia, October 25, 2008, at http://www.parliament.ge/index.php?lang_id=ENG&sec_id=1329&info_id=20940.

7. Interview with Alexander Lomaia. Lomaia also refers to this conversation in his testimony before the Parliamentary Temporary Commission on Military Aggression and Other Acts of Russia against the Territorial Integrity of Georgia on October 27, 2008. See the transcript of the testimony at http://www.parliament.ge/index.php?lang_id=ENG&sec_id=1329&info_id=21134.

8. For further details on Georgian planning, see the excellent essay by Lt. Col. Robert E. Hamilton, "The Bear Came through the Tunnel: An Analysis of Georgian Planning and Operations in the Russo-Georgian War." Hamilton was chief of the U.S. Office of Defense Cooperation from July 2006 to 2008.

9. For further details see Hamilton, "The Bear Came through the Tunnel."

10. Interview with Stephen Hadley, former U.S. National Security Advisor.

11. See, for example, the essay by Pavel Felgenhauer, "After August 7: The Escalation of the Russia-Georgian War," in Svante E. Cornell and S. Frederick Starr, eds., *The Guns of August 2008* (New York and London: M. E. Sharpe), p. 171.

12. Interview with former secretary of state Condoleezza Rice, May 19, 2009.

13. As quoted by Omid Memarian in "Saakashvili Asked to Step Down," Inter Press Service News Agency (IPS), August 12, 2008.

14. See the transcript of Saakashvili's address, Civil Georgia, August 11, 2008, at http://www.civil.ge/eng/article.php?id=19051&search=.

15. See "President Bush Discusses Situation in Georgia" at www.whitehouse.gov/news/releases/2008/08print/20080811–1.html.

CHAPTER 7

1. As quoted in Samantha Shields, "Russian Pullout Fulfills Georgia Pledge," *Wall Street Journal*, October 9, 2008. http://online.wsj.com/article/SB122345021244814657.html.

2. For a good overview of Sarkozy's critical views on Russia on the eve of his election, see his interview with Pascal Bruckner, André Glucksmann, Michaël Prazan, and Yasmina Reza in *Le Meilleur des mondes*, no. 2 (Autumn 2006). The lunch with leading French Russian experts at which Sarkozy discussed his strategy of focusing on Medvedev rather than Putin is referred to by Vincent Jauvert in "Sarko le Russe: histoire secrète d'un revirement," *Le nouvel observateur*, November 13, 2008. For a more general overview of the French debate on Russia see Laure Mandeville, "Russie: l'empire contre-attaque," *Politique internationale* no. 121 (Autumn 2008), and at http://www.politiqueinternationale.com/revue/article.php?id_revue=121&id=752&content=synopsis.

3. In mid-November Sarkozy boasted at a ceremony in the Élysée Palace: "I remember the American president's call the day before our departure for Moscow. 'Don't go there, they [the Russians] want to go to Tbilisi, they're 40 kilometers away. Don't go, [just] condemn it.'" As quoted in AFP, November 13, 2008, at http://afp.google.com/article/ALeqM5g4Xu-k5Pg5t-BswZ-H22uBExGLQQ. The White House subsequently denied that such an exchange had ever occurred.

4. As quoted by Gleb Pavlovsky in discussion "Vseh pod tribunal?" Radio Ekho Moskvy, August 12, 2008, at http://echo.msk.ru/programs/klinch/533352-echo/.
5. The exchange is recalled in Jauvert, "Sarko le Russe." Putin's spokesman Dmitry Peskov subsequently confirmed the essence of the exchange when he said, "Putin spoke in words very similar to what is written in the article." As quoted in Steve Gutterman, "Putin Described Hanging Georgian Leader," *Associated Press,* November 14, 2008.
6. Interview with French foreign minister Bernard Kouchner.
7. See the transcript of the Medvedev-Sarkozy press conference, Moscow, August 12, 2008, at http://www.un.int/russia/new/MainRoot/docs/warfare/statement120808en4.htm.
8. See "Text of Bush's Statement on the Georgia Conflict," AFP, August 13, 2008.
9. As quoted in Steven Lee Myers and Thom Shanker, "Bush Aides Say Russia Actions in Georgia Jeopardize Ties," *New York Times,* August 15, 2008. http://www.nytimes.com/2008/08/15/world/europe/15policy.html.
10. See John McCain, "We are All Georgians," *Wall Street Journal,* August 14, 2008.
11. See "Bush and Georgia," *Wall Street Journal,* August 13, 2008.
12. See the transcript of the Saakashvili-Rice press conference, August 15, 2008, at http://www.president.gov.ge/?l=E&m=0&sm=2&st=10&id=2712.
13. Interview with former secretary of state Condoleezza Rice, May 19, 2009.
14. By September 5, 2008, the Russian army had established some thirty checkpoints that had not existed when the ceasefire was signed. The vast majority of them were located outside of the security zones around both South Ossetia and Abkhazia.
15. See "Medvedev's Statement on South Ossetia and Abkhazia," *New York Times,* August 26, 2008. http://www.nytimes.com/2008/08/27/world/europe/27medvedev.html.
16. See Dimitry Medvedev, "Why I Had to Recognize Georgia's Breakaway Regions," *Financial Times,* August 27, 2008.
17. See the interview given by Dimitry Medvedev to Television Channel One, Russia, NTV, August 31, 2008 at http://www.kremlin.ru/eng/speeches/2008/08/31/1850_type82912type82916_206003.shtml.
18. "Saakashvili 'No Longer Exists' as Georgia's President: Medvedev," AFP, September 2, 2008. http://afp.google.com/article/ALeqM5jVDUlJhriAoLoWvbKCC6g5lsy1yA.
19. See Steven Erlanger, "European Union Struggles to Hold Moscow to Promises," *International Herald Tribune,* September 7, 2008. http://www.nytimes.com/2008/09/07/world/europe/07iht-union.4.15954445.html.
20. See the transcript of the Medvedev-Sarkozy press conference at the Maiendorf Castle outside of Moscow at http://www.kremlin.ru/eng/speeches/2008/09/08/2208_type82912type82914type82915_206283.shtml.
21. See President Sarkozy's comments at his press conference with Georgian president Mikheil Saakashvili at https://pastel.diplomatie.gouv.fr/editorial/actual/ael2/bulletin.gb.asp?liste=20080911.gb.html&submit.x=8&submit.y=8&submit=consulter.
22. Ibid.

ACKNOWLEDGMENTS

I would like to thank Craig Kennedy, president of the German Marshall Fund of the United States (GMF), for giving me the opportunity to write this book. Craig has not only been my boss but a friend. He and GMF have provided the freedom and creative environment that enabled me to develop the ideas reflected in these pages. Karen Donfried, executive vice president at GMF, has also been a steadfast pillar of support throughout all the ups and down of this book. GMF's work on and activities in the wider Black Sea region were critical in helping me deepen my understanding of events in Georgia and its neighbors in the region.

I would also like to thank Richard C. Holbrooke and Strobe Talbott for their friendship, encouragement, and support of this project. Richard has been a comrade-in-arms and collaborator on the Georgia issue from the beginning. He, too, saw what was coming and predicted with great accuracy the events that would lead to the Russo-Georgian war of 2008. Strobe Talbott and I have been colleagues and friends since the mid-1990s when we wrestled with the challenge of building a Europe whole, free, and at peace in the State Department. Our ongoing discussions about Russia and its policy toward its neighbors have been invaluable in sharpening my own thinking. Their comments on earlier versions of the manuscript were invaluable.

I have benefited from the support and assistance of many friends in Georgia. Many of them granted or arranged interviews or access to sources and are listed in the Note on Bibliography and Sources. But a special thanks for their friendship goes to Natalia Kancheli, Daniel Kunin, Alex Rondeli, Shota Utiashvili, and Temuri Yakobashvili. The same is true for a handful of colleagues and friends on both sides of the Atlantic who put up both with my repeated and at times pointed questions and criticism, read various drafts of this manuscript, or debated and sparred with me over this or that interpretation of an event, often late into the evening and over the occasional glass of Georgian wine. They include Carl Bildt, Matt Bryza, Dan Fried, Alex Rondos, Peter Semneby, John Tefft, and Damon Wilson.

Authors receive the credit—as well as the criticism—their books generate. But writing a book is a lot of work and requires a lot of support. My special assistant Iveta Kruma did a marvelous job in providing that support by helping to keep me organized, tracking down numerous details and facts, checking drafts, translating Russian sources, and contributing to this project in countless other ways. I would also like to thank my Deputy in Brussels, Dr. Corinna Horst, who took enough work off my desk in Brussels so that I could focus and actually finish this project on time.

My agent, Andrew Stuart, was a true professional in assisting me through the stages of completing a book. Jake Kilisvitch and the team at Palgrave Macmillan were effective at sharpening my prose and were a pleasure to work with. My friend Dietmar Mueller-Elmau provided a quiet and comfortable setting at Schloss Elmau in Bavaria for me to complete the final edits to the manuscript.

I wrote this book while battling a relapse of cancer. My decision to do so reflected the faith I had in and the encouragement I received from my doctors to continue to pursue my passions and dreams while undergoing treatment. I would like to thank Professor Michael Keating of the Leukemia Department at M.D. Anderson Cancer Center in Houston, Texas, and Dr. Eric van den Neste from the Centre d'Hematologie at the Cliniques Universitaires Saint Luc in Brussels, Belgium. Professor Keating heads a transatlantic coalition working to cure this form of cancer. I have benefited enormously from his vision, inspiration, and contagious confidence and friendship.

A final and heartfelt word of thanks goes to my wife, Barbara, and my son, Erik, for their support, patience and humor over the past year as this book has gone from what seemed a crazy idea to a real project to completion. Once again they have endured a steady stream of trips to the region, visits from Georgians to our home, and long debates into the wee hours of the morning with all sorts of visitors in the cause and hope of expanding the frontiers of freedom to this small but beautiful country on the eastern shore of the Black Sea. This book is dedicated to them.

Elmau, Germany
August 2009

INDEX